Problem Solving and Learning Disabilities

Problem Solving and Learning Disabilities
An Information Processing Approach

Melinda Parrill-Burnstein, Ph.D.
Director
Institute for Child and Family Development and Research
Atlanta, Georgia;
Clinical Appointment
Department of Psychiatry
Emory University School of Medicine
Atlanta, Georgia

Grune & Stratton
A Subsidiary of Harcourt Brace Jovanovich, Publishers
New York   London   Toronto   Sydney   San Francisco

© 1981 by Grune & Stratton, Inc.
All rights reserved. No part of this publication
may be reproduced or transmitted in any form or
by any means, electronic or mechanical, including
photocopy, recording, or any information storage
and retrieval system, without permission in
writing from the publisher.

**Grune & Stratton, Inc.
111 Fifth Avenue
New York, New York 10003**

Distributed in the United Kingdom by
**Academic Press Inc. (London) Ltd.
24/28 Oval Road, London NW 1**

Library of Congress Catalog Number 81-81501
International Standard Book Number 0-8089-1340-9

Printed in the United States of America

To Robert

Contents

General Considerations 1
1. **Attention** 15
2. **Concept Organization** 55
3. **Memory** 91
4. **Language** 117
5. **Cognitive Mapping** 149
6. **Social Cognition** 176
7. **Issues** 198
   Index 207

Preface

Problem Solving and Learning Disablities: An Information Processing Approach organizes accumulated research in the field of learning disabilities within the context of education and psychology. To accomplish this, Chapters 1 through 6 include a review of relevant research and theories of child development, cognitive development, and learning disabilities with the intent to provide a better understanding of the relationship between normal development and learning disabilities. Learning disabilities are viewed as reflecting a *difference* in processing rather than simply a *delay* in processing. This is not to exclude, however, the possibility that a subsample of children with learning disabilities demonstrates a delay in development or that other subsamples of children demonstrate both delays and differences in performance.

The chapters are arranged in order of complexity (e.g., attention basic to concept organization; attention and concept organization basic to memory; and so forth). In addition to the hierarchical sequencing implied here, these processes are simultaneously reciprocal. For example, as the attention process affects memory, it is affected by memory. These relationships between processes (simultaneous and hierarchical) are not easily distinguished.

Problem Solving and Learning Disabilities is designed for advanced courses in psychology, education, and learning disabilities, especially those that emphasize diagnostics, remediation, and research. It provides a much needed reference source that reviews and integrates data about information processing and learning disabilities for the purpose of evaluating present research and remedial procedures. Private practitioners, professors, teachers, and researchers alike will find this text instructive in their work with and study of children with learning disabilities.

Acknowledgments

Many people have contributed to the preparation of this book.

I owe a great deal to Lynn Baker-Ward, who edited the manuscript several times, to Dr. Ted Miller, who provided invaluable comments, to Dr. Joan Laughton, who gave me her support, and to the members of the staff of Grune & Stratton, who were responsible for the editorial and production stages of the book.

My former students and research assistants from the Communicative Disorders Department at Emory University, particularly Randi Vassil, Eileen Hazan-Ginzburg, Judy Lyttle, Janis Sayre, Bev Bergman, Renee Becker, Susan Haas, Evelyn Pesiri, Patti Ruffin, and my brother Dr. Forrest Novy, served as sounding boards. Their insights and energy enhanced the perspective of the book and helped to develop its theoretical construct.

I also would like to acknowledge the contributions of Dr. Forrest Novy, and Drs. Blanche Podhajski and Barbara Bruno Haskins, who, while graduate students at Northwestern University, critiqued the chapter on language and provided invaluable comments.

For participation in our research for the past five years, I would like to thank Carol Goldsmith of the Atlanta Speech School, Dr. Barbara Dunbar-Bianchi of the Paideia School, and Dr. Mary Ben McDorman of the Howard School.

For the typing and retyping of the manuscript, I wish to thank Julia Bridger—not only for the skill and speed of her work but for her friendship as well.

To Dr. Doris Johnson, my master's professor, and Dr. Boyd McCandless, my dissertation advisor, I owe a great deal. Dr. Johnson provided the foundation for my future work in learning disabilities. Through Dr. McCandless's guidance, training, and understanding of the field of learning disabilities and psychology, I was encouraged to integrate my work in both these areas. Dr. Gagné, with his treasured letters, helped shape the understanding of the role of instruction presented in this book. Drs. Shanna Richman and Barry Gholson helped clarify the hypothesis testing paradigm early in my work. This paradigm provided the conceptual and theoretical framework that is further developed in this text.

Last, but not least, I wish to thank my family. Without the support of my husband, Robert, this book would not have been possible. To my parents, Selma and Ben Parrill, and my grandmother, Ruth Leaf, as well as to the children who participated in our research, remediation programs, and diagnostic clinic, I owe a special thanks.

General Considerations

Information processing theory provides a framework for the study of problem solving and learning disabilities. The information processing theorist sees humans as analogous to complex machines, like modern computers, with elaborate "programs" that enable them to deal with information about the world in adaptive ways (Flavell, 1977). Information processing is the method by which this information is analyzed and synthesized in sequential steps (Neisser, 1976). Information processes involved in problem solving are attention, concept organization, memory, language, cognitive mapping, and social cognition. These problem-solving activities are the topics of the chapters of this book. The topics are discussed within the context of the problem-solving analysis of stimulus differentiation, selective attention, response generation, response execution, and appropriate response to feedback. Each chapter includes definitions, an overview of current theory, a summary of the development of the process, a review of relevant research, and suggestions for research and remediation. In this chapter, the organization of the book is described briefly; theories of cognitive development and instruction are reviewed; and theories of learning disabilities and cognitive processing are discussed.

TOPIC ORGANIZATION

Chapter topics are arranged from the simple to the complex. These problem-solving activities are interrelated. For example, attention is necessary for the higher level skill acquisition of concept organization; concept organization depends on selective attention to relevant features and prior experience, hence memory; *cognitive* mapping is a specific form of memory, and its development overlaps with that of social cognition. Language facilitates and influences learning at all levels.

These problem-solving activities are discussed in the context of the problem-solving analysis shown in Figure 1. This problem-solving analysis is cumulative; at each level of problem solving, the skills involved in the preceding component(s) are required. At the first level, that of stimulus differentiation, the child recognizes the existence of a problem. The child identifies and discriminates the relevant aspects of the problem from the irrelevant aspects. At the second level, that of selective attention, the child learns to attend to certain aspects or attributes of stimuli, and to ignore others. At the third level, that of response generation, it is necessary for the child to generate alternative responses or hypotheses about solutions to the problem. At the fourth level, that of response execution, the child tests a hypothesis.

At the fifth level, that of appropriate response to feedback, it is necessary for the child to test or evaluate the feasibility or correctness of the hypothesis selected. Not all responses are correct; not all responses are incorrect. Some

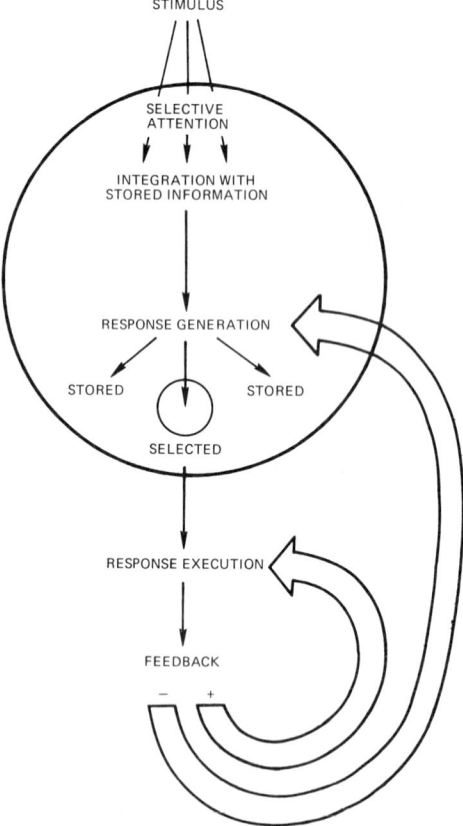

Fig. 1. Problem-solving analysis. The skills needed in the previous component(s) are required at each level of problem solving.

responses are reinforced all of the time; others some of the time; and still others infrequently. The child determines what to do and how to proceed on the basis of the feedback or reinforcement received. At this level, the child learns how to incorporate the information provided by the feedback received. Consequently, the child learns to respond as expected to by those who provide the feedback, or to respond appropriately. Generally, if the child is told that a response is correct, he or she continues testing that response. If the child is told that a response is incorrect, a new response is selected and the original response eliminated. This analysis is one way of describing how the skills of attention, concept organization, memory, language, cognitive mapping, and social cognition are learned. This is an analysis of hypothesis testing behaviors.

THEORIES OF NORMAL CHILD DEVELOPMENT

There are different theories that describe how children proceed and progress through the various levels of stimulus differentiation, selective attention, response generation, response execution, and appropriate response to feedback. Three of these theories are discussed below: Piaget's Stage Theory; Instructional Theory, as posited by Bruner (1973) and Gagné (1975; Gagné & Briggs, 1979); and Levine's (1975) Hypothesis Testing Theory.

Case (1978) differentiates between theories of cognitive development and theories of instruction. A theory of cognitive development describes the learning process; a theory of instruction provides information regarding how this process can be accelerated and facilitated. Learning theories can provide a beginning point in the formulation of educational remediation. For each of the theories discussed below, the theory's implications for remediation are emphasized.

Stage Theory

A theorist prominent in cognitive developmental psychology is the stage theorist Piaget (1969). Case (1978) discusses a neo-Piagetian theory that bridges the gap between Piaget's theory of learning and an educational or instructional theory. Piaget's theory is described in detail through the remainder of this book and is summarized only briefly here.

In general, children develop through stages that are defined by different intellectual requirements and accomplishments (Piaget, 1969). At the sensorimotor stage from birth to about 2 years of age, the child interacts with the environment at a motor level. At the preoperational stage (about 2 to 7 years), the child deals with beginning forms of symbolic behavior; at the concrete operational stage (about 8 to 12 years), reasoning increases and certain acts are achieved that require more flexible thought processes. At the formal operation stage (12 years through adulthood), abstract logic predominates.

The child moves from one stage to the next by changes in cognitive structure. Three processes that allow change from one stage to another are assimilation, accommodation, and equilibrium. When the child accommodates information, additional information is added to an already existing set of knowledge; during assimilation, new information changes this existing knowledge or schema. Accommodation and assimilation occur simultaneously. Equilibrium is the balance between assimilation and accommodation.

Case (1978) suggests three major implications of Piaget's theory. First, the child should be taught at his or her level or stage of development; second, exercises should be designed that encourage transition from one stage to the next; and, third, operational structures that underlie specific tasks should be identified. Piaget does not specify how to teach information or knowledge.

Case (1978) proposes a neo-Piagetian theory, including a theory of instruction. Case suggests instruction designed to take into account three aspects of components: (1) structure analysis (task analysis); (2) assessment of the child's current functioning; and (3) instructional design (sequence of instruction). Case describes in detail each of these aspects and suggests very specific designs of strategies to change or facilitate changes in cognitive structure.

Instructional Theory

Bruner (1966, 1973) considers his theory a theory of development and instruction. The child develops from an enactive representation of the word, requiring total motor involvement, to symbolic representation enabling the mental manipulation of abstract symbols. Bruner's theory is rich with implications for the processes of learning and teaching. The school, according to this conceptualization, should be an active facilitator of learning. Rules, rather than specific skills, should be learned. Further, teaching should be directed to the child's present developmental level and should convey new skills in progression from simple to more complex. Bruner's theory is also described in greater detail throughout this book.

Gagné (1968) considers his model of learning as a description rather than a theory. Further, he states that this model is not the only description of the way in which information can be learned. More recently, Gagné and Briggs (1979) revamped the conditions for learning. These conditions include, in sequence: discriminations, concrete concepts, defined concepts, rules, and higher order rules.

At the level of discriminations, Gagné describes the process of differentiating between stimuli on the basis of physical dimensions. At the next level, that of concrete concepts, the child classifies a group stimulus on the basis of common characteristics. Next, defined concepts are established. Defined concepts are differentiated from concrete concepts in that the child must attach and demonstrate the meaning of some particular object, event, or relationship to the concrete concepts. Rules are learned when the child responds consistently to regularities occurring across a variety of situations. Higher order rules are complex combinations of simpler rules. Many similarities between this analysis and Gagné's original analysis (Gagné, 1968) are apparent.

General Considerations

Gagné and Briggs (1979) expand this description of learning to include principles of instructional design. Basic assumptions about instructional design are that: (1) the individual benefits; (2) long- and short-term goals are planned; (3) the design is systematic (e.g., a systems approach); and (4) instruction is based on knowledge of how children learn (e.g., contiguity, repetition, and reinforcement).

Gagné and Briggs describe categories of learned capabilities. These are intellectual skills, cognitive strategies, verbal information, motor skills, and attitude. Gagné and Briggs advocate the teaching of cognitive strategies, defined as internally organized plans that select and guide problem-solving behavior. A cognitive strategy is an internally controlled process by which the child attends, learns, remembers, modifies, and thinks (Gagné, 1975). This process involves such skills as analysis and synthesis and deductive and inductive reasoning. Gagné and Briggs (1979) elaborate how to design cognitive strategies in detail.

Hypothesis Testing Theory

In the 1970s, there was a resurgence of interest in the hypothesis testing theory of cognitive development (Gholson, Levine, & Phillips, 1972, Levine, 1975). The hypothesis-testing task, employing the blank trials procedure, was widely extended to research with children (Eimas, 1969, 1970; Gholson et al., 1972).

The procedure involves presenting the child with a pair of stimuli similar to those shown in Figure 2. Each stimulus differs on one of four dimensions (e.g., color, size, detail, form) from the other stimulus. For example, the top left stimulus in Figure 2 is big, triangular, yellow, and dotted. The left stimulus differs from the one on the right on a cue on each of four dimensions. The child's task is to determine the cue the experimenter has determined as solution. During the procedure, the child is given feedback only on certain trials, referred to as feedback trials. Four blank-trial probes, where the child is not told the consequences of his or her choice, are interspersed between two feedback trials. The order in which the child chooses one member of the stimulus pair on the blank-trial probe reveals the hypothesis tested. The child may test hypotheses, defined in this task as stimulus attributes (e.g., yellow, triangle) or response sets. Three responses to either the left or the right side of the card, and one choice to the alternate side correspond to stimulus attribute. Two responses to one side and two responses to the other, or four responses to one side, do not correspond to hypotheses.

Levine (1975) outlines assumptions underlying Hypothesis Testing Theory. First, hypotheses are sampled, at random, from a pool of hypotheses. Second, a hypothesis is selected and tested; if feedback is positive, that choice is retained; if feedback is negative, that choice is changed and another selected. Third, strategies are inferred from response patterns. Fourth, responses are organized so as to lead to solutions of problems. Hypothesis Testing Theory uses the following

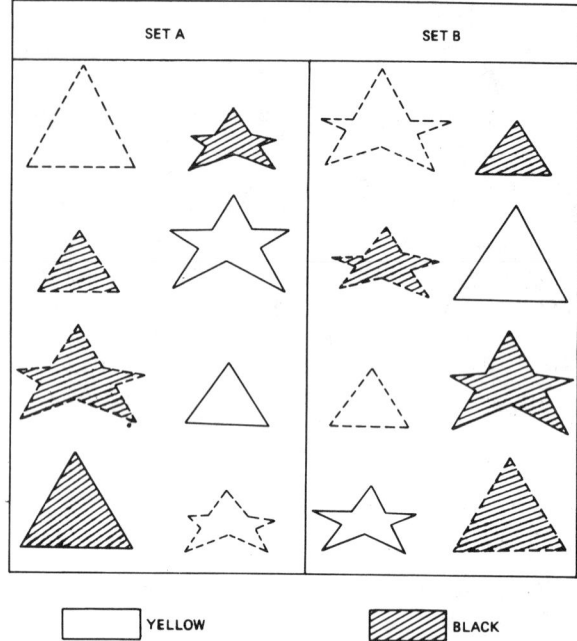

Fig. 2. Hypothesis testing stimuli for feedback trials (Set A) and blank-trial probes (Set B).

problem-solving analyses: stimulus differentiation, selective attention, response generation, response execution, and response to feedback (Parrill-Burnstein, 1978). Hypothesis Testing Theory is the main theoretical position stressed in this book.

To summarize, general implications from theories described suggest that learning is an active process, is systematic, and proceeds through various information processing levels. Instructional frameworks emphasizing the consideration of the level at which the child is currently functioning, an analysis of the types of stimulation presented, and the teaching of sequences of steps are reviewed. Particular attention is paid to the role of task or component analysis, with an emphasis on teaching strategies rather than isolated skills. In the next section, theories regarding children with learning disabilities are described and discussed. When possible, educational implications are drawn from the theoretical orientations discussed above.

THEORIES OF CHILDREN WITH LEARNING DISABILITIES

In this section, theories of the impact of learning disabilities on the processes of attention, concept organization, language, memory, cognitive mapping, and social cognition are discussed. Learning disabilities as a problem-solving difference affecting the organization of behavior, that is, the formation and use of efficient strategies due primarily to information processing deficits is proposed.

Attention

Attention is the process of stimulus selection (Neiseer, 1976) or selective perception (Gibson, 1969). Strauss and Lehtinen (1947) provide educational implications for teaching many of the first children who were identified as having intact intelligence but attentional problems. These authors identify what they refer to as a general disruption in attention. More specifically, behavioral disruptions are posited as arising from three factors: disinhibition, hyperactivity, and distractibility. Disinhibition is defined as the child's distraction by inner factors; distractibility is defined as attention to irrelevant factors within the environment; and, hyperactivity is defined as excessive motor performance. Their teaching techniques are designed to tap undamaged resources and control such overt behaviors as inattention and motor drive.

This early approach by Strauss and Lehtinen (1947) is reflected in the *Diagnostic and Statistics Manual of Mental Disorders*, 3rd ed. *(DSM* III; 1980). In the *DSM* III, a problem with attention, referred to as Attention Deficit Disorder, is described. Characteristics associated with this disorder may or may not include hyperactivity, but do include such behavior descriptions as inattention and impulsivity. This presentation is described in greater detail in the chapter on attention.

Strauss and Lehtinen also discussed four educational goals. These were to (1) maintain and control external factors; (2) help the child develop voluntary control; (3) encourage cooperation; and (4) teach the child to accept the contributions of other classmates. Cruickshank (1966) designed specific conditions modeled after Strauss and Lehtinen to modify and maximize such information-processing problems as inattention.

Cruickshank (1966) outlined external factors, such as the specific physical organization of the classroom, that should be considered in the design of educational programs for children with behavior problems. Cruickshank described such concepts as overstimulation, perceptual dysfunction, and multisensory processing. Overstimulation referred to the presentation of so much information that the child was distracted by irrelevant features or was unable to attend to selective aspects of any of the stimulus features. A perceptual dysfunction implied a basic problem in perception. Multisensory processing was to provide information that was processed through more than one sensory modality simultaneously (e.g., audition and taction). Today, researchers such as Ross (1976), and Dykman et al. (1971) focus more on defining the limits imposed by attentional factors than on educational implications. These theories are described in detail in the chapter on attention.

Concept Organization

Concept organization is the combination of concepts in different relationships. Researchers studying concept organization have examined information processing in children with learning disabilities (e.g., Farnham-Diggory, 1978). Pertinent researchers are Torgesen and Goldman (1977), Keogh (1977), and Parrill-Burnstein and Baker-Ward (1979). General conclusions are that children with learning disabilities actively process and organize information, and formulate strategies based on that information.

Information processing theorists provide a slightly different perspective about how the child with learning disabilities learns. There is a stronger focus on overt behavior, and on experimentally manipulating conditions to document changes in behavior. Implications for remedial planning stem from this orientation.

Memory

Memory is retention of information. Theories of memory suggest that children with learning disabilities demonstrate problems attending selectively to relevant information (Tarver et al., 1976); generating verbal encoding strategies spontaneously (Bryan, 1972; Parrill-Burnstein & Baker-Ward, 1979; Tarver et al., 1976); and responding appropriately to feedback (Parrill-Burnstein & Baker-Ward, 1979). It is generally assumed that deficits in information processing affecting memory capabilities underlie learning disabilities. Some researchers suggest that this deficit is manifested as a developmental delay (e.g., Tarver et al., 1976); others suggest an information processing difference (e.g., Parrill-Burnstein & Baker-Ward, 1979).

Language

Theorists interested in language and language disorders are Johnson and Myklebust (1967) and Myklebust (1954). In a classic textbook, *Learning Disabilities: Educational Principles and Practices*, Johnson and Myklebust define and delineate language; outline the psychoneurologic theoretical position; and, most importantly, suggest a philosophical framework for designing and implementing remedial techniques for children with learning disabilities.

Language functioning is defined in terms of receptive, inner, and expressive abilities. Receptive language abilities are involved in the understanding of spoken or written words, phrases, and sentences. Inner language abilities are involved in the symbolic representations of experience. Expressive language abilities are those involved in verbal output.

Johnson and Myklebust describe in detail techniques to remediate learning disabilities and language deficits. They suggest that children with learning disabilities demonstrate psychoneurologic dysfunctions that affect their language performance, but not their potential. The "psychological" part of the term psychoneurologic refers to a dysfunction in overt behavior. This behavioral disruption provides data to aid in the formulation of inferences about "neurologic" integrity, hence the term *psychoneurological*. Behavioral deviations are attributed to neurologic causes, regardless of the age of onset of the child's learning difficulties. These neurologic determinants of learning disabilities are believed to exist despite the child's intact appearance (e.g., normal EEG), and are considered congenital in etiology (Myklebust & Boshes, 1960). This theoretical perspective influences principles for remediation.

Generally, the scientists originally associated with the psychoneurologic dysfunctions theory were major contributors to the field of remediation and educational planning. Consistent with contemporary perspectives, they suggested that the teaching of strategies rather than specific skills should be the goal of educating children with learning disabilities. The control of both external and internal factors is generally implied, and sometimes specified, within the design of the remedial procedures suggested by the proponents of psychoneurologic dysfunctions theory.

Johnson and Myklebust (1967) outlined 11 principles for remediation: These were (1) individualize the problem; (2) teach to the level of involvement; (3) teach to the type of involvement;(4) teach according to readiness; (5) structure the task so that input precedes output; (6) teach to the child's tolerance levels; (7) take into account the effects of multisensory stimulation; (8) use integrities (i.e., the child's strengths) when modifying the child's processing deficits; (9) control other important variables (e.g., rate of presentation); (10) improve both verbal and nonverbal skills; and (11) take into account neurologic considerations.

Additional principles to consider in planning remediation include the following: (1) determine the changes the child encounters in moving from group instruction to a clinical working relationship; (2) identify the child's present strategies; (3) when possible, pair verbal and visual information during instruction; (4) determine the impact of the learning disability on social cognition; and (5) design teaching techniques based on task analysis (employed by Johnson and Myklebust when designing remedial suggestions).

Lerner (1976) further articulates the task analysis format used in remediation. She suggests that both the task presentation (stimulus) and response be analyzed; that is, broken down into a series of steps or components that lead to solution of problems. Lerner specifies five questions that must be answered in analyzing a task: (1) What does the task require in terms of receptive and expressive abilities? (2) What type of sensory involvement does the child have? (3) What is the nature of the task (verbal or nonverbal)? (4) What are the social and nonsocial contributions of the task? (5) What skills are acquired in performing and how does the child's learning disability involve these skills?

Cognitive Mapping

Cognitive mapping is the ability to represent through spatial imagery concepts and knowledge. Kephart (1975), Getman (1965), Frostig (1972), and Barsch (1967) have constructed theories based on the perceptual motor factors that underlie the appropriate development of cognitive mapping skills. Generally, these theories posit that higher level processing develops out of the adequate development of perceptual motor systems. Further, they suggest that motor development influences the acquisition of many other learned behaviors. Motor responses are the first behaviors learned, and are initially used to express output. Body movement in space is stressed when discussing motor movement.

Kephart (1975), a major proponent of this theoretical position, emphasizes normal motor development of children without learning problems. Kephart suggests that problems in school are related to difficulties in assimilating critical experiences related to time, space, and movement.

Getman (1965), an optometrist, specifies educational implications stemming from the investigation of motor and visual motor processes. Getman (1946), describes developmental stages of perception that can be facilitated through training. These stages progress from innate reflexes to locomotion to more coordinated movements, (such as eye-hand movements), to occular motor to speech motor to visual to perceptual to abstraction based on elaboration and integration of information. A child must acquire a stable foundation at the earlier stages in order to function well at the later stages (Gearheart, 1973).

Barsch (1967) formulates a theory of education that reflects his background as a teacher of physically handicapped and neurologically impaired children (Gearheart, 1973). Barsch's theory is referred to as *movigenics*, which emphasizes that proper motor development is essential to the appropriate development of perception and cognition. Barsch provides specific training exercises designed within the context of his theory of movement as a critical component.

These perceptual motor theorists suggest that techniques based on motor development, and the interrelationship between motor and the development of visual and perceptual capabilities, are important contributions to school learning. Most stress the importance of movement and ignore, for the most part, the role of language in development.

Social Cognition Theory

Children with learning disabilities are observed to have problems interacting with others, leading to the hypothesis that learning disabilities have an impact on social cognition. Basically, problems in social cognition are difficulties interpreting the behaviors of others. This affects the child's skill when interacting appropriately with others. To date, most of the emphasis in the study of the social cognitive skills of children with learning disabilities has been on the impressions of others (e.g., Bryan, 1978). Kronick (1976) points out the importance of a sociologic perspective of children with learning disabilities. She implies that the child's interpretation of social circumstances be taken into account when attempting to understand the problems of children with learning disabilities. Parrill-Burnstein and Baker-Ward (1979) emphasize the importance of the learning disabled child's response to social stimuli in various contexts. From most of this research, it is apparent that the child's abilities to generate hypotheses and utilize feedback are particularly relevant when discussing the social cognitive inferences.

SUMMARY

The perspective taken in this book is that information processing analyses provide necessary data for the study, design, and implementation of educational remediation. To accomplish this, research in the fields of education, psychology, and learning disabilities is integrated. Furthermore, this book is organized sequentially into the topics of attention, concept organization, memory, language, cognitive mapping, and social cognition. A simultaneous relationship between processes is also stressed. These research topics are presented in the context of the problem-solving sequence of selective attention, response generation, response execution, and appropriate response to feedback. It is proposed that learning disabilities is a problem-solving difference affecting the organization of behavior, that is, the use and formation of strategies, due to information processing deficits.

REFERENCES

Barsch, R. H. *Achieving perceptual motor efficiency*. Seattle, Washington: Special Child Publications, 1967.

Bruner, J. S. *Toward a theory of instruction*. Cambridge: Harvard University Press, 1966.

Bruner, J. S. *Beyond the information given*. New York: W. W. Norton, 1973.

Bryan, T. The effects of forced mediation upon short-term memory of children with learning disabilities. *Journal of Learning Disabilities*, 1972, 5, 605–609.

Bryan, T. Social relationships and verbal interactions of learning disabled children. *Journal of Learning Disabilities*, 1978, 10(8), 107–115.

Case, R. Piaget and beyond: Toward a developmentally based theory of instruction. In R. Glaser (Ed.), *Advances in instructional psychology*. Hillsdale, New York: Halsted Press, 1978.

Cruickshank, W. M. *The teacher of brain-injured children*. New York: Syracuse University Press, 1966.

Diagnostic and statistics manual of mental disorders. (DSM-III), 3rd ed). Washington D.C.:American Psychiatric Association, 1980. New York: Syracuse University Press, 1966.

Dykman, R. A., Ackerman, P. T. Clements, S. D., et al. Specific learning disabilities. In H. R. Myklebust (Ed.), *Progress in learning disabilities* (Vol. II). New York: Grune & Stratton, 1971.

Eimas, P. D. A developmental study of hypothesis behavior and focusing. *Journal of Experimental Child Psychology*, 1969, *8*, 1960–1972.

Eimas, P. D. Effects of memory aids on hypothesis behavior and focusing in young children and adults. *Journal of Experimental Child Psychology*, 1970, *10*, 319–336.

Farnham-Diggory, S. Learning disabilities. In J. Bruner, M. Cole, & B. Lloyd (Eds.), *The developing child series*. Cambridge: Harvard University Press, 1978.

Flavell, J. H. *Cognitive development*. Englewood Cliffs, N.J.: Prentice-Hall, 1977.

Frostig, M. Visual perception, integrative functions, and academic learning. *Journal of Learning Disabilities*, 1972, *5*, 1–15.

Gagné, R. M. Contributions of learning to human development. *Psychological Review*, 1968, *75*, 177–191.

Gagné, R. M. *Essentials of learning for instruction*. Hinsdale, Illinois: The Dryden Press, 1975.

Gagné, R. M., & Briggs, L. J. *Principles of instructional design*. New York: Holt, Rinehart & Winston, 1979.

Gearheart, B. C. *Learning disabilities: Educational strategies*. St. Louis: C. V. Mosby, 1973.

Getman, G. The visual-motor complex in the acquisition of learning skills. In J. Hellmuth (Ed.), *Learning disorders* (Vol. 1). Seattle: Special Child Publications, 1965.

Gholson, B., Levine, M., & Phillips, S. Hypothesis strategies and stereotypes in discrimination learning. *Journal of Experimental Child Psychology*, 1972, *13*, 423–446.

Gibson, E. J. *Principles of perceptual learning and development*. New York: Appleton-Century-Crofts, 1969.

Johnson, D. J., & Myklebust, H. *Learning disabilities: Educational principles and practices*. New York: Grune & Stratton, 1967.

Keogh, B. *Implications of research on attentional problems*. Paper read at the International Conference of the Association for Children with Learning Disabilities, Washington, D.C., 1977.

Kephart, N. C. The perceptual-motor match. In W. M. Cruickshank & D. P. Hallahan (Eds.), *Perceptual and learning disabilities in children: Psychoeducational practices* (Vol. 1). New York: Syracuse University Press, 1975.

Kronick, D. The importance of a sociological perspective towards learning disabilities. *Journal of Learning Disabilities*, 1976, *9*(2), 115–119.

Lerner, J. W. *Children with learning disabilities*. Atlanta: Houghton Mifflin, 1976.

Levine, M. *A cognitive theory of learning: Research on hypothesis testing*. Hillsdale, New York: Lawrence Erlbaum Associates, 1975.

Myklebust, H. R. *Auditory disorders in children: A manual for differential diagnosis*. New York: Grune & Stratton, 1954.

Myklebust, H. R., & Boshes, B. Psychoneurological learning disorders in children. In E. C. Frierson & W. B. Barbe (Eds.), *Educating children with learning disabilities (II)*. New York: Appleton-Century-Croft, 1967, pp 26–35.

Neisser, U. *Cognition and reality*. San Francisco: W. H. Freeman, 1976.

Parrill-Burnstein, M. Teaching kindergarten children to solve problems: An information processing approach. *Child Development*, 1978, *49*(3), 700–706.

Parrill-Burnstein, M., & Baker-Ward, L. Learning disabilities: A social cognitive difference. *Learning Disabilities: An Audio Journal for Continuing Education,* vol. III (10), 1979.
Piaget, J. *The child's conception of the world.* Paterson, N.J.: Littlefield, 1969.
Strauss, A., & Lehtinen, L. *Psychopathology and education of the brain-injured child.* New York: Grune & Stratton, 1947.
Ross, A. O. *Psychological aspects of learning disabilities and reading disorders.* New York: McGraw-Hill, 1976.
Tarver, S. G., Hallahan, D. P., Kauffman, J. M., et al. Verbal rehearsal and selective attention in children. *Journal of Experimental Child Psychology,* 1976, *22*(3), 375–385.
Torgesen, J., & Goldman, T. Verbal rehearsal and short-term memory in reading disabled children. *Child Development,* 1977, *48*(1), 56–60.

FURTHER READINGS

Baldwin, A. L. *Theories of child development.* New York: John Wiley & Sons, 1967.
Bower, T. G. R. *Human development.* San Francisco: W. H. Freeman, 1979.
Braga, J. S., & Braga, J. *Growing with children: The early childhood years.* Englewood Cliffs, N.J.: Prentice-Hall, 1974.
Bryan, T. H., & Bryan, J. H. *Understanding learning disabilities* (2nd ed.). Sherman Oaks, N.Y.: Alfred Publishing Company, 1978.
Duke, M., & Norwicki, S. *Abnormal psychology: Perspectives on being different.* Monterey, California: Brooks/Cole, 1979.
Farnham-Diggory, S. *Learning disabilities: A psychological perspective.* Cambridge, Mass.: Harvard University Press, 1978.
Flavell, J. H. *Cognitive development.* Englewood Cliffs, N.J.: Prentice-Hall, 1977.
Gibson, E. J. *Principles of perceptual learning and development.* New York: Appleton-Century-Crofts, 1969.
Gottlieb, M. I., Zinkus, P. W., & Bradford, L. J. (Eds.). *Current issues in developmental pediatrics: The learning-disabled child.* New York: Grune & Stratton, 1979.
Hallahan, D. P., & Kauffman, D. P. *Introduction to learning disabilities: A psychobehavioral approach.* Englewood Cliffs, N.J.: Prentice-Hall, 1976.
Haring, N. G., Bateman, B., Gleason, G. B., et al. *Teaching the learning disabled child.* Englewood Cliffs, N.J.: Prentice-Hall, 1977.
Hammill, D. D., & Bartel, N. R. (Eds.). *Educational perspectives in learning disabilities.* New York: John Wiley & Sons, 1971.
Hoffman, M. L., & Hoffman, L. W. (Eds.). *Child development research* (Vol. 1). New York: Russell Sage Foundation, 1964.
Hoffman, M. L., & Hoffman, L. W. (Eds.). *Child development research* (Vol. 2). New York: Russell Sage Foundation, 1966.
Johnson, S. W., & Morasky, R. L. *Learning disabilities* (2nd ed.). Boston: Allyn & Bacon, 1980.
Lerner, J. W. *Children with learning disabilities: Theories, diagnosis, teaching strategies* (2nd ed.). Boston: Houghton Mifflin, 1976.

McCarthy, J. J., & McCarthy, J. F. *Learning disabilities*. Boston: Allyn & Bacon, 1969.

Mussen, P. H. (Ed.). *Handbook of research methods in child development*. New York: John Wiley & Sons, 1960.

Mussen, P. H. (Ed.). *Manual of child psychology* (3rd ed.; Vol. I). New York: John Wiley & Sons, 1970.

Mussen, P. H. (Ed.). *Manual of child psychology* (3rd ed; Vol. II). New York: John Wiley & Sons, 1970.

Myers, P. I., & Hammill, D. D. *Methods for learning disorders*. New York: John Wiley & Sons, 1976.

Rosner, J. *Helping children overcome learning difficulties: A step-by-step guide for parents and teachers*. New York: Walker, 1975.

Ross, A. O. *Learning disability: The unrealized potential*. New York: McGraw-Hill, 1977.

Sabatino, D. A., & Miller, T. L. (Eds.). *Describing learner characteristics of handicapped children and youth*. New York: Grune & Stratton, 1979.

Weiner, I. B., & Elkind, D. *Readings in child development*. New York: John Wiley & Sons, 1972.

White, B. L. *The first years of life*. New York: Avon Books, 1975.

Yussen, S. R., & Santrock, J. W. *Child development*. Dubuque, Iowa: William C. Brown, 1978.

1
Attention

Attention is a basic information process that is frequently defined within the context of perception. Attention is the process of stimulus selection (Ross, 1976) or selective perception (Pick, Frankel, & Hess, 1975). Perception is the integration of sensory stimulation with the anticipatory schema of the perceiver (Neisser, 1976). Attention is part of three ongoing processes: *attention and perception, attention and memory,* and *attention and cognition* (Pick et al., 1975). Research is organized according to these processes.

In a recent review of the findings on attention of infants and young children, Pick et al. (1975), suggested guidelines for research: the roles of the perceiver, the environment, and development. Pick pointed out that although data were available about the effects of environmental stimulation on attention, there were few studies regarding the behaviors and development of the perceiver.

Developmental trends associated with attention are not clear-cut; perception changes with age and experience. Wright and Vlietstra (1975) summarize the development of attention within the context of their search-exploration theory. Preschool children tend to attend to the most salient characteristics of the stimulus, to position cues, and to random items. Between 5 and 7 years of age, children scan a visual array more systematically, though scanning is still erratic. Around 6 years of age, children can direct attention toward a recognized goal. Older children, 10 to 14 years, increase instrumental or instructional learning and recall more central or task-relevant information (Hagen & Kail, 1975). A number of theories are proposed to describe these changes in development.

THEORIES OF ATTENTION

Central to all theories of perception reviewed in this discussion are the following aspects: the role of the perceiver (active-passive); the acquisition of stimulation (filter-pickup); and the concept of capacity (limited-unlimited). Theories are organized according to the Theory of Specificity (Gibson, 1969; Pick et al., 1975), the Gestalt Perceptual Theory of Learning (Asch, 1969; Kohler, 1941), the Information Processing Theory (Broadbent, 1958; Neisser, 1976), and the Theory of Orienting Responses (Wright & Vlietstra, 1975).

Theory of Specificity

Pick et al. (1975) describe attention as a process of selection. They suggest that the study of attention is the study of how this selection process occurs. Attention is treated not as an isolated construct, but as an ongoing process that is part of the cognitive activities of perception, memory, and thought. Their review of selective perception is consistent with data summarized in the next chapter under the topic of Simple Concept Selection (page 000-000) and is not dealt with here.

Similar to Pick et al., Gibson (1969) defines perception as a selective process. During information processing, perceptions become more specific; that is, more differentiated and precise (Gibson & Gibson, 1955). The perceiver does not learn to process previously unavailable stimuli; rather, an increase in the ability to extract additional information occurs. Although this information was previously available in the environment, it was not picked up by the perceiver. In this way, changes in perception stem from children's inward responsivity to cues they did not previously utilize. Perceivers are limited by both the environment and their stage of development in the amount and type of information processed.

Gibson describes three processes as basic to the mechanism of perceptual learning: abstraction or recognition of critical properties which differentiate stimuli; filtration of irrelevant stimuli; and integration of perceived information. Perceptual learning is an increase in the ability to obtain new information from stimuli in the environment (Gibson, 1969).

Gestalt Perceptual Theory of Learning

Gestalt Perceptual Theory is a theory of selectivity. Similar to Gibson (1969), the gestalt psychologists emphasize the process of differentiation in perceptual development (e.g., Kohler, 1959). Attention is viewed as an ongoing part of perception. Perceptual learning is the result of the reorganization or dynamic redistribution of neurologic activity. Insight or learning occurs through perceptual reorganization as well (Postman & Riley, 1957). The major focus of the Gestaltists is on the nature or formation of associations (Asch, 1961; Asch,

Ceraso, & Heimer, 1960). Associations are differentiated and articulated rather than simply added together (Kohler, 1941). Associations are the aftereffects of perception which may persist as memory traces to be activated later (Asch, 1969). The formation of associations is directly determined by perceptual relationships (Asch, 1961). Perceptual relationships are a function of the total configuration of the situation (the gestalt, or the whole; Koffka, 1931). Gestalt theory was a predominating theory of the 1950s and early 1960s.

Information Processing Theory

In sharp contrast to the Theory of Selectivity and Gestalt Perceptual Theory of Learning, Information Processing Theory takes into account the cognitive or internal aspects of attention. Broadbent (1958), a major information processing theorist, assumes that irrelevant information is filtered out at multiple levels of processing. Broadbent suggests that the perceiver is limited in the capacity to process all peripherally available information. Furthermore, what is processed is processed through a single central center.

Neisser (1976) suggests that the Gibsonian Theory of Selectivity is incomplete in describing attention; cognitive structuring or internalization of information is not addressed. To deal with cognition, Neisser proposes the concept of a perceptual cycle. The focus of this concept is on the active participation of the child and the continuous process of perception. This perceptual cycle consists of an initial stimulus, pre-existing structures or schema, and overt and covert processing. The diagram of the perceptual cycle, describing visual perception, is shown in Fig. 1-1. This diagram can be applied to describe the perception of other sensory information, and illustrates a complex interrelationship expressed as schema.

This schema and available stimulation determine what information is perceived. Schema is the internal organization of information. This allows the anticipation of certain kinds of stimulus input, and directs the exploration of the sensory organs in preparing the perceiver for active learning. What is picked up during exploration modifies existing schema, which in turn modifies further exploration. Unlike traditional information processing theorists (i.e., Broadbent, 1958), Neisser (1976) proposes that unwanted information is not filtered out—it is simply not attended to. Selection is a positive process, internal to the organism, which is manifested in covert behavior.

Neisser also criticizes the assumptions of a single processing center and limited capacity to process information. He suggests that the concept of limited capacity implies both a passive participant and limitations in brain capacity. To refute both assumptions, Neisser notes the abilities to learn new information in new ways throughout life, as well as the ability to process simultaneously or attend selectively to information for more than one modality or within the same modality.

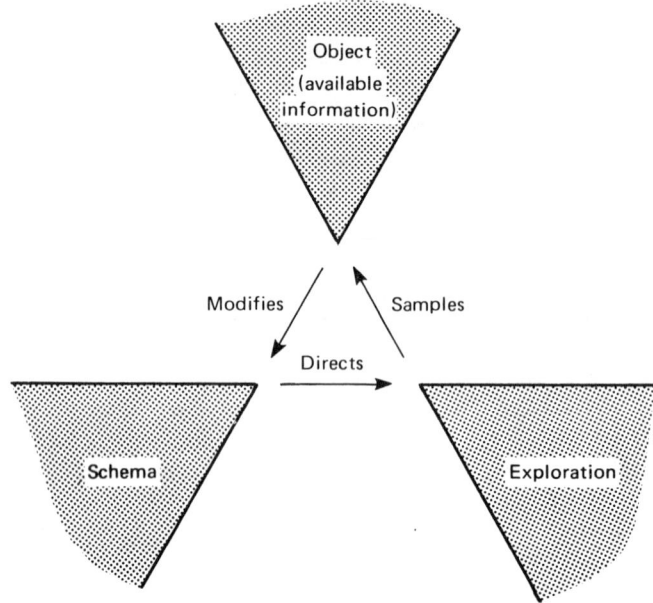

Fig. 1-1. Neisser's perceptual cycle (From *Cognition and Reality* by Ulric Neisser. W. H. Freeman and Company. Copyright © 1976. Reprinted with permission.)

Theory of Orienting Responses

Wright and Vlietstra (1975) discuss the development of systematic information processing in children. These authors suggest that major shifts in development occur with a change in the nature of the stimulus variables that control behavior. Two information processes are discussed. These are exploration and search, which are reflected in observing behaviors. During both exploration and search, the organism acquires information from the environment. How this information is acquired distinguishes these two processes. Exploration is motivated by curiosity and guided by stimulus salience. Exploration (1) is more spontaneous and less systematic; (2) consists of shorter sequences; (3) shows less continuity from one sequence to another; (4) is more divergent; and (5) is influenced by salience of stimulation. Search behavior, on the other hand, (1) is more task- and goal-oriented; (2) consists of instrumental responding; and (3) is of two types—perception and logic. Wright and Vlietstra propose that the development of both search and exploration progress from general to more specific and systematic processing.

In general, most of the theorists reviewed concluded that processing of global characteristics to more specific attributes occurs with development. This was referred to as selective attention (Neisser, 1976), or selective perception (e.g., Pick et al., 1975), reflecting the interrelationship between attention and perception. The most prevalent view, with respect to the role of the perceiver, was that stimulation was perceived and processed by an active participant rather than passive observer. The question of limited capacity is not yet resolved, although Neisser's view represents the most recent opinion.

THEORIES OF LEARNING DISABILITIES AND ATTENTION

The Attention Deficit Disorder was recently listed in the latest edition of the *Diagnostic and Statistics Manual of Mental Disorders (DSM*-III). This term was used to describe the behaviors of children with and without hyperactivity who were experiencing learning problems. Cardinal characteristics associated with this disorder are inattention, impulsivity, and, possibly, hyperactivity. Onset is before the age of 7; the duration of the disorder is at least 6 months. The Attention Deficit Disorder is not due to schizophrenia, affective disorder, or severe or profound mental retardation.

Kopell (1979) summarizes the Attentional Deficit Hypothesis position. Proponents of this position suggest that children with learning disabilities differ from children without learning problems in their abilities to select or allocate processing capacity. Another common conclusion is that these children have problems sustaining attention (Douglas, 1974; Dykman et al., 1971; Keogh & Margolis, 1976; Ross, 1976).

The Attentional Deficit Hypothesis, as applied to learning disabilities, is not a new concept and data are available (e.g., Strauss & Lehtinen, 1947). There are also a number of recent reviews of theory and research (Harris, 1976; Koppell, 1979; Torgesen, 1977). The focus of much of this research is on the role of attention and perception in learning (e.g., Dykman et al., 1971).

Children with adequate capabilities and inadequate performance were described as having attentional deficits as early as the 1940s by Strauss and Lehtinen (1947). These pioneers focused on three aspects of attention: hyperactivity, distractibility, and disinhibition. Hyperactivity referred to excessive motor activity. Distractibility referred to attention to irrelevant or extraneous variables, as well as difficulty sustaining attention. Disinhibition referred to internal distraction rather than external distraction. (Later, the term perseveration was introduced to describe excessive repetitive behaviors.) Texts in the early 1960s reflected this position and stressed the importance of providing uncomplicated and understimulating educational environments for learning disabilities children (Cruickshank, 1966).

During the late 1960s and early 1970s the study of attention shifted to evaluation of physiologic changes (e.g., Dykman et al., 1971) and information processes (Clements, 1966). Dykman and his associates (Dykman et al., 1970;

Dykman et al., 1971) suggested that learning disabilities resulted from an organically based deficit in attention. These deficits were attributed to neurologic immaturity and were manifested as a developmental lag. Specific deficits in the ability to inhibit responding and in responding to irrelevant stimuli were noted. Deficits in attention were found at the levels of alertness, stimulus selection, and/or vigilance. These problems were symptoms of a more generalized deficit, sustaining attention, which was accompanied by a decrease in physiologic activity. It was concluded that attention and physiologic deficits changed as a function of maturation and experience.

Along these same lines, Douglas (1972, 1974) described attentional problems as involving one or more of the following: (1) impulsive control; (2) the ability to analyze information; (3) the ability to plan information; (4) the ability to organize information. Working with hyperactive children, Douglas (1972) suggested that the core symptoms were (1) the inability to sustain attention and (2) the inability to control impulses.

Recently, Ross (1976) suggested learning disabilities as a developmental lag in selective attention, that is, in the ability to use and sustain attention. Selective attention was defined as an adaptive capacity enabling responsivity to certain stimuli or to a combination of stimuli at any given time. The capacity of selective attention changed with age. Ross described three primary aspects of attention. These were arousal, attentiveness, and concentration. Arousal was associated with a physiologic dimension (i.e., a continuum in which sleep is at one extreme and wakefulness is at the other). Attention referred to the readiness of the organism to perceive and process incoming stimulation. Concentration referred to whether or not attention was global or specific.

Ross (1976) also summarized Berlyne's (1970) analysis of the processes involved in selective attention. These were attention in learning, attention in remembering, and attention in performance. Attention in learning referred to stimulus response associations, that is, learning to respond to specific stimuli. Attention in memory referred to the information that was attended to and retained. Attention in performance referred to attention to certain stimuli that elicited previously reinforced responses.

The ability to sustain attention was also mentioned within an educational context by Keogh and Margolis (1976). These researchers analyzed attention into three components. These were (1) coming to attention; (2) making decisions; and (3) sustaining attention. Coming to attention involved two aspects—extraneous and possibly disruptive motor activity, and the selection and organization of salient irrelevant aspects of the task. Keogh (1971) suggested that hyperactive children demonstrated deficits at this level of attention. Decision making referred to the tempo or speed of the response. Maintaining attention referred to sustained attention. Keogh and Margolis suggested that children with learning disabilities may have problems with any of these components.

In summary, the Attentional Deficit Hypothesis gained support when physiologic responses were examined (e.g., Dykman et al., 1971; Rourke & Czudner, 1972), overt actions evaluated (Douglas, 1972; Strauss & Lehtinen, 1947), and particularly when sustained attention was measured (e.g., Ross, 1976). Recent research findings support this hypothesis in describing the problems of some children with learning disabilities.

RESEARCH REVIEW

Most of the research reviewed in this section employed a normal control or comparison group rather than providing set norms for performance; therefore, the literature regarding children with and without learning problems are presented together. Research is organized according to the topics *Attention and Perception, Attention and Memory,* and *Attention and Cognition.*

Attention and Perception

The literature reviewed here is subcategorized according to the type of task presented. These tasks are simple reaction time, dysjunctive reaction time, and vigilance. Particular attention is paid to the dependent measures used (e.g., heart rate). Selected studies regarding children diagnosed as having minimal brain dysfunction (MBD) and being hyperactive are included in this review. Here, the terms MBD and learning disabilities are used interchangeably. Not all hyperactive children have learning disabilities and not all children with learning disabilities are hyperactive. However, many children that are hyperactive are not able to pay attention, and have problems acquiring incidental and instructional information. One possible result of hyperactivity may be a discrepancy between potential and achievement, hence, a learning disability.

SIMPLE REACTION TIME TASKS

A simple reaction time task consists of a warning signal and a response stimulus. The period between the warning signal and the onset of the response stimulus is the preparatory interval (PI). The PI starts with the onset of the warning signal and alerts the subject to prepare for the presentation of the response stimulus. During this period, until the onset of the response stimulus, the child is required to maintain attention. With the onset of the response stimulus, the child is required to press a lever or switch as quickly as possible. This simple reaction time task is also referred to as a "speed of motor performance measure." The dysjunctive reaction time task differs from the simple reaction time task in that the subject must respond quickly to certain stimuli and inhibit responding to other stimuli (Sroufe, 1971). Dependent measures associated with these reaction time tasks are cardiac acceleration, response latency, response latency variability, and activity level (Sroufe et al., 1973).

Cardiac deceleration is used as a physiologic measure for assessing developmental changes in the ability to maintain attention. In general, heart rate slows during attention. Sroufe et al. (1973) summarize the conditions under which heart rate deceleration occurs. Heart rate deceleration has been associated with the presence of novel or surprising stimuli, fixation or systematic scanning, anticipation of stimuli, and other circumstances. During anticipation of stimuli, cardiac deceleration is greatest with the stimulus onset, but varies greatly as a function of the length of the preparatory interval.

Cardiac deceleration is calculated in different ways. Sroufe (1971) uses a formula where the heart beat rate occurring at the stimulus onset is subtracted from the heart beat rate occurring three beats from the stimulus response onset. Latency is the time between the presentation of the stimulus and the motor response. Response latency variability is the time differences of the same child across trials. Activity level is the number of switches actively set off by the child's gross motor movements (Sroufe et al., 1973).

Sroufe studied developmental changes in cardiac deceleration using both a simple reaction time task and a dysjunctive reaction time task. The dysjunctive reaction time task required the subject to respond quickly to certain stimuli and inhibit responding to other stimuli. Sroufe's subjects were 6-, 8-, and 10-year-old children. One half of the children in each group received a 5-second PI and one half of the children received a 10-second PI. All received both reaction time tasks. The results showed that reaction time was positively correlated with cardiac deceleration, particularly with 10-year-olds. Children age 6 to 8 did not differ significantly.

Sroufe's (1971) results indicated that the length of the PI affected performance. Reliable deceleration was not found for any group with 10-second PIs. With 5-second PIs, 10-year-old children showed more consistent cardiac deceleration than either 6- or 8-year-old children, who did not differ from each other. The type of the reaction time task was also significant. Ten-year-old children showed greater cardiac deceleration than either the 6- or 8-year-olds when the task was a dysjunctive reaction time task. Eight-year-olds differed significantly from 6-year-olds in the expected direction. With respect to the response latency, 8- and 10-year-olds were significantly faster than 6-year-olds. These findings were consistent with earlier reports relating cardiac deceleration to the quickness of the response (Lacey & Lacey, 1970). Faster reaction times were correlated with greater cardiac deceleration. Deceleration was more consistent at the older ages.

Children with learning disabilities did not respond as expected when cardiac deceleration and reaction time measures were employed. Sroufe et al. (1973) worked with 38 boys between the ages of 7 and 10 years. Of these, 17 children were without learning problems and served as a normal comparison group. The other 21 children were referred to the Pediatric Neurology Clinic of the University of Minnesota Health Science Center for attention deficits and learning disabilities. The majority of these children were taking medication (Ritalin) and made up the experimental group. A simple reaction time task was administered. The warning signal was an auditory tone, and the response stimulus was a bright light. The PI was 5 seconds. The dependent measures were cardiac deceleration, response latency, response latency variability, and activity level of the child. Cardiac deceleration was calculated according to Sroufe's (1971) criteria. Children in the experimental group were tested on or off Ritalin (placebo administered) 6 weeks after the initial testing session to evaluate the effects of medication on attention.

Results obtained for the normal comparison group were similar to those found by Sroufe (1971). Children in this group showed significantly greater cardiac deceleration than those in the experimental group. The two groups did not differ with respect to response latency; however, latency variability did differ between the groups; it was greatest for those in the experimental group. Activity levels were greatest for the children in the experimental group as well. When children in the experimental group were tested 6 weeks later, more appropriate responses were obtained with children on medication but not for those in the placebo group. With respect to the relationship between reaction time and cardiac deceleration, the expected relationship—an increase in cardiac deceleration with an increase in reaction time—was found with the control group but not for the experimental group. Significant age trends were not found.

These findings were interpreted as suggesting that cardiac deceleration associated with the anticipation of a stimulus reflect an attentional process, specifically, that of maintaining attention. This was supported when children referred for attentional problems or learning disabilities did not show the expected responses on reaction time tasks and measures of cardiac deceleration.

Czudner and Rourke (1970, 1972) suggested that the standard reaction time task could be used as a measure of brain damage while varying the PI intervals. They presented data to suggest that simple reaction time was an index of brain damage, and that latency was an index of the severity of the brain damage. In their first study, Czudner and Rourke (1970) used visual stimuli for both the warning signal and the response stimulus. The warning signal was a white light; when illuminated, this light signaled that the children were to maintain attention. The white light was followed by a red light. When the red light was illuminated, it signaled that the children were to press the lever quickly. The PIs were varied. There were eight 2-, 4-, or 8-second intervals presented in blocks of ten trials (regular condition) or randomly distributed over a series of trials (irregular condition). Subjects were 30 children (mean age approximately 10 years; mean I.Q. approximately 105). In the experimental group, 15 children were diagnosed as brain damaged; all but one child had abnormal EEG's. In the comparison group, the 15 children were without learning and behavior problems. Both groups were matched on age and IQ.

Significant differences between the two groups were obtained. Generally, children in the experimental group did significantly better in the regular condition, but only with the 2-second PI. For the comparison group, significant differences were obtained with PI's of 2, 4, and 6 seconds. Longer PIs produced longer latencies. Children in the comparison group also did significantly better in the regular condition. Further analyses indicated that latencies were shorter for blocked presentations when compared to random presentations.

Czudner and Rourke concluded that an increase in latency, with an increase in PI in the regular condition, indicated increased difficulty in maintaining attention. The opposite effect, a decrease in latency with an increase in PI in the irregular condition, was interpreted as indicating that subjects adopted a specific response strategy. They became aware that the longer the PIs, the greater the probability that the onset of the response stimulus would soon occur. Czudner and Rourke also suggested that the relatively ineffective performance of children in the experimental group when short PIs were presented was due to reactive inhibition, which interfered with readiness to respond. With respect to establishing a learning set over trials, it was suggested that children with brain damage did not learn response sets. This conclusion was supported by the increased variability observed within this group.

Using this same paradigm, Rourke and Czudner (1972) investigated reaction time using auditory stimuli. The warning signal was a high-pitched tone. The response stimulus was a low-pitched tone. To activate the warning signal, the child pressed a telegraph key. The warning signal remained on until the onset of the response stimulus. The child's task was to lift his or her finger as quickly as possible when the low tones were presented. Lifting rather than pressing the lever and activating the response signal were the procedural differences from Czudner and Rourke (1970). PI was either 2, 4, or 6 seconds, and was either presented as part of a regular interval (blocked) or as irregular intervals (random). There were two groups of children. The experimental group was made up of 24 children (out of 600 screened), who were diagnosed as having brain damage. The comparison group was made up of 24 children without learning problems. These two groups were further subdivided into younger (average age of the brain-damaged children was 7 years, 7 months, with a range of 7 years, 1 month to 9 years) and older (average age of the brain-damaged children was 11 years, 7 months, with a range of 10 years, 2 months and 13 years, 7 months). Comparison and experimental groups were matched for mean age and for full-scale WISC IQs. Definitions of brain damage described in the first experiment (Czudner & Rourke, 1970) were adhered to in selecting these children.

Results indicated that during the regular condition, reaction time increased as PI increased. With irregular presentations, the relationship was less clear-cut. These findings were similar to those obtained using visual stimuli (Czudner & Rourke, 1970). Age findings indicated that older brain-damaged children reacted faster than younger brain-damaged children. Furthermore, brain-damaged children and children without learning problems did better when the presentation of the stimuli was blocked. Younger brain-damaged children had significantly slower reaction time than either older brain-damaged children or younger normals; these latter two groups did not differ from older children in the normal comparison group.

Rourke and Czudner (1972) interpreted their findings as indicating that older brain-damaged children may indeed compensate or recover from deficits in the ability to maintain attention. Czudner and Rourke (1970, 1972) concluded that the deficits observed with the children with brain damage were not modality-specific and did improve with age.

To summarize, both the reliability of cardiac deceleration response (Sroufe, 1971) and response latencies (Czudner & Rourke, 1970; Rourke & Czudner, 1972) increased after age 10 when children without learning problems were studied. Children with learning problems did not show these increases. In addition to a lack of appropriate physiologic change until after age 11 (Rourke & Czudner, 1972), younger children with brain damage had slower reaction times (Czudner & Rourke, 1970; Rourke & Czudner, 1972). These differences persisted across modalities (Czudner & Rourke, 1970; Rourke & Czudner, 1972). These results were interpreted as indicating that (1) the processing of information for young children with learning problems as well as those with brain damage was slower or delayed; (2) that after age 11, children with brain damage compensated for the effects of the deficit; and (3) children with learning problems have basic difficulties in maintaining or sustaining attention.

DYSJUNCTIVE REACTION TIME OR CONDITIONAL DISCRIMINATION

Dykman and associates (1971) employed a dysjunctive reaction time task or a conditional discrimination task. The term "conditional discrimination" is used in that the subject's response is conditional or dependent upon more than one dimension or cue (e.g., ignore green; react to red). Dykman et al. (1970) studied the performance of 82 boys with learning disabilities (designated as the experimental group) and compared their performance to 34 boys without academic problems (designated as the comparison group). Children with learning disabilities ranged in age from 8 years to 11 years, 11 months with a mean age of 9 years, 3 months.

These children all had at least a 90 full-scale IQ on the WISC and 75% had reading disabilities. Children with learning disabilities were either in special classes for children with learning disabilities or were being screened regarding such placement. From this sample 20 children were classified as hyperactive (median age: 9 years, 3 months); 19 as hypoactive (median age: 9 years, 2 months); and 34 as normoactive (median age: 10 years, 2 months). Mental ages for the children with learning disabilities were (1) 9 years, 10 months for children subclassified as hyperactive; (2) 9 years, 6 months for children subclassified as hypoactive; and (3) 10 years, 8 months for children subclassified as normoactive. Medication was discontinued for 3 to 5 days prior to the experiment. Approximately 23 children in the comparison group (median age: 10 years, 6 months) had WISC intelligence scores in the bright-normal or superior range. Eleven had IQ scores in the 90s. The comparison group had a median mental age of 11 years, 6 months. Chronological age and mental age differences between the groups made these results difficult to interpret.

The experiment was conducted in three phases: conditioning; differentiation; and differentiation and distraction. The procedure was a standard conditional discrimination reaction time task. The stimuli were three lights: red, green, and white. During conditioning, the child was told to press a lever as quickly as possible when a red light was illuminated, and to release the lever as quickly as possible when the white light was illuminated. During the differentiation phase, the same procedure was followed except the green light was sometimes presented alone with the instructions to ignore it. In the differentiation and distraction phase, the child was exposed to a loud hoot that sounded prior to or during the illumination of the colored lights. Children in this phase were told to disregard both the green light and the hoot. Actually, there were distracting stimuli occurring during both differentiation and differentiation and distraction phases. During the differentiation phase, the distracting stimulus was visual; and during the differentiation and distraction phase, the distractions were visual and auditory. Three levels of instruction were provided, each more specific in information.

During the conditioning phase, the results showed that significantly more hyperactive children than comparison children required extra instruction. In general, hyperactive and hypoactive children performed similarly and made more errors than either the normoactive or comparison group. These latter two groups did not differ from each other. The most frequent errors made were between trials (e.g., key playing). In order, from the most to the least errors produced, the groups were hyperactive, hypoactive, normoactive, and comparison. This was interpreted as indicating that hyperactive children had the greatest difficulty maintaining attention, and children without learning problems had the least. With respect to latency data, lever release was faster than lever press. The order of the groups from the slowest to fastest reaction time was hypoactive, normoactive, hyperactive, and comparison. With the introduction of the green light (differentiation phase) and hoot (differentiation and distraction phase), release latencies increased, particularly for children with learning disabilities. Press latencies increased most during differentiation and hooter presentation, particularly for children with learning disabilities.

Dykman et al. (1970) further subdivided the children with and without learning disabilities by age: 8 to 10 years versus 10 to 11 years, 11 months and older. In general, older children have faster reaction times than younger children. Differences as functions of the presence and absence of a learning disability were found. Generally, hypoactive children were significantly slower than children in the other groups under most conditions. Hyperactive children in the youngest group accounted for most of the differences due to age. Fewer differences were observed with older children. With respect to age, a sharp decrease in reaction time was observed with an increase in age.

Because of initial problems in subject sampling, another group of children with learning disabilities was selected with more appropriate IQs and ages. With these children, similar trends were noted, but clear-cut differences were not obtained.

Dykman et al. (1970) interpreted these findings as suggesting that children with learning disabilities processed information at a slower rate than children without learning problems; this slower processing rate hindered performance in academic and nonacademic settings; further, the ability to arouse or maintain attention was deficient in children with learning disabilities, particularly hyperactive children.

In another study, Dykman et al. (1971) worked with 52 children between the ages of 6 and 12 years. Twenty-six were diagnosed as brain damaged and 26 were without learning or behavior problems. Children in the former group made up the experimental group, while those in the latter group made up the comparison group. The apparatus used in the procedure was similar to that described by Dykman et al. (1970. Physiologic measures were skin resistance, cardiac deceleration, and muscle activity. Generally, the task was to press the lever in response to the green light; lift in response to the white light; and ignore in response to the red light.

Results showed that children in the brain-damaged group had slower reaction times, made more impulsive errors, and were less reactive on physiologic measures. Dykman et al. (1971) interpreted these results as indicating that when beginning a task, children with brain damage were at least as alert as those without learning problems. However, children in this group were not able to sustain or maintain that alert state. The deficits were in inhibiting responding and ignoring irrelevant stimuli, which reflected problems sustaining attention. Dykman et al. (1970, 1971) suggested that the observed deficits were due to neurologic immaturity. This was manifested in developmental delays, which changed as a function of experience and physical maturity.

In summary, 10-year-old children without learning disabilities showed consistent physiologic changes during condition discrimination tasks. Children 6 and 8 years of age responded less consistently (Sroufe, 1971). Dykman et al. (1970, 1971) found that children with learning disabilities showed a general decrease in physiologic reactivity, which improved with age. Deficits observed were attributed to neurologic immaturity and reflected psychologic problems in maintaining attention. These results were consistent with those of studies using simple reaction time tasks (Sroufe, 1971; Sroufe et al., 1973).

VIGILANCE

Vigilance is defined as the physiologic and psychological readiness to respond (Anderson, Halcomb, & Doyle, 1973). Attention of this type is reflected in the ability to detect changes in stimuli over a period of sustained observation (Frankmann & Adams, 1962). Vigilance performance is usually assessed by requiring the subject to detect infrequently occurring signals over a given period of time, usually 30 minutes. These infrequently occurring stimuli are presented in the context of regularly occurring stimuli (Anderson et al., 1973). Most research has been conducted with adults. The most frequent findings are that vigilance performance declines over time, and improves with interruptions and regular and consistent presentations of stimuli (e.g., Whittenburg, Ross, & Andrews, 1956).

Kirchner and Knopf (1974) used a vigilance task with 64 second graders classified as either high or low achievers in reading. Their stimulus was a movie of a stationary jet fighter plane against a blue background. A star, which changed colors, was affixed to the jet. The child's task was to push the button whenever the star changed colors. Color changes were random and occurred every 30, 60, 90, or 120 seconds for a half second in duration. Results showed that high achievers made significantly more correct detections than low achievers. The number of correct detections decreased significantly across trials. No sex differences or differences as a function of interval length between presentations were found.

Anderson et al. (1973) studied vigilance performance with 30 children diagnosed as learning disabled, and 30 without learning problems (age range: 8 years, 2 months to 11 years, 4 months; mean age: 9 years, 4 months). Unlike those in the study by Dykman et al. (1971), if the children were taking medication, they continued to do so throughout the experiment.

The apparatus was a panel with red and green lights positioned next to each other on the horizontal plane. Children were placed in front of the panel and told to press a button as quickly as possible when the red-green combination flashed on. Other light combinations (e.g., red-red, green-green) were to be ignored. Dependent measures were the number of correct detections, number of false alarms, and activity level of the subject. Number of correct detections was used to evaluate attention to relevant stimuli; number of false alarms was used to evaluate responses to irrelevant stimuli. Activity level was determined by observing motor behavior during the experiment and reviewing the subjects' educational data.

Anderson, Holcomb, and Doyle (1973) found that children with learning disabilities differed from children without learning problems on all dependent measures. Children with learning disabilities made more false alarms and fewer correct detections than children without learning problems. On the basis of the examiners' subjective judgment, the children with learning disabilities were subgrouped according to activity levels: Hyperactive, hypoactive, and normoactive. Further analysis indicated that those in the hyperactive group made fewer correct detections and more false alarms than either those in the hypo- or normoactive learning disabilities groups.

Anderson et al. (1973) interpreted their results as indicating that the vigilance task differentiated language-impaired children with learning disabilities from those with activity problems. Their data do not substantiate such interpretations because a language/learning disabilities population was not differentiated. They also suggested that these data, and those of Dykman et al. (1971), supported the hypothesis that hyperactive children had difficulty inhibiting responses and therefore were more impulsive.

In another study, Doyle, Anderson, and Halcomb (1976) studied the effects of distraction on vigilance task performance. The standard vigilance task was employed and was 30 minutes in duration. The subjects were 70 boys between the ages of 8 years and 12 years. Thirty-five of these children were diagnosed as having learning disabilities; 17 were receiving resource help and 18 were in self-contained classrooms for children with language problems and learning disabilities. The children were late subclassified by activity level as either hyperactive, hypoactive, or normoactive. A comparison group of 35 boys in regular classes was included. Data regarding this group were incomplete and most comparisons were made within the learning disabled populations.

The apparatus used was a panel with red and green lights. To the right of the red and green lights were 7 distractor lights. The child's task was to press a button in response to any red-green combination. The dependent measures were number of correct responses and number of false alarms.

Results indicated that children with learning disabilities made more false alarms and detected fewer correct signals than those without learning problems. Differences between the three learning disabilities groups were not obtained for the number of correct detections; however, these groups did differ significantly when false alarm data were analyzed. Hyperactive children made more false alarms than did the hypoactive or normoactive children with learning disabilities. With respect to vigilance performance, only the comparison group demonstrated the classic finding of a decrease in vigilance performance over time or trials. Performance in the learning disabled group was variable and unsystematic. Furthermore, children with learning disabilities were affected most by the visual distractors.

Doyle et al. (1976) interpreted these results as indicating that children with learning disabilities, particularly hyperactive children, paid more attention to extraneous visual stimuli than children without learning problems. It was also suggested that hyperactive children showed evidence of disinhibition, poor stimulus selection, and problems sustaining attention. These interpretations were consistent with Dykman et al. (1970), but were inconsistent with the findings reported by Browning (1967).

Browning (1967) introduced distractor stimuli during a concept learning task. His subjects were children diagnosed as minimally brain damaged (MBD) and children without learning problems. Browning found that normal children were more easily distracted than MBD children. Task and population differences may account for this discrepancy between Browning's findings and those of Doyle et al. (1976).

In another study, Grassi (1970) investigated the vigilance performance of 25 children with sustained brain damage (e.g., cerebral palsy), 25 diagnosed as behavior disordered, and 25 without learning problems. The age range was 11 to 15 years, with a mean age of approximately 13 years. The children in the three groups were matched on both age and average IQ. The task was an auditory vigilance task. The children listened to a 20-minute tape consisting of randomly placed numbers presented at approximately 1 per second. The children were to draw an "X" on a sheet of paper every time the number "6" was detected.

The results indicated that normal children detected significantly more correct signals than those in the behavior-disordered group, followed by those in the brain-damaged group. These latter two groups differed significantly from each other. These findings were interpreted as indicating that reactive inhibition occurred over time for all groups, but much more so for the behavior-disordered and brain-damaged groups. These differences reflected an inability to maintain and sustain attention. Practical implications were for short work periods and interspersed rest periods during a long task.

In summary, lower-achieving children made more false alarms and detected fewer correct stimuli during vigilance task performance (Anderson et al., 1973; Doyle et al., 1976 Kirchner & Knopf, 1974). In particular, hyperactive children had the greatest difficulty (Anderson et al., 1973; Doyle et al., 1976). Reasons for this were that hyperactive children were more impulsive (Anderson et al., 1976; Grassi, 1970), more easily distracted (Doyle et al., 1976), and had problems sustaining attention (e.g., Doyle et al., 1976).

With respect to attention and perception, children with learning problems had difficulty sustaining attention (e.g., Anderson et al., 1973; Dykman et al., 1970, 1971), processing or reacting to information quickly (e.g., Grassi, 1970), and responding only to relevant stimuli over time (e.g., Anderson et al., 1973).

Attention and Memory

The research reported here is mentioned only briefly. Terms are defined, studies reviewed, and developmental trends discussed in detail in Chapter 3.

Ross (1976) suggests attending and remembering as a separate form of selective attention. Examination of data in terms of what and how much is recalled provides information regarding selective attention. To assess *attention and memory*, the child is briefly presented with a series of lists of items and then asked to recall or recognize these items. Attention is inferred from the difference between what is remembered and what is presented (Pick et al., 1975). Serial position curves, incidental-central paradigm, and dichotic listening studies provide information about attention and memory.

HAGEN'S CENTRAL-INCIDENTAL ATTENTION TASK

A frequently used measure of selective attention and memory is Hagen's task assessing memory for incidental and central information (Hagen, 1967; Hagen & Hale, 1973). The child is shown a series of cards with two figures on each card. After each card is shown, it is placed face down in front of the child, forming an array. To evaluate central recall, the child is told to point to the location of a specific target item. To evaluate incidental recall, the child is presented with both figures on the card and asked to match the ones that go together.

Results showed that incidental learning occurred at all ages but decreased at about the seventh grade (Hagen, 1967); central recall increased between fifth and seventh grades (Hallahan, Kauffman, & Ball, 1973). These findings were interpreted as indicating an increase in selectivity (Pick et al., 1975), in skill (Hagen & Kail, 1975), and in the ability to eliminate quickly irrelevant or unwanted stimuli (MacCoby, 1969).

Tarver et al. (1976) compared children with learning disabilities to children without learning problems. They also found that children with learning disabilities recalled less central information and similar amounts of incidental information. When children with learning disabilities rehearsed (i.e., repeated aloud the items to be remembered), central recall was facilitated; the differences between these children and those without learning problems were eliminated. Bryan (1972) did not replicate this finding.

SERIAL POSITIVE CURVES

Attention is also inferred from the order in which items are remembered. This relationship is graphed as a serial position curve. Both total number of items retained and the sequence in which the items are retained are studied. Usually, the child is presented with a series of items or lists (verbal or nonverbal stimuli); after a short delay, the child is asked to recall or recognize those items. Enhanced retention of items presented at the end of the list is referred to as a *recency effect*. These items are stored in short-term memory. Retention of the items presented at the first of the list is stored in long-term memory and is referred to as a *primacy effect*. A primacy effect indicates active rehearsal (Flavell, 1970). Rehearsal is a type of strategy that increases in use with age (Flavell, 1970).

Developmental findings associated with rehearsal and serial position curves are as follows: Children as young as 8 years use rehearsal strategies. By age 10, rehearsal is used with more elaborate forms of organization (e.g., chunking or grouping together to-be-remembered items; Pick et al, 1975). Similar trends are observed when the serial position curves are examined. Recency effects are obtained before age 7 and primacy effects after age 7 (Pick et al., 1975). Reasons offered for such changes are an increase in the ability to (1) formulate and use strategies (Flavell & Wellman, 1976); (2) organize information (Miller, 1956); and (3) encode information about order (Huttenlocher & Burke, 1976).

In summary, during serial recall, 8-year-old children with learning disabilities do not remember items presented first in the list. This is a lack of a primacy effect. Older children with learning disabilities remember items presented first and last in the list; both recency and primacy effects were obtained (Tarver et al., 1976). Bauer (1977) used visual stimuli and found similar effects. These findings were interpreted as indicating that younger children with learning disabilities rehearsed less than older children with learning disabilities.

DICHOTIC LISTENING

Dichotic listening tasks are structured so that the subject receives more than one set of information simultaneously. The child's task is to attend to only one set (target information) and to ignore the remaining set(s) (distractor information). Stimuli may be auditory, verbal, visual, or a combination of these.

Doyle (1973) summarized developmental findings of selective attention using the dichotic listening task with children without learning problems. Children improved in the ability to focus attention and ignore distractors. Older elementary school children did better at recalling target information than younger children. When errors were made, older children made fewer errors of intrusion than younger children. (Intrusion errors were inclusion of distractor or parts of distractor information.) When younger children made errors, these included distractor information but also tended to combine distractor information with target information (e.g., chair/brush equals CHUSH.) Doyle concluded that younger and older children differ in the ability to inhibit intrusions from distractor material rather than in filtering out irrelevant information.

Conners, Kramer, and Guerra (1969) worked with children identified as high and low achievers. Dichotic listening performance and the ability to synthesize or blend sounds into words was studied. The subjects were 140 children in the sixth grade. Children were matched on age, sex, and IQ. On the blending task, children were required to blend a series of sounds to form a word (i.e., d- o- g, dog). On the dichotic listening task, children were presented with a series of digits and required to recall as many as possible. Ordering was not specified by the examiner; however, incorrect orderings were scored as failures.

Conners et al. (1969) found significant differences when performance on the auditory synthesis test was evaluated. Low achievers had more difficulty than high achievers. Low achievers also recalled less target information during the dichotic listening task. Conners et al. (1969) interpreted these findings as indicating that the role of short-term memory in auditory synthesis and dichotic listening was limited, and that their results reflected differences in selective attention.

To summarize, children with learning disabilities recalled similar amounts of incidental information, but not as much central information when the central-incidental task paradigm was used as well as when dichotic listening tasks were used. When ordering was a factor, children with learning disabilities had the greatest difficulty. The implications were that children with learning disabilities attended to information but not necessarily the most relevant information; further, they failed to attend to the order of presentation.

Attention and Cognition

Two research areas of attention and cognition are cognitive tempo and self-regulation. Cognitive tempo refers to the rate of learning; self-regulation refers to control during learning. Both topics provide information about learning styles and the ability to evaluate and respond appropriately to task characteristics. Research is organized according to the topics of cognitive tempo and self-regulation.

COGNITIVE TEMPO

Kagan et al. (1964) introduced the reflective-impulsive dimension to describe differences in children's problem-solving abilities not accounted for by IQ or verbal skills (Zelniker & Jeffrey, 1976). The most frequently used task to evaluate this dimension was the Matching Familiar Figures Test (MFFT), developed by Kagan (1966).

MFFT involves presenting the child with a standard figure and six other figures. One of the six other figures is identical to the standard. The child's task is to select the figure identical to the standard. The distractor items differ from the standard in subtle ways. Dependent measures are latency to the first response and total number of errors made (Kagan et al., 1964).

Using the MFFT, children are classified as either reflective or impulsive by means of a double median split. Those above the median on number of errors and below the median on response latency are classified as impulsives or fast-inaccurates. Kagan describes impulsives as hyperactive, more easily distractible, and less concerned about performance (Block, Block & Harrington, 1974). Those below the median on number of errors, and above the median on response latency, are classified as reflectives, or slow-accurates. Kagan describes these children as ponderous, careful, and thoughtful (Block et al., 1974). Children with other combinations of response latency and number of errors are usually not included in further analyses.

A great deal of research has been generated using the MFFT. These findings are summarized elsewhere and only reviewed briefly here (see Block et al., 1974; Epstein, Hallahan, & Kauffman, 1975). Research suggests that the impulsive-reflective dimension is moderately stable over time and generalizes to other tasks. A negative relationship between response latency and error score exists. Research with the MFFT suggests differences in cognitive tempo as a function of accuracy (Block et al., 1974); reinforcement history (Messer, 1970b); expectations about the task (Kagan, 1966); reading achievement (Kagan, 1965); and strategy preference (Zelniker & Jeffrey, 1976). There are a number of criticisms of this task and theory.

Block et al. (1974) and others (Ault, Mitchell, & Hartmann, 1976; Becker, Bender, & Morrison, 1978) present strong evidence suggesting limitations of the MFFT as a measure of impulsivity-reflectivity. Block et al. (1974) discuss problems using an accuracy score as a measure of classification. Block et al. (1974)

point out that the MFFT deviates from Hagen's conceptualization and operationalization of cognitive tempo. In concept, Block questions Kagan's use of the accuracy as one of two criteria for classification. (Latency as a measure of cognitive tempo was not criticized.) For example, latency and number of errors are negatively correlated (average correlation about .40). Block suggested that this correlation is too low to justify such an emphasis on classification. Inclusion of accuracy also confounds results obtained; it is not possible to assess whether differences between reflective-impulsive children's performance are due to accuracy or decision time. In addition, support for construct validity of the MFFT is discrepant as is the lack of information regarding alternate form reliability.

Ault, Mitchell, and Hartman (1976) also address methodologic problems associated with the measurement of cognitive tempo. Though their tone is more optimistic than Block et al. (1974), they elaborate similar criticisms. Two major concerns were the low negative correlations between latency and total number of errors, and the low reliability of error scores.

Zelniker and Jeffrey (1976), who worked with normal children, hypothesized that children classified as reflective or impulsive differed in information processing strategies. Four experiments were conducted. Stimuli were manipulated to require either detailed analysis or global analysis of the figures presented. Third-, fourth-, and sixth-grade children were worked with. In experiment one, fourth graders were the subjects. Stimuli were the standard MFFT and a new MFFT. The new MFFT was constructed in such a way as to evaluate attention to internal detail or external detail. Examples of the standard MFFT and the modified MFFT are seen in Figures 1-2 and 1-3.

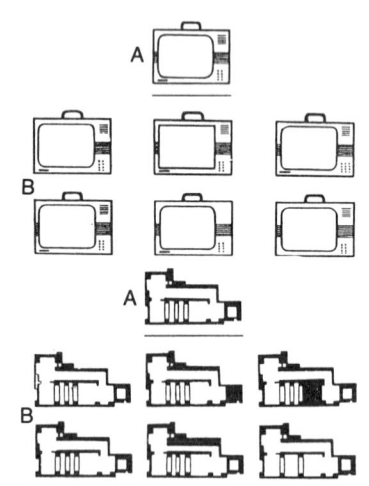

Fig. 1-2. (A): A meaningful detail problem. (B): An abstract detail problem. (From Zelniker, T., and Jeffrey, W. E. Reflective and impulsive children: Strategies of information processing underlying differences in problem solving. *Monographs of The Society for Research in Child Development,* 1976, *41*. Reprinted by permissions.)

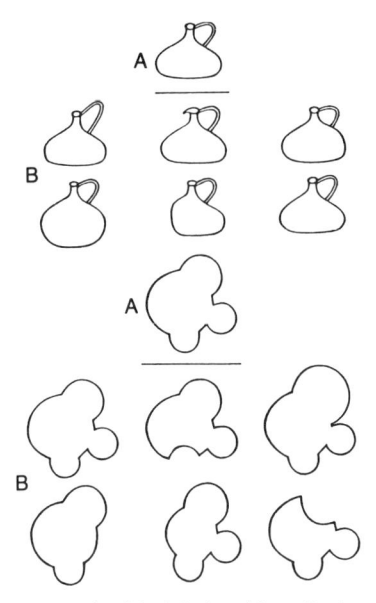

Fig. 1-3. A: A meaningful global problem. B: An abstract global problem. (From Zelniker, T., and Jeffrey, W. E. Reflective and impulsive children: Strategies of information processing underlying differences in problem solving. *Monographs of The Society for Research in Child Development,* 1976, *41*. Reprinted by permission.)

In the first experiment, children were presented with the standard MFFT. Six weeks later, the new MFFT was administered. Latency to the first response and total number of errors were the dependent measures. Results were similar when the standard and the new MFFT were used. When the accuracy scores of reflective and impulsive children were compared using the new MFFT, reflectives did significantly better on those figures requiring internal detail analysis. The two groups did not differ on those figures requiring global analysis of external details. Furthermore, latency was significantly longer on the detailed analysis task than on the global analysis tasks. Reflectives took significantly longer times on the detailed figures than on the global figures. Impulsives did not differ significantly on the type of figure and had significantly shorter response latencies on both types of tasks. In this way, impulsives were superior to reflectives. These authors concluded that the type of strategy employed was at least one of the variables underlying the reflective-impulsive dimension. They also concluded that response latency was an indicator of cognitive style.

In the second experiment, instructions were manipulated in order to encourage either an analytical or global approach when dealing with the figures. The subjects were 60 sixth-grade children. The stimuli were the MFFT and the Conceptual Style Test (CST). The CST required children to associate two of three pictures, which could be grouped on either fine details (e.g., stripes) or global characteristics (e.g., form).

Using the CST, reflective children made more analytical responses than impulsive children; this difference, however, was not statistically significant. Impulsive children, on the other hand, made nonanalytic responses faster than reflective children. Analytic responses were associated with slower latencies. The results were interpreted as indicating that children performed best when task characteristics and strategies employed were compatible.

During experiment three, memory and organization of reflective and impulsive children were studied using both verbal and visual stimuli. Verbal stimuli were sentences and the visual stimulus was a picture of an ongoing activity involving people. Generally, the results showed that reflective children recalled more details than impulsive children when not trained to a criterion (a certain number correct). When trained to a criterion, both groups performed similarly. This was interpreted as indicating that the rate of decay of long-term memory traces was similar for both groups.

During experiment four, strategies were assessed using a concept learning task. Subjects were the same as those in experiment two. Reflective and impulsive children performed similarly in terms of the number of problems solved, response latencies, and total number of cards or trials to solution. Results were interpreted as indicating that cognitive tempo was not a factor when the child could select and implement his or her own strategy efficiently.

Zelniker and Jeffrey (1976) concluded that (1) under certain conditions, impulsive children were more accurate than reflective children; (2) an analytic style was associated with reflective children and a global style was associated with impulsive children; and (3) task demands interacted with cognitive style.

Modification of cognitive style was successful in altering response latency but not error scores. Modeling techniques were employed (Debus, 1970) as well as special training procedures (Kagan, Pearson, & Welch, 1966). An example of such a study is that conducted by Zelniker and Oppenheimer (1973).

Zelniker and Oppenheimer (1973) modified the information processing of impulsive children. Their subjects were 60 kindergarten children identified as impulsives using the MFFT. One half of the children were assigned to one of two training conditions. Thirty of the children received training on matching a standard to a variant that was identical. The remaining 30 children received training on matching a standard to a variant that was different. Training was followed by one of three transfer tasks assessing different types of information processing techniques: (1) distinctive features; (2) prototype; and (3) control. Results indicated that children receiving differentiation training learned to process the features of distinguishing stimuli, while those in the matching condition did not show such a preference. These findings were interpreted as suggesting that directing attention to differences between variants encouraged the learning of distinctive features while the other training procedures did not.

Block et al. (1974) studied the relationship between accuracy, cognitive tempo, and personality factors. Their subjects were 100 children between the ages of 4 and 5 years. Personality data were gathered by means of a modification of the California Q-Sort, employing judges as raters of personalities of the children. All four classifications (reflective-accurate, reflective-inaccurate, impulsive-accurate, and impulsive-inaccurate) were included. Results indicated that accuracy was related to personality factors while latency was not. Differences between reflective and impulsive children were primarily a function of accuracy rather than cognitive tempo. In contrast to Kagan's interpretation of personality factors associated with impulsive performance, Block et al. concluded that impulsive children were hypersensitive, vulnerable, and structure-seeking.

Messer (1970a, 1970b) studied both the stability of the MFFT and the effects of experimentally induced failure. Messer (1970b) found that with experimentally induced failure, an increase in time and a decrease in errors was observed for impulsive children. In another study, Messer (1970a) studied impulsive and reflective children over a 2½-year period. At the beginning of the study, the children were in first grade; they were tested again in the third grade. The MFFT was one of the tests administered. Messer found moderate stability over time; children identified as impulsive or reflective in the first grade were still considered as such in the later grade. Those children who had failed a grade were more impulsive during grade one and remained more impulsive after 2½ years. Messer suggested that a lack of anxiety on the part of the impulsive child accounted for these differences. In both studies, Messer suggested that anxiety, or lack of anxiety, influenced cognitive styles.

Weiner and Adams (1974) replicated Messer's (1970b) findings. These authors studied the effects of failure, success, and frustration more directly. Ninety-two fourth-grade children were administered the MFFT. Three weeks later, these same children were exposed to either a successful, frustrated, failure, or control condition. Children in the four conditions were given anagrams and told to make a meaningful word (e.g., cta/cat). In the success condition, the words were easily constructed. In the frustration condition, half of the anagrams were solvable and half were not; in the failure condition, none of the anagrams was solvable. The control group was not given any manipulables or anagrams. The results showed that the frustration group changed significantly less over the 3-week period than either the failure or control group. These latter groups did not differ from each other. Greater increases in MFFT latency scores were observed for failure and control groups. Greater decreases in MFFT error scores were observed with impulsives; an increase in latency was associated with a decrease in errors and latency was modified by instructions while accuracy was not. Weiner and Adams concluded that prior reinforcement history affected the responses of reflective and impulsive children.

Kagan (1966) manipulated expectations toward performance. Subjects were 136 boys and 107 girls in the third grade. Serial recall lists were stimuli. Expectations were encouraged through instruction. One third of the children were told their performance on the MFFT was poor; another third was told that the lists to be presented were difficult; and another third, the control group, was not told anything. Children classified as reflective reported more correct words than impulsives under all three conditions. When the impulsives made errors, they were errors of commission or inclusion. Reflective boys were influenced most by instruction. These children made more errors when they were told that the list was difficult. Kagan's study provided only minimal support for his hypothesis regarding anxiety and impulsive children.

Reading ability and cognitive tempo were studied by Kagan (1965). His subjects were 65 boys and 65 girls who were tested using a variety of tasks including the MFFT. Children classified as reflective did better at reading recognition at the end of both first and second grades than those identified as impulsives.

To summarize, work with children without learning problems suggests that problems in the conceptualization and methodology of the MFFT exist (Ault et al., 1976; Becker et al., 1978; Block et al., 1974). The major criticisms were the use of an accuracy score to classify children, the low negative correlation between latency and error, and the low reliability of error scores. It was suggested that children classified as impulsive or reflective differed in the strategies they employed (Zelniker & Jeffrey, 1976), and in personality factors (e.g., Messer, 1970b); further, they were influenced by task characteristics and instruction (e.g., Weiner & Adams, 1974). Modification techniques were successful in altering response latencies but not error scores (Kagan, 1965).

Cognitive tempo has also been investigated in children with learning disabilities. The construct is subject to the same criticism with this group as with normal children. Becker, Bender, and Morrison (1978) discuss the limitations of the MFFT with children with learning disabilities. They suggest problems in concurrent validity, test-retest reliability, predictive validity, and the relationship between response time and errors.

To address the above issues, Becker et al. undertook an extensive study of 371 first-grade children. A year later, 206 of these same children were available for retest. Results indicated that the relationship between MFFT performance and school performance was positive and significant, as was test-retest reliability. Higher correlations were obtained for latency than for error scores.

Consistencies in classification over time were also considered. Sixty percent of the children who were classified as reflectives and 56 percent of the children classified as impulsives were classified as such a year later. Predictive validity was assessed by correlating various aspects of the MFFT with the Wide Range Achievement Test. Though correlations were significant, they were low. General conclusions were that results with children with learning disabilities using the MFFT as a measure of reflective-impulsive dimensions should be interpreted with caution.

Regarding the performance of children with learning disabilities on the MFFT (1) hyperactive children and impulsive children responded similarly (Keogh, 1971); (2) a significant and positive relationship between cognitive tempo and academic achievement was obtained (Hallahan et al., 1973); (3) high-risk children had difficulty switching or changing cognitive tempo (Becker, 1976); and

(4) modeling techniques affected the latency but not the accuracy of responding (Nagle & Thwaite, 1979). These findings were consistent with those obtained for children without learning problems.

Keogh (1971) suggested cognitive tempo, more specifically impulsivity, as a means of describing the behaviors of hyperactive children. She hypothesized that the speed of response with hyperactive children contributed to their learning problems (Epstein et al., 1975). Other authors have also suggested a relationship between impulsivity and hyperactivity (Campbell, 1973), and a relationship between impulsivity and learning disabilities (Epstein et al., 1975).

Hallahan, Kauffman, and Ball (1973) demonstrated a relationship between cognitive tempo and academic achievement. Their subjects were 2,000 sixth-grade boys. From this group, subjects were identified as high or low achievers. Criteria for selection as a low achiever were appropriate age, at least 1 year below grade level in reading and/or arithmetic, and an average IQ. High achievers were performing at grade level. Hagen's Central-Incidental Task and the MFFT were used. The first task was used as a measure of selective attention and the second as a measure of cognitive tempo. The results showed that high achievers, compared to low achievers, recalled more central but not more incidental information. On the MFFT, high achievers made significantly fewer errors than low achievers. Differences in latency scores were not significant. These findings were interpreted as indicating that better selective and sustained attention are associated with high achievement.

Keogh and Donlan (1972) studied the relationship between cognitive style and cognitive tempo. Their subjects were 62 boys with learning disabilities (age range: 8 years to 13 years, 9 months). Twenty-seven of the children had learning disabilities and were either in full-time programs for children with learning disabilities or were receiving resource learning disabilities help. Twenty-five children were identified as mildly or moderately learning disabled and received remediation during the summer for reading only. The three measures selected were designed to measure perceptual and spatial organization were the Rod Frame Test, the MFFT, and a pattern walking test.

The Portable Rod Frame Test was a modification of Witkin's (1972) original test designed for use with adults. The child's task was to set a rod at a true vertical position against the fixed frame. In this way, field-dependence and field-independence were assessed. The second test, Kagan's MFFT, was used to determine cognitive style and tempo. Finally, a pattern walking test (Keogh, 1971) was presented where the child walked through the organization of geometric forms.

Keogh and Donlan (1972) found that the two learning disabilities populations did not differ from each other on either the Rod Frame Test or the walking pattern test. However, when compared to available data for children without learning problems, Keogh and Donlan concluded that learning disabilities children were field-dependent. On the MFFT, children with severe learning disabilities were significantly more impulsive than children with moderate learning disabilities. Children with severe learning disabilities were both field-dependent and impulsive, while those with less severe learning disabilities were only field-dependent. Keogh and Donlan (1972) interpreted these results as supporting the view of learning disabilities as a perceptual-spatial organization deficit. Further, these results suggested that children with learning disabilities have a global rather than analytic style when processing information.

As part of a larger study, Becker (1976) studied the cognitive style of 60 kindergarten children identified as high-risk or nonrisk. The MFFT was administered as one of the six tasks. The other tasks involved motor responses (e.g., walking and drawing) and involved the child's ability to increase or decrease speed as the situation required. No significant differences were found between risk and nonrisk children on the MFFT. Other results indicated that high-risk children had difficulty changing tempo, particularly on complex tasks.

Nagle and Thwaite (1979) used the MFFT to evaluate the effects of different modeling conditions. Their subjects were 30 children in the third and fourth grades who were diagnosed as learning disabled and classified as impulsive on the basis of the MFFT. These children were assigned to one of three conditions. The child either observed a model who was reflective on a matching task, a model who was impulsive on a matching task, or a model who played an unrelated game. The child was exposed to one of these conditions weekly for three consecutive weeks. The matching to sample tasks were presented at the end of each session and one week after the final session. Response latency and changes in error scores were the dependent measures.

Consistent with other research, the latency scores of the children with learning disabilities were modified by observing the reflective model, but errors made did not change significantly. Children with learning disabilities who observed the impulsive model responded with shorter latencies than the control group. These differences in performance increased over training sessions.

In summary, similarities between hyperactive children and impulsive children were noted (Keogh, 1971). The relationship between academic achievement of children with learning disabilities and cognitive tempo was also suggested (Hallahan et al., 1976). As with children without learning disabilities, training techniques facilitated and affected latency scores but not accuracy scores (Nagle & Thwaite, 1979).

VERBAL REGULATION

Verbal regulation of overt responding refers to a shift in control from the verbalizations of others (external) to the child's internal planning or self-regulatory behaviors (Wozniak, 1972). A child's success on a variety of problem-solving tasks (e.g., memory, concept formation) requires this transition from external to internal control of overt behavior. Luria (1961), a Soviet theorist, discusses the development of this change in control (Wozniak, 1972). Before the age of 2 to 3, external speech exerts little control over motor activity. Between the ages of 3 and 4½ years, children respond correctly to verbal commands directed at a single, distinct signal. After 4½ to 5 years, the child regulates future behavior by internally retained verbal rules.

Two tasks that allow study of impulsive behaviors and/or the effects of verbal cueing are the Simon Says Game and a matching-to-sample task. Data with children without learning problems are reviewed first.

Stronmen (1973) used the Simon Says Game with children without learning problems. His task required children to inhibit a motor response through verbal regulation. The experimenter's external speech, "Simon says," exerted control over the nonverbal commands/demonstrations. The child was told to perform a specific motor activity or action, but only if it was prefaced by the command, "Simon says." If "Simon says" did not preface the command, the child's task was to inhibit the motor response. The experimenter performed all commands regardless of whether or not they were prefaced by "Simon says." Strommen's subjects were 71 children in preschool, kindergarten, first grade, and third grade. He found that errors decreased significantly over grades. This decrease was linear. All children improved across trials except for preschool children and kindergarten males. When errors were made, younger children did not seem to recognize inconsistencies between their motor responses and the verbal stimulus. This was not the case with older children.

Using a different task, Birch (1966) studied verbal control over nonverbal behavior. The subjects were 47 children between the ages of 2 years, 2 months and 7 years. All were enrolled in a nursery school program. Birch's task required the children to depress a lever when told to do so, or when given a nonverbal signal, which was a buzzer. The buzzer or verbal command was issued every 15 seconds (periodic condition) or whenever the subjects released the lever (contingent condition). This resulted in four conditions: (1) verbal contingency; (2) buzzer contingency; (3) buzzer periodic; and (4) verbal periodic. The dependent measures were the extent of depression of the lever, length of time depressed, and type of command issued.

The results showed that when told to depress the lever, 3½-year-old children pressed the lever significantly less often than children of 3½ to 7 years. Also, the length of the lever press was significantly longer for verbal commands. Young children in the buzzer condition released the lever faster than those in the other groups. The type of motor presentation (periodic or contingent) was not significant.

Birch (1966) interpreted these results as indicating that external verbal commands increased the tendency to persist in an activity, and that repeating the verbal command was necessary to maintain an appropriate overt response.

The Simon Says task and the matching-to-sample task were employed to investigate impulsive responses and verbal regulation of children with learning disabilities. In addition, training techniques to increase control of impulsive responses were studied (for a review, see Abikoff, 1979).

Parrill-Burnstein (1980) studied performance on the Simon Says Game with children with and without learning disabilities. Participating were 140 children:

two groups, each consisting of 45 children with learning disabilities, were from different private schools for children with learning disabilities and 50 without learning problems were included as a comparison group. Children were in grades one through five and were worked with individually. The experiment was conducted in two phases, which were spaced approximately 24 to 36 hours apart. During phase one, the Simon Says Game was played as described by Strommen (1973). During phase two the verbal commands were spoken by the experimenter, but the actions were not demonstrated. The dependent measure was the number of errors, that is, responses to commands not prefaced by "Simon says."

Parrill-Burnstein (1980) found that during the standard Simon Says Game, the groups differed significantly. Further analysis indicated that children from one group with learning disabilities made more impulsive errors than those in the other two groups. These latter two groups did not differ from each other. Significant age effects were also obtained. Children in the first grade made more errors than those in the other grades. These effects were consistent with Strommen's (1973). When demonstration was eliminated, the three groups performed similarly. Differences as a function of age where still significant.

Parrill-Burnstein interpreted these results as indicating that children from one group with learning disabilities may have included more children with nonverbal and attentional problems than those in the other group of children with learning disabilities. These children were distracted by demonstration and had difficulty attending selectively to the relevant verbal commands. In other words, these children were hindered by the presence of competing cues. This hypothesis was supported by the lack of a statistical difference when only verbal cues were presented.

Weithorn and Kagen (1979) studied the effects of verbal regulation on a matching-to-sample task. Their subjects were 94 first-grade children (age range: 5 years, 11 months to 7 years, 11 months). These children were selected on the basis of two criteria: They received either a high or low score on the Grammatic Closure Subtest of the Illinois Test of Psycholinguistic Abilities (ITPA) and were identified by two teachers as having either high- or low-activity levels. There were four groups: high-activity level, low language; high-activity level, high language; low-activity level, low language; and low-activity level, high language. Each of these groups was further subdivided into control and experimental groups.

Children in all groups were given matching-to-sample problems. Those in the experimental group were taught to verbalize the criteria, as well as to evaluate verbally each choice as either correct or incorrect. Children in the control group were given unrelated language tests in place of the instructions given to those in the experimental group. Results indicated that training affected the performance of children in the high-activity level group more than those in the low-activity level group. After training, children in the high-activity level group made fewer errors and did not differ significantly from those in the other groups. Significant differences were not obtained when language level was considered.

To summarize, impulsive errors of children without learning problems decreased with an increase in age (Strommen, 1973). Preschool children did not always recognize inconsistencies between external verbal commands and their motor responses (Strommen, 1973). External commands also increased the tendency of younger children to engage in an activity already initiated (Birch, 1966).

The performance of children with learning problems differed significantly when compared to the performance of children without learning problems. One group of children with learning disabilities were more impulsive and more easily distracted by nonverbal cues than children without learning problems (Parrill-Burnstein, 1980). Verbal mediation reduced impulsive behaviors of children with high-activity levels (Weithorn & Kagen, 1979). These results were consistent with those obtained when cognitive tempo was studied.

CONCLUSIONS

Children with learning disabilities had problems inhibiting responses, sustaining attention, and tuning out irrelevant information. These results were obtained when perception, memory, and cognition were studied. Deficits in selective attention and response execution were substantiated when physiologic measures were employed, when cognitive tempo and style were assessed, and when reaction time tasks were used. Problems in selective attention, more specifically, arousal (Ross, 1976), impulsive control (e.g., Parrill-Burnstein, 1980), decision-making (Keogh & Margolis, 1976), stimulus selection, focusing (Dykman, 1972), and concentration (e.g., Anderson et al., 1973) were proposed to describe these deficits.

With respect to response execution, children with learning disabilities had problems imitating others, responding to designated information when presented simultaneously with irrelevant information, and using available feedback. Differences in response execution were interpreted as reflecting more basic problems in attention. The type of learning problem influenced responses made and the extent of the deficits observed.

IMPLICATIONS FOR REMEDIATION AND RESEARCH

Implications for remediation and research are (1) segmenting work periods; (2) using training techniques to focus attention and facilitate rehearsal; (3) avoiding the presentation of competing cues with relevant information; and (4) using instructions to increase self-monitoring skills. Suggestions are organized according to the topics of attention and perception, attention and memory, and attention and cognition.

Remediation

ATTENTION AND PERCEPTION

Using reaction time measures, vigilance tasks, and physiologic measures, it was found that children with learning disabilities responded at slower rates, were distracted by task-irrelevant information, and had problems sustaining and focusing attention. The implications were for intermittent breaks, changes in the responses required, limiting input in terms of length and complexity, and changes in the types of tasks assigned. Each of these was incorporated in the following suggestions.

Provide the child with a piece of paper folded in half on which a series of digits and numbers is randomly ordered (approximately 30 on each line with 20 lines). Have the child move the piece of paper in a sliding fashion, exposing the series in order at about 8 to 10 figures per second. This encourages correct sequencing. The child's task would be to mark all the numbers for approximately 10 to 15 minutes. At the end of 10 minutes, the task is switched in that the child is asked to mark all the letters if he had done the number of the first task. At the end of 10 more minutes, the child is instructed to stand up and perform simple exercises such as stretching or bending for approximately 30 seconds. At each break, the number of items correctly marked is recorded. This sequence is presented, increasing the time between breaks, until the child can sustain attention for approximately 20 minutes.

This procedure can be extended to include academic content as well. For example, when completing math assignments such as addition, give the child a signal to begin, stop after 5 to 10 minutes, change the task from addition to subtraction, switch again after another 10 minutes have passed. Gradually, the time spent on the activity can be increased.

Another activity designed to facilitate sustaining attention is to provide the child with a systematic way of approaching academic and nonacademic problems. If the child has difficulty reading without supervision for 10 minutes or less, this activity would be appropriate. Give the child a paragraph to read. At the end of each paragraph, have ready for the child a series of comprehension questions requiring determination of cause-and-effect relationship. For example, questions might include the following: "What will the next paragraph be about?" "What cues within that paragraph provide that information?" "Write down those answers."

Using self-monitoring skills and providing immediate feedback also enables children to sustain attention for longer periods of time. Sit the child before a language master with a list of cards with vocabulary words on each. As each word is either read or defined, the child runs the card through the language master and evaluates his or her own performance. Another activity may be to give the child a paragraph with various types of errors (e.g., misspellings or mispunctuations). The child's task is to correct the paragraph in a given amount of time working in sequence (using a scanning sheet if necessary). If some children require more supervision, teachers may have to work with those children on a one-to-one basis before the children can work either by themselves at a language master or with other children.

ATTENTION AND MEMORY

Children with learning disabilities retained less central information and similar amounts of incidental information. Younger children with learning disabilities did not remember initially presented information and had problems attending to and remembering simultaneously presented information.

Suggestions to improve recall of central information and initially presented information are described in the chapter on memory, Chapter 3. Implications for dichotic listening tasks are presented here. Children who have problems processing information simultaneously and focusing on the most relevant information would benefit from the following instruction.

To direct or focus attention, it is suggested that information presented be short and explicit. When possible, verbal and nonverbal information should be paired; that is, presented simultaneously. If the child becomes overloaded with simultaneous input, information from more than one modality should be faded in gradually rather than presented from both modalities at one time immediately. For example, some children understand more when they read aloud; others show little tolerance for this type of verbal feedback. Have the child read parts aloud and parts silently. Gradually increase the amount of verbal feedback until the child is either reading aloud with comprehension or reading without verbal cues but still decoding information.

Many times, social interactions occur where subgroups form or more than one person is speaking at once. Mock situations such as these could be set up in classrooms. Children should be cued to social cues that direct attention, such as loudness of the message, proximity of the speaker, and the relative importance of the speaker or the message.

Simultaneous processing also occurs during academic subjects such as reading and spelling and may facilitate math performance if integrated appropriately, taking into account the child's level of functioning. In reading or spelling, a child learns to associate a sound (verbal) with a letter (visual). Furthermore, some children perform better at analyzing this relationship (spelling) or at synthesizing this relationship (reading).

If a child is having difficulty acquiring this skill of associating sounds and letters or of sequencing sounds within the word, the next task suggested might be appropriate. When teaching initial reading skills, the sequencing of sound-letter associations might be five consonants (e.g., *c, t, m, b,* and *s*) and one vowel (e.g., the short vowel *o*).

The child is placed before a mirror and is asked to imitate the clinician's modeling of various facial expressions, such as when saying the short vowel "o." Once the child can imitate this expression without sound, the sound of the letter is made, the child looks in the mirror at the facial configuration (the mouth in the form of an *o*), and imitates. A short *u* can be taught next by drawing the child's arm quckly down to his or her stomach and pretending to hit and make the sound "uh."

ATTENTION AND COGNITION

Children with learning disabilities were frequently categorized as fast-inaccurate when cognitive tempo was investigated. Children with learning disabilities also have problems self-pacing or regulating input and output. These children did not use verbal cues to regulate motor responses or cognitive responses.

Vigilance. To facilitate vigilance performance, it is suggested that the child be given a 10- to 15-minute assignment with a 2- to 3-minute break (to stretch, etc.) every 5 minutes.

Self-regulation. To encourage the processing of relevant information only and to improve verbal regulation, the following are suggested. Children should be told what the relevant cues are and be required to focus on those cues only. A task designed using the Simon Says Game format would be to line children up facing the teacher. Have one child state the verbal command, a second child give the third child (who is playing the game) feedback regarding the correctness or incorrectness of that child's response. Have the child rotate through each role. Eventually, fade in the nonverbal demonstration of each command as spoken.

A similar task would be to give the child a series of verbal commands while demonstrating each command and to have the child note when the demonstration and the verbal input are discrepant (e.g., the verbal statement, "Turn to page 134," made while sharpening a pencil, versus opening a book while saying, "Turn to page 134 ").

Reflective and impulsive. Children with learning disabilities may be more impulsive and less accurate than children without learning problems. Also, when attempts to change performance have been made, latency rather than accuracy was modified. To increase accuracy, verbal demonstration and providing additional cues are suggested. Encouraging the child to systematically evaluate each figure as well as compare visual figures to the model is stressed.

Provide the child with a sheet of paper. Ask him or her to cover up all the figures except the standard and the figure being compared. Ask the child to take a second sheet of paper and cover up half of the exposed figures. The child is to compare each section of the figure (e.g., top half, then bottom half) to the standard prior to moving on to the next figure. Also, having the child circle the part of the figure that differs from the standard might be helpful. Differences between the standard and the figure may be in terms of size perception, directionality, color perception, and external or internal detailing.

To modify both latency and accuracy it is suggested that a stopwatch be used. The child is to explore the figures for a minimum time, circling as before the part of the figure that differs from the standard or is the odd figure in the group.

Research

Implications for research are the same as those for remediation except that each implication is further investigated or studied systematically. For all experiments, it is suggested that a normal comparison group be included; that differentiation within the learning disabilities population be attempted; and that children with and without learning disabilities be equated on IQ, and either achievement level or chronological age.

ATTENTION AND PERCEPTION

To evaluate whether short breaks do enable children with learning disabilities to process information more accurately, that is, sustain attention, the following task is suggested. Present the child with a series of sheets on which numbers and letters are randomly ordered. Have the child mark all the numbers or letters for a 15-minute period, recording the number completed at each minute interval. Next, present the child with the same task. At every 2-minute interval, the child is required to stretch. Performance under these two conditions is compared.

To determine whether providing preparatory cues facilitates the readiness to attend, it is suggested that children be told verbal cues such as "Wait; ready; begin," before beginning an activity (such as completing math problems or reading a sentence). This is compared to the number correct and the time necessary to complete the task without such cues.

ATTENTION AND MEMORY

To investigate the simultaneous processing of information to be remembered, the following two studies are suggested.

Recall, without instructions to direct attention, is assessed. Initially, the child is presented with words spoken by a female voice to one ear and a male voice to the other ear. Testing of recall of the information given by those voices is recorded. Then, the child is told to attend only to one of the two voices. Recall of information is again tested and compared to previously acquired information.

In the second task, recall of related and unrelated information in a multisensory presentation is evaluated. Verbal information is presented and is either a sentence or unrelated words (e.g., the red cat is on the chair, versus cat, red, chair). During the auditory presentation, the child is presented with either a series of unrelated words or sentences written on cards.

ATTENTION AND COGNITION

Variations of the Simon Says Game allow study of another type of skill at self-regulation. The first question posed is whether or not verbal mediation facilitates self-regulation. The standard Simon Says Game is played. Before the child demonstrates a command, he or she is required to verbalize the command started prior to the movement. This is compared to the child's performance without such verbalization.

An experiment designed to study the effects of reducing cognitive tempo would involve (1) presenting the standard MFFT; (2) asking the child to study each figure for 10 seconds and then marking the figures that differ from the standard; and (3) providing the child with a sheet of paper and requiring that he or she cover all other figures and study the exposed figure for 10 seconds, then revealing each of the other figures in sequence, and finally marking the figures that differ from the standard.

REFERENCES

Abikoff, H. Cognitive training interventions in children: Review of a new approach. *Journal of Learning Disabilities*, 1979, *12*(2), 123–136.

Anderson, R. P., Halcomb, C. G., & Doyle, R. B. The measurement of attentional deficits. *Exceptional Children*, 1973, *39*, 534–539.

Asch, S. E. Perceptual conditions of association. In M. Hendle (Ed.), *Documents of gestalt psychology*. Berkeley and Los Angeles: University of California Press, 1961.

Asch, S. E. A reformulation of the problem of associations. *American Psychologist*, 1969, *24*, 92–102.

Asch, S. E., Ceraso, J., & Heimer, W. Perceptual conditions of association. *Psychological Monographs*, 1960, *74*, 1–48.

Ault, R. L., Mitchell, C., & Hartman, D. P. Some methodological problems in reflection-impulsivity research. *Child Development*, 1976, *47*, 227–231.

Bauer, R. H. Memory processes in children with learning disabilities: Evidence for deficient rehearsal. *Journal of Experimental Child Psychology*, 1977, *24*, 415–430.

Becker, L. D. Conceptual tempo and the early detection of learning problems. *Journal of Learning Disabilities*, 1976, *9*(7), 433–442.

Becker, L. D., Bender, N. N., & Morrison, G. Measuring impulsivity-reflection: A critical review. *Journal of Learning Disabilities*, 1978, *11*(10), 626–632.

Berlyne, D. E. Attention as a problem in behavior theory. In D. I. Mostofsky (Ed.), *Attention: Contemporary theory and analysis*. New York: Appleton-Century-Crofts, 1970, pp. 25–49.

Birch, D. Verbal control of nonverbal behavior. *Journal of Experimental Child Psychology*, 1966, *4*, 266–275.

Block, J., Block, J., & Harrington, D. Some misgivings about the Matching Familiar Figures Test as a measure of reflection-impulsivity. *Developmental Psychology*, 1974, *10*, 611–632.

Broadbent, D. E. *Perception and communication.* New York: Pergamon Press, 1958.

Bryan, T. The effects of forced mediation upon short-term memory of children with learning disabilities. *Journal of Learning Disabilities,* 1972, 5, 605–609.

Browning, R. M. Effects of irrelevant peripheral visual stimuli on discrimination learning in minimally brain-damaged children. *Journal of Consulting Psychology,* 1967, 31, 371–376.

Campbell, S. B. Cognitive style in reflective, impulsive, and hyperactive boys and their mothers. *Perceptual and Motor Skills,* 1973, 36, 747–752.

Clements, S. D. *Minimal brain dysfunction in children: Terminology and identification.* PHS Publication 1415, U.S. Department of Health, Education and Welfare, 1966.

Connors, C. K., Kramer, K., & Guerra, F. Auditory synthesis and dichotic listening in children with learning disabilities. *Journal of Special Education,* 1969, 3, 163–170.

Cruickshank, W. M. (Ed.). *The teacher of brain-injured children.* Syracuse, New York: Syracuse University Press, 1966.

Czudner, G., & Rourke, B. P. Simple reaction time in brain-damaged and normal children under regular and irregular preparatory interval conditions. *Perceptual and Motor Skills,* 1970, 31, 767–773.

Czudner, G., & Rourke, B. P. Age differences in visual reaction time of "brain-damaged" and normal children under regular and irregular preparatory interval conditions. *Journal of Experimental Child Psychology,* 1972, 13, 516–526.

Debus, R. L. Effects of brief observation of model behavior on conceptual tempo of impulsive children. *Developmental Psychology,* 1970, 7, 22–32.

Douglas, V. I. Stop, look, and listen: The problems of sustained attention and impulse control in hyperactive and normal children. *Canadian Journal of Behavioral Science,* 1972, 4, 259–282.

Douglas, V. I. *Sustained attention and impulse control: Implications for the handicapped child.* Department of Health, Education and Welfare, Publication No. 73-0500. U.S. Department of Health, Education and Welfare, 1974.

Doyle, A. B. Listening to distraction: A developmental study of selective attention. *Journal of Experimental Child Psychology,* 1973, 15, 100–115.

Doyle, R. B., Anderson, R. P., & Halcomb, C. G. Attentional deficits and the effects of visual distractions. *Journal of Learning Disabilities,* 1976, 9(1), 48–54.

Diagnostic and statistics manual of mental disorders (3rd ed.). American Psychiatric Association, 1980.

Dykman, R. A., Ackerman, P. T., Clements, S. D., et al. Specific learning disabilities: An attentional deficit syndrome. In H. R. Myklebust (Ed.), *Progress in learning disabilities* (Vol. II). New York: Grune & Stratton, 1971.

Dykman, R. A., Walls, R., Suzuki, T., et al. Children with learning disabilities: Conditioning, differentiation, and the effect of distraction. *American Journal of Orthopsychiatry,* 1970, 40, 766–781.

Epstein, M. H., Hallahan, D. P., & Kauffman, J. M. Implications of the reflectivity-impulsivity dimension for special education. *The Journal of Special Education,* 1975, 9(1), 11–25.

Flavell, J. H. Developmental studies of mediated memory. In H. W. Reese & L. P. Lipsitt (Eds.), *Advances in child development and behavior* (Vol. 5). New York: Academic Press, 1970.

Flavell, J. H., & Wellman, H. M. Metamemory. In R. V. Kail & J. W. Hagen (Eds.), *Memory in cognitive development*. Hillsdale, New Jersey: Lawrence Erlbaum Associates, 1976.

Frankmann, J. P., & Adams, J. A. Theories of vigilance. *Psychological Bulletin*, 1962, 59, 257–272.

Gibson, E. J. *Principles of perceptual learning and development*. New York: Appleton-Century-Crofts, 1969.

Gibson, J. J., & Gibson, E. J. Perceptual learning: Differentiation or enrichment? *Psychological Review*, 1955, 62, 32–41.

Grassi, J. Auditory vigilance performance in brain damaged, behavior disordered, and normal children. *Journal of Learning Disabilities*, 970, 3, 302–304.

Hagen, J. W. The effects of distraction. *Child Development*, 1967, 38, 685–694.

Hagen, J. W., & Hale, G. A. The development of attention in children. In A. Pick (Ed.), *Minnesota symposium on child psychology* (Vol. 7). Minneapolis: University of Minnesota Press, 1973.

Hagen, J. W., & Kail, R. V. The role of attention in perceptual and cognitive development. In W. Cruickshank and D. P. Hallahan (Eds.), *Perceptual and learning disabilities in children* (Vol. II). Syracuse, N.Y.: Syracuse University Press, 1975.

Hallahan, D. P., Kauffman, J. M., & Ball, D. W. Selective attention and cognitive tempo of low achieving and high achieving sixth grade males. *Perceptual and Motor Skills*, 1973, 36, 579–583.

Huttenlocher, J. & Burke, D. Why does memory span increase with age. *Cognitive Psychology*, 1976, 8(1), 1–31.

Kagan, J. Reflection-impulsivity and reading ability in primary grade children. *Child Development*, 1965, 36, 609–628.

Kagan, J. Reflection-impulsivity: The generality and dynamics of conceptual tempo. *Journal of Abnormal Psychology*, 1966, 1, 17–24.

Kagan, J., Pearson, L., & Welch, L. Modifiability of an impulsive tempo. *Journal of Educational Psychology*, 1966, 57, 359–365.

Kagan, J., Rossman, B. L., Day, D., et al. Information processing in the child: Significance of analytic and reflective attitudes. *Psychological Monographs: General and Applied*, 1964, 78.

Keogh, B. K. Hyperactivity and learning disorders: Review and speculation. *Exceptional Children*, 1971, 38, 101–110.

Keogh, B. K., & Donlan, McG. Field dependence, impulsivity, and learning disabilities. *Journal of Learning Disabilities*, 1972, 5, 331–336.

Keogh, B. K., & Margolis, J. Learn to labor and to wait: Attentional problems of children with learning disorders. *Journal of Learning Disabilities*, 1976, 9(5), 276–286.

Kirchner, G. L., & Knopf, I. J. Difference in the vigilance performance of second-grade children as related to sex and achievement. *Child Development*, 1974, 45, 490–495.

Koffka, K. *The growth of the mind* (2nd ed.). New York: Harcourt, 1931.

Kohler, W. On the nature of associations. *Proceedings of the American Philosophic Society*, 1941, 84, 489–502.

Kohler, W. Gestalt psychology today. *American Psychologist*, 1959, 14, 727–734.

Koppell, S. Testing the attentional deficit notion. *Journal of Learning Disabilities*, 1979, 12(1), 43–48.

Lacey, J. & Lacey, B. Some automatic central nervous system inter-relationships. In P.

Black (Ed.), *Physiological correlates of emotion.* New York: Academic Press, 1970, pp., 205–227.

Luria, A. R. *The role of speech in the regulation of normal and abnormal behavior.* New York: Liveright, 1961.

MacCoby, E. E. The development of stimulus selection. In J. P. Hill (Ed.), *Minnesota symposia on child psychology* (Vol. 3). Minneapolis: University of Minnesota Press, 1969.

Messer, S. Reflection-impulsivity: Stability and school failure. *Journal of Educational Psychology,* 1970a, *61*(6), 487–490.

Messer, S. The effect of anxiety over intellectual performance in reflection-impulsivity in children. *Child Development,* 1970b, *41,* 723–735.

Miller, G. A. The magical number seven, plus or minus two: Some limits on our capacity for processing information. *Psychological Review,* 1956, *63,* 81–97.

Nagle, R. J., & Thwaite, B. C. Modeling effects on impulsivity with learning disabled children. *Journal of Learning Disabilities,* 1979, *12*(5), 331–336.

Neisser, U. *Cognition and reality: Principles and implications of cognitive psychology.* San Francisco: W. H. Freeman and Company, 1976.

Parrill-Burnstein, M. *Simon Says Game and learning disabilities: A study of distractibility.* Paper presented at the Southeastern Psychological Association, Washington, D.C., March 1980.

Pick, A. D., Frankel, D. G., & Hess, V. L. Children's attention: The development of selectivity. In E. M. Hetherington (Ed.), *Review of child development research* (Vol. 5). Chicago: University of Chicago Press, 1975.

Postman, L., & Riley, D. A. A critique of Kohler's theory of association. *Psychological Review,* 1957, *64*(1), 61–72.

Ross, A. O. *Psychological aspects of learning disabilities and reading disorders.* New York: McGraw-Hill Book Company, 1976.

Rourke, B. P., & Czudner, G. Age difference in auditory reaction time of brain damaged and normal children under regular and irregular prepartory interval conditions. *Journal of Experimental Child Psychology,* 1972, *14,* 372–378.

Sroufe, L. A. Age changes in cardiac deceleration within a fixed foreperiod reaction-time task: An index of attention. *Developmental Psychology,* 1971, *5*(2), 338–343.

Sroufe, L. A., Sonies, B. C., West, W. D., et al. Anticipatory heart rate deceleration and reaction time in children with and without referral for learning disabilities. *Child Development,* 1973, *44,* 267–273.

Strauss, E., & Lehtinen, L. B. *Psychopathology and education of the brain-injured child.* New York: Grune & Stratton, 1947.

Strommen, E. A. Verbal self-regulation in a children's game: Impulsive errors on "Simon Says." *Child Development,* 1973, *44,* 849–853.

Tarver, S. G., Hallahan, D. P., Kauffman, J. M., et al. Verbal rehearsal and selective attention in children. *Journal of Experimental Child Psychology,* 1976, *22*(3), 379–385.

Torgesen, J. K. The role of nonspecific factors in the task performance of learning disabled children: A theoretical assessment. *Journal of Learning Disabilities,* 1977, *10*(1), 27–34.

Weiner, A. S., & Adams, W. V. The effect of failure and frustration on reflective and impulsive children. *Journal of Experimental Child Psychology,* 1974, *17,* 353–359.

Weithorn, C. J., & Kagen, E. Training first graders of high-activity level to improve performance through verbal self-direction. *Journal of Learning Disabilities*, 1979, *12*(2), 82–88.

Whittenburg, J. A., Ross, S., & Andrews, T. G. Sustained perceptual efficiency as measured by the Mackworth "Clock" Test. *Perceptual and Motor Skills*, 1956, *6*, 109–116.

Witkin, H. A., Goodenough, D. R., & Karp, S. A. Stability of cognitive style from childhood to young adulthood. *Journal of Personality and Social Psychology*, 1967, *7*(3), 291–300.

Wozniak, R. H. Verbal regulation of motor behavior: Soviet research and non-Soviet replications. *Human Development*, 1972, *15*, 13–57.

Wright, J. C., & Vlietstra, A. G. The development of selective attention: From perceptual exploration to logical search. In H. Reese (Ed.), *Advances in child development and behavior* (Vol. 10). New York: Academic Press, 1975.

Zelniker, T., & Jeffrey, W. E. Reflective and impulsive children: Strategies of information processing underlying differences in problem solving. *Monographs of the Society for Research in Child Development*, 1976, *41*(5), Serial No. 168.

Zelniker, T., & Oppenheimer, L. Modification of information processing of impulsive children. *Child Development*, 1973, *44*, 445–450.

FURTHER READINGS

Alabiso, F. Inhibition functions of attention in reducing hyperactive behavior. *American Journal of Mental Deficiency*, 1972, *17*, 259–282.

Alabiso, F. P., & Hansen, J. C. *The hyperactive child in the classroom*. Springfield, Delaware: Charles C. Thomas, 1977.

Alwitt, L. F. Attention in a visual task among non-readers and readers. *Perceptual and Motor Skills*, 1966, *23*, 361–362.

Ault, R. L. Problem-solving strategies of reflective, impulsive, fast-accurate, and slow-inaccurate children. *Child Development*, 1973, *44*, 259–266.

Boxley, G. B., & LeBlanc, J. M. The hyperactive child: Characteristics, treatment, and evaluation of research design. In H. Reese (Ed.), *Advances in child development and behavior* (Vol. 11). New York: Academic Press, 1976.

Brich, H., & Belmont, L. Auditory-visual integration in normal and retarded readers. *American Journal of Orthopsychiatry*, 1964, *34*, 852–861.

Birch, H., & Lefford, A. Intersensory development in children. *Monographs of the Society for Research in Child Development*, 1963, *28*, Serial #89.

Block, G. H. Hyperactivity: A cultural perspective. *Journal of Learning Disabilities*, 1977, *10*(4), 236–240.

Boydstun, J. A., Ackerman, P. T., Stevens, D. A., et al. Physiological and motor conditioning and generalization in children with minimum brain dysfunction. *Conditional Reflex*, 1968, *3*, 81–104.

Campanelli, P. A. Sustained attention in brain damaged children. *Exceptional Children*, 1970, *1*, 317–323.

Chalfant, J., & Scheffelin, M. *Central processing dysfunctions in children: A review of research*. NINDS Monograph No. 9. Bethesda, Maryland: U.S. Department of Health, Education and Welfare, 1969 (Task Force III).

Cohen, N. J., & Douglas, V. I. Characteristics of the orienting response in hyperactive and normal children. *Psychophysiology,* 1972, *9*(2), 238–245.

Cruickshank, W. M., & Hallahan, D. P. *Perceptual and learning disabilities in children: Psychoeducational practices*. Syracuse, New York: Syracuse University Press, 1975.

Cunningham, C. E., & Barkley, R. A. Hyperactive behavior, drugs, and academic failure. *Journal of Learning Disabilities,* 1978, *11*(15), 274–280.

Farnham-Diggory, S. *Information processing in children*. New York: Academic Press, 1972.

Firestone, P., Poitras-Wright, H., & Douglas, V. The effect of caffeine on hyperactive children. *Journal of Learning Disabilities,* 1978, *11*(3), 133–141.

Gibson, E. J. Trends in perceptual development: Implications for reading. In A. D. Pick (Ed.), *Minnesota symposia on child development* (Vol. 8). Minneapolis: University of Minnesota Press, 1974.

Gibson, J. J. *The senses considered as perceptual systems*. Boston: Houghton-Mifflin, 1966.

Hallahan, D. P., Gajar, A. H., Cohen, S. B., et al. Selective attention and locus of control in learning disabled and normal children. *Journal of Learning Disabilities,* 1978, *4*, 47–52.

Hallahan, D. P., Lloyd, J., Kosiewicz, M. M., et al. Self-monitoring of attention as a treatment for a learning disabled boy's off-task behaviors. *Learning Disabilities Quarterly,* 1979, *2*(3), 24–32.

Hallahan, D. P., Tarver, S. G., Kauffman, J. M., et al. The effect of reinforcement and response cost on selective attention. *Journal of Learning Disabilities,* 1978, *11*(7), 430–438.

Harris, L. P. Attention and learning disordered children: A review of theory and remediation. *Journal of Learning Disabilities,* 1976, *9*(2), 100–110.

Howie, A. M. Effects of brief exposure to symbolic model behavior on the information processing behavior strategies of internally and externally oriented children. *Developmental Psychology,* 1975, *11*, 325–335.

Joynt, D., & Cambourne, D. Psycholinguistic development and the control of behavior. *British Journal of Educational Psychology,* 1968, *38*, 249–260.

Katz, P. A., & Deutsch, M. Relation of auditory-visual shifting to reading achievement. *Perceptual and Motor Skills,* 1963, *17*, 327–332.

Margolis, H. Auditory perceptual test performance and the reflection-impulsivity dimension. *Journal of Learning Disabilities,* 1977, *10*(3), 164–172.

Meichenbaum, D., & Goodman, J. Reflection-impulsivity and verbal control of motor behavior. *Child Development,* 1969, *40*, 785–797.

Mondani, M., & Tutko, T. Relationship of academic underachievement to incidental learning. *Journal of Consulting and Clinical Psychology,* 1969, *33*, 558–560.

Ott, J. N. Influence of fluorescent lights on hyperactivity and learning disabilities. *Journal of Learning Disabilities,* 1976, *9*(7), 417–422.

Palkes, H., Stewart, M., & Kahava, B. Porteus maze performance of hyperactive boys after training in self-directed verbal commands. *Child Development,* 1968, *39*(3–4), 817–826.

Prout, H. T. Behavioral intervention with hyperactive children: A review. *Journal of Learning Disabilities,* 1977, *10*(3), 141–146.

Pribram, K. H. Effort and the control of attention. *Journal of Learning Disabilities,* 1977, *10*(10), 632–634.

Quay, L. C., Popkin, M., Weld, G., et al. Responses of normal and learning disabled children as a function of the stopwatch in the matching figures testing situation. *Journal of Experimental Child Psychology,* 1978, *26,* 383–388.

Rapp, D. J. Does diet affect hyperactivity? *Journal of Learning Disabilities,* 1978, *11*(6), 383–389.

Richey, D. D., & McKinney, J. D. Classroom behavioral styles of learning disabled boys. *Journal of Learning Disabilities,* 1978, *11*(5), 297–302.

Sabatino, D. A., & Ysseldyke, J. E. Effect of extraneous "background" on visual-perceptual and performance of readers and non-readers. *Perceptual and Motor Skills,* 1972, *35,* 323–328.

Stevens, D. A., Boydstun, J. A., Dykman, R. A., et al. Presumed minimal brain dysfunction in children. *Archives of General Psychiatry,* 1967, *16,* 281–285.

Tarver, S. G., & Hallahan, D. P. Attention deficits in children with learning disabilities: A review. *Journal of Learning Disabilities,* 1974, *7,* 560–569.

Vellutino, F. R., Steger, B. M., Moyer, S. C., et al. Has the perceptual deficit hypothesis led us astray? *Journal of Learning Disabilities,* 1977, *10*(6), 375–385.

Wilson, C. D., & Lewis, M. The cardiac response to a perceptual cognitive task in young children. *Psychophysiology,* 1970, *6*(4), 411–420.

Zelniker, T., Jeffrey, W., Ault, R., et al. Analysis and modification of search strategies of impulsive and reflective children on the Matching Familiar Figures Test. *Child Development,* 1972, *43,* 321–335.

Zelniker, T., Renan, A., Sorer, I., et al. Effects of perceptual processing strategies on problem solving of reflective and impulsive children. *Child Development,* 1977, *48*(4), 1436–1442.

Zentall, S. S., Zentall, T. R., & Barack, R. C. Distraction as a function of within task stimulation for hyperactive and normal children. *Journal of Learning Disabilities,* 1978, *11*(9), 540–548.

2
Concept Organization

Concept organization is the combination of concepts in different relationships. Concepts, concept learning, and concept attainment are terms used to describe concept organization. Concepts (e.g., red, dog, freedom) are regularities in the environment that are identified and grouped (Bruner, 1973; Bruner, Olver, & Greenfield, 1966). Concept learning or discrimination learning is responding selectively in the presence of multiple stimuli (Reese, 1976). Concept attainment is the process by which other examplars of a concept are identified (i.e., furniture: chair, sofa, table; Bruner, Goodnow, & Austin, 1956). Concept organization is a problem-solving activity that requires, in sequence: selection attention; response generation; response execution; and appropriate response to feedback. This problem-solving analysis is emphasized when reviewing tasks used to study concept organization.

Three types of concept organization tasks are Simple Concept Selection, Concept Formation, and Complex Concept Selection. Simple Concept Selection tasks involve two dimensional stimuli and require the child to demonstrate a preference for a hypothesis (i.e., stimulus attributes) or identify instances of a predetermined concept (Restle, 1962). Concept Formation tasks involve stimuli that can be grouped in a variety of ways and require the child to select a specific relationship over other possible relationships (Bruner et al., 1966). Complex Concept Selection tasks involve multidimensional stimuli. When two-dimensional stimuli are used, the solution is changed without the subject's knowledge after the child has determined the relevant dimension (e.g., Kendler & Kendler, 1962). When four-dimensional stimuli are used, increases in cognitive demands (i.e., the amount of attention and memory necessitated by the task) require that concepts be ordered and evaluated simultaneously (e.g., Gholson & Beilin, 1978).

Research is organized according to these three types of tasks with particular emphasis placed on the child's formulation and application of strategies.

DEVELOPMENT OF STRATEGIES

The study of concept organization allows for the study of strategies (Bruner, Goodnow, & Austin, 1956; Johnson, 1978a&b). Implicit in attaining a concept is the underlying plan or strategy of the problem solver (e.g., Bruner et al., 1966; Johnson, 1978). Strategies are inferred from observable behavior; are associated with consistencies or regularities in decisions (Bruner, 1973); are systematic and orderly; and lead to solutions of problems (Gholson, Levine, & Phillips, 1972).

Johnson (1978) suggests three main reasons why the study of concept learning is particularly appropriate for the investigation of strategies. First, the study of concept learning requires the selection of a novel task; consequently, performance is not influenced greatly by prior experience. Second, the design of the task (e.g., segmented into a series of trials) allows inferences to be made about the type of strategy employed by the subject. Finally, the task formats make it possible to determine which hypotheses are eliminated and retained following feedback.

Strategy development parallels conceptual development. Concept organization depends on the information processing strategies formulated and used. The efficiency of the strategy used is determined by the number of trials necessary to reach criterion or solution. In general, developmental changes in strategies are observed at first, second, and sixth grades.

Preschool and kindergarten children tend to perseverate on a specific aspect or position of the stimulus during many of the concept organization tasks. For example, on the hypothesis-testing task, young children respond to a position of the stimulus or a specific stimulus feature. Though they do not solve the problems, their response choices are systematic and orderly (Gholson et al., 1972). Between the ages of 5 and 7 years, a transitional period occurs. Frequently, inconsistent or random responding increases (Rieber, 1969); physical quantities are not successfully manipulated; and literal interpretations of stimuli are made (Piaget & Inhelder, 1969).

Sometime between the ages of 7 and 8 years, the child begins to respond to specific stimulus aspects and formulates plans that lead to solutions of problems (e.g., Bruner, 1973; Gholson & McConville, 1974). The responses of the child become more logical, and the consequences of these responses become more predictable and anticipated (Piaget & Inhelder, 1969). After age 8, selective attention to dimensions occurs, and the child's solutions of problems increase, as does the efficiency of the strategy employed (e.g., Gholson et al., 1972).

Around sixth grade, or at about 10 years of age, children use more sophisticated strategies and, on certain tasks, perform similarly to adults. Also during this time, attention to central information increases (Hallahan, Kauffman, &

Ball, 1973) and attention to incidental information decreases (Hagen, 1967); accurate cognitive maps are formed (Hardwick, McIntyre, & Pick, 1976); mutual role-taking occurs (Shantz, 1975); and responses to feedback are more appropriate in that the children learn to retain a response when correct and change a response when told it is incorrect (Gholson et al., 1972).

To summarize, cognitive shifts in performance occur around the first, second, and sixth grades. The efficiency of the strategies used increases with age, that is, older children solve more problems in fewer trials.

THEORIES OF STRATEGY DEVELOPMENT

Theories of strategy development are theories of concept learning. The most influential theorist is Bruner (1973; Bruner et al., 1956; Bruner et al., 1966). Bruner suggests that concept learning is a hierarchical process that is interrelated with the development of language. Bruner uses the term concept attainment to describe the constructive and active process of encountering, generating, and evaluating hypotheses or instances. The instances encountered are either confirming or infirming and are either negative or positive. This results in four types of instances encountered: positive confirming; negative confirming; positive informing; and negative informing. For example, the following is hypothesized: "Kindergarten children perseverate on the position of a stimulus when the hypothesis testing task is employed." A positive confirming instance is encountered when kindergarten children respond repeatedly to the position of a stimulus or a specific attribute of the stimulus, regardless of feedback (Gholson et al., 1972). A negative confirming instance is encountered when second graders do not perseverate, but use strategies. A negative informing instance is encountered when kindergarten children do not perseverate. A positive informing instance is encountered when second graders perseverate on a position or stimulus attribute.

Hypotheses generated about the problem-solving situation are a function of the specific instances encountered. Once generated, hypotheses are evaluated. This evaluation occurs with reference to an internal model. This internal model represents our orienting theory toward our environment and is based on the regularities or consistencies encountered in the environment.

The sequence of encountering, generating, and evaluating instances with respect to an internal model requires that decisions be made. Bruner (1973) describes patterns of decisions as strategies involving acquisition, retention, and utilization of information in order to meet certain objectives (e.g., solution of the problem in the fewest number of trials possible). Most strategies described by Bruner are receptive in nature. A receptive strategy is a plan that is formulated by the child as instances are encountered. Receptive strategies are employed during concept organization and do not vary across tasks (e.g., Bruner, 1973; Mosher & Hornsby, 1966). Receptive strategies, however, do change as a function of the efficiency of the problem solver.

Bruner (1973) identifies two types of ideal strategies that are only approximated by problem solvers. The first and most efficient is the focusing or wholist strategy. This strategy is observed when the child selects and evaluates an initial hypothesis on the basis of all the information encountered. The second and less efficient strategy is the scanning strategy. Problem solvers employing this strategy may either process instances simultaneously or in parts. However, all the information encountered is not processed at one time. Generally, those employing the scanning strategy encounter more negative infirming instances, while those employing the focusing strategy encounter more negative confirming instances. Bruner's descriptions of these two types of strategies are elaborated and further defined by more recent theorists (e.g., Gholson et al., 1972).

To summarize, Bruner (1973) suggests that the child uses strategies to solve concept learning problems. Initially, the child identifies temporal and spatial similarities in the environment. More efficient problem solvers learn to focus on more relevant and abstract relationships while ignoring the irregularities or inconsistencies in information. This increase in efficiency is a function of both the problem solver's underlying plan and internal mode.

Offering a somewhat different perspective, Restle (1962) discusses the process involved in the selection of strategies in Simple Concept Selection tasks. Consistent with Bruner, Restle defines a strategy as a particular pattern of responses to stimuli that are inferred over a series of trials. In the strategy selection process, hypotheses are tested one at a time until the correct strategy is selected. In other words, what the child learns is to select the correct strategy. Emphasis is placed on retesting a hypothesis when feedback is positive and changing it when feedback is negative. This description of appropriate response to feedback is a basic assumption of Hypothesis-Testing Theory (e.g., Gholson, 1980; Levine, 1975).

In summary, similar strategies are applied across concept organization tasks (e.g., Annett, 1959; Gholson et al., 1972; Mosher & Hornsby, 1966). Changes in strategies are observed with children at different ages. More efficient strategies are used by older children, and reflect an increase in at least two abilities: the ability to attend and process hypotheses simultaneously, and the ability to compare feedback information across trials. Various reasons are offered to account for such changes and suggest differences in theoretical orientation. In the next section, these theories are briefly discussed within the context of the tasks employed to study concept organization.

CONCEPT ORGANIZATION OF CHILDREN WITHOUT LEARNING PROBLEMS

Except for a few isolated studies, researchers stopped investigating concept organization in traditional ways (e.g., shift behavior, transposition, and stimulus preference) some time during the 1960s and early 1970s. During the early 1970s, focus shifted to the study of hypothesis testing behaviors and the pragmatics of language. (For more information on language, see Chapter 4.) Recent theorists have adopted some of the basic theoretical constructs associated with this earlier work, but have modified others. Relevant theory and data substantiating these assumptions are reviewed under the topics of Complex Concept Selection, Concept Formation, and Simple Concept Selection.

Complex Concept Selection

Various theories have been formulated to describe concept organization. Two of these theories stem from research in the areas of concept shift learning and hypothesis-testing. The most researched area is concept shift learning. Therefore, it is not unexpected that major theoretical frameworks for the study of concept organization are from that literature. These theories, and pertinent research, are discussed under the subcategories of stimulus differentiation, selective attention, mediation, hypothesis-testing, and feedback. In this way, data are related to the problem-solving analysis proposed in the Introduction.

STIMULUS DIFFERENTIATION

Kendler and Kendler's (1962) analysis of concept shift learning is presented in detail under *Mediation;* other perspectives of concept shift learning are elaborations of their position. Tighe and Tighe (1972) discuss the importance of stimulus control in children's concept shift learning. Stimulus control occurs through differential reinforcement and results in predictable responding in the presence of specific cues. Tighe and Tighe present an analysis of shift performance referred to as Sub-Problem Analysis. Tighe and Tighe (1972) designed the Sub-Problem Analysis procedure to determine if the children responded to each stimulus pair as an independent problem, or if they responded to relationships between pairs.

The traditional concept learning problem is presented in Figure 2-1. In Figure 2-1, the reward situation is reversed for both pairs during a reversal shift. In contrast, for the extradimensional shift, the reward for one pair remains the same, is unchanged, and is changed for the other pair. According to the subproblem analysis, the subject learns twice as much information in order to complete the reversal shift. The extradimensional shift requires the learning of only one subproblem on each trial. In this way, the extradimensional shift is easier to learn than the reversal shift.

When very young children without learning problems and infrahumans nonhumans were studied, both learned extradimensional shifts faster than reversal shifts (Tighe, 1973). Tighe, Glick & Cole (1971) found that 4-year-old youngsters solved the problems in fewer trials when the unchanged pair was correct, and showed a slow, gradual acquisition of the correct response to the changed pair.

SINGLE UNIT THEORY

Reversal Shift

$$S \begin{matrix} \nearrow R_{large} \\ \searrow R_{small} \end{matrix}$$

Nonreversal Shift

$$S \begin{matrix} \nearrow R_{large} \\ \searrow R_{black} \end{matrix}$$

MEDIATIONAL THEORY

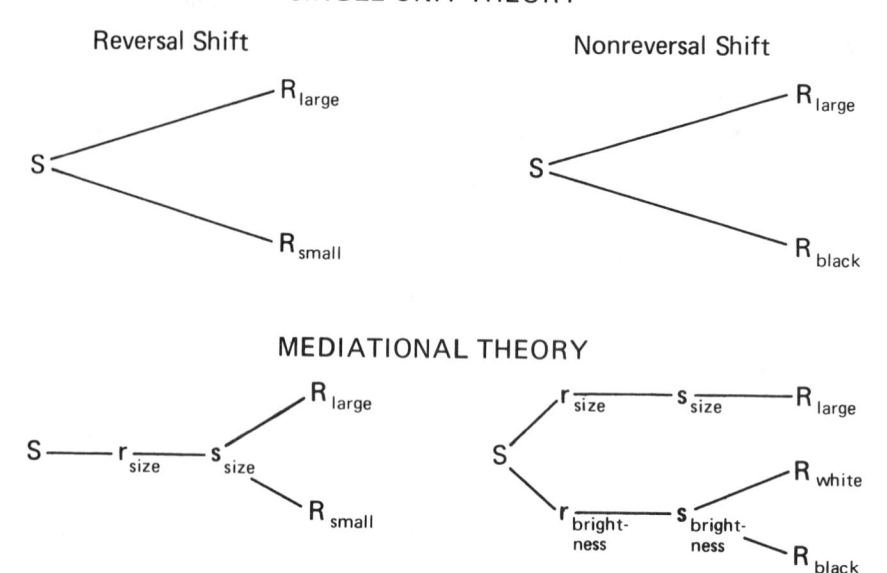

$$S \longrightarrow r_{size} \longrightarrow s_{size} \begin{matrix} \nearrow R_{large} \\ \searrow R_{small} \end{matrix}$$

$$S \begin{matrix} \nearrow r_{size} - s_{size} \begin{matrix} \nearrow R_{large} \\ \searrow R_{white} \end{matrix} \\ \searrow r_{brightness} - s_{brightness} \begin{matrix} \nearrow \\ \searrow R_{black} \end{matrix} \end{matrix}$$

Fig. 2-1. Kendler and Kendler's Cognitive analysis of a reversal and nonreversal shift. (From Kendler, H. H., & Kendler, T. S. Vertical and horizontal processes in problem solving. *Psychological Review,* 1962, 69(1), 1–16. Copyright [1962] by the American Psychological Association. Reprinted by permission.)

This occurred regardless of whether or not the shift was reversal or extradimensional. Ten-year-old children learned the reversal shift faster than the extradimensional shift; these children solved extradimensional shift problems at a slower rate regardless of whether or not the changes or unchanged pair was presented. Tighe and Tighe (1972) concluded that young children learned each pair as an individual subproblem, while older children and adults learned the relationship between pairs. Tighe and Tighe suggested that differences in shift performance were the function of the child's ability to differentiate distinguishing features of the task, which was related to the degree of dimensional control.

In terms of development, changes in concept shift performance occurred before age 5 (Caron, 1970; Tighe & Tighe, 1970), between 5 and 7 years (e.g., Kendler & Kendler, 1972), and after age 10 (Tighe & Tighe, 1970). Before the age of 5, extradimensional shifts were accomplished more easily than reversal shifts. Between the ages of 5 and 7 years, reversal and nonreversal shifts were learned with equal difficulty. After age 10, and during early childhood, reversal shifts were learned faster than extradimensional shifts. Reasons suggested for these changes in performance were differences in the ability to use verbal mediations (Kendler & Kendler, 1962); to focus attention (Zeaman & House, 1963); and to respond to stimulus relationships (Tighe & Tighe, 1972).

Concept Organization

SELECTIVE ATTENTION

Zeaman and House (1963) studied how retarded children learned to solve reversal and extradimensional shift problems. These authors proposed that this type of learning required the acquisition of a chain of responses. First, the child oriented toward, or observed, the relevant dimension. This was referred to as observer response. Next, the child approached the correct cue on the relevant dimension. This was referred to as the instrumental response. In both of these activities, the stimulus dimension elicited attention; children either attended to one dimension at a time, or more than one dimension simultaneously. If the selected cue was reinforced, both the instrumental and observer responses were strengthened. If the cues were not reinforced, both of these responses were weakened. In this way, attention was directed to the relevant cue through differential reinforcement.

If the child had difficulty solving the problems, it was proposed that the information was processed, but not necessarily information about the relevant dimension. To gather support for their position, Zeaman and House (1963) compared the performance of retarded children on three shift tasks: reversal shift; extradimensional shift; and intradimensional shift. An intradimensional shift was when the solution was changed to a new cue (e.g., blue) within the same relevant dimension as the previously reinforced cue (e.g., black). Results showed that transfer of learning was negative when an extradimensional shift was instituted. Reversal shifts were learned faster than extradimensional shifts when the relevant dimension was varied within trials. These findings were interpreted as indicating that shift learning was both a function of the relationship between the stimuli (Zeaman & House, 1963), and the presentation of the stimuli (Caron, 1970).

Dickerson (1966) also studied concept shift behavior of preschool children. In his procedure, the relevant dimension was varied from trial to trial. Dickerson found that reversal and intradimensional shifts were learned faster than extradimensional shifts. These results were interpreted as indicating positive transfer of learning from the reversal to the intradimensional shift. Caron (1970) found the opposite effect with a group of 3-year-olds. These children learned the extradimensional shift faster than the reversal shift when presentation of the irrelevant dimension was constant within trials. These studies emphasize the importance of stimulus presentation on concept shift learning.

MEDIATION

Kendler and Kendler (1962) studied the role of mediation in concept shift learning. Kendler and Kendler developed a standard procedure used to assess concept shift learning. In concept shift learning, the child was presented with a pair of two-dimensional stimuli, similar to those shown in Figure 2-2. Referring to Figure 2-2, the stimuli differ on two dimensions, such as color and size. The

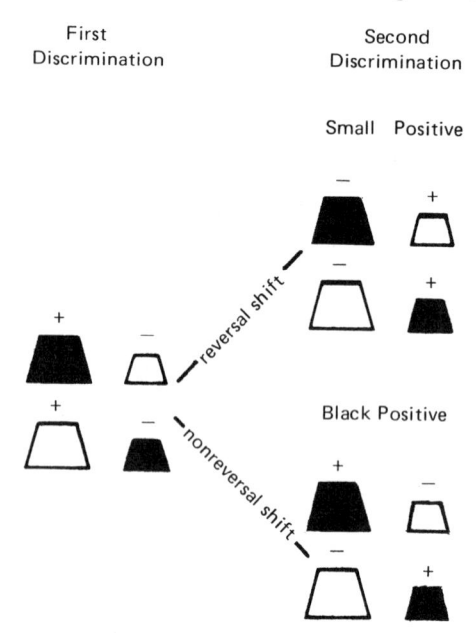

Fig. 2-2. Kendler and Kendler's example of reversal and nonreversal shift. (From Kendler, H. H., & Kendler, T. S. Vertical and horizontal processes in problem solving. *Psychological Review*, 1962, 69(1), 1–16. Copyright [1962] by the American Psychological Association. Reprinted by permission.)

child is reinforced for responding to a specific cue on a dimension, such as black on the color dimension. When black is reinforced, color becomes the relevant dimension; the other dimension, size, becomes the irrelevant dimension. Cues on the irrelevant dimension are reinforced some of the time, that is, when they are associated with the stimulus containing the cue from the relevant dimension. After the child attains the solution and selects consistently the correct stimulus or relevant cue, the relevant cue is changed without the subject's knowledge. In this way, a new problem is posed (Tighe & Tighe, 1972). If white becomes the correct cue, the shift is referred to as a reversal shift; both the previously reinforced cue and the new reinforced cue are from the same dimension. If the cue on the irrelevant dimension (i.e., small-size) becomes correct and is reinforced, the shift is referred to as a nonreversal or extradimensional shift; the now-reinforced cue is from a different dimension than the previously reinforced cue.

Kendler and Kendler (1962) propose that mediation occurs when a reversal shift is learned faster than a nonreversal shift. This is not the case when a nonreversal shift is learned faster than a reversal shift. During mediation, the external or overt stimulus leads to an implicit response. This implicit

Concept Organization

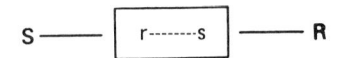

```
S ———— [ r--------s ] ———— R
```

Fig. 2-3. A schematic representation of the mediational hypothesis.

response produces an implicit cue, which is linked to the overt response. The implicit cue and stimulus are inferred from the overt response. When a subject mediates, the implicit response-stimulus (R-S) relationship is maintained, that is, if never reinforced after the reversal shift, the child who mediates will shift to white. Both of these cues are from the same dimension and were generated during the reversal shift problem. In this way, the cue white is still available and does not need to be generated. During the nonreversal shift, the child who mediates must generate a new implicit response-stimulus relationship that is associated with the previously irrelevant dimension.

Kendler and Kendler (1962) found that older children, approximately age 7, benefited most from mediating responses, such as verbal rehearsal. Four-year-old children who were able to generate spontaneously the correct verbal response only benefited when that verbal response was associated with the relevant and dominant dimension. These same children were hindered when the irrelevant dimension was verbalized.

Reese (1962) summarized early findings regarding the effects of verbal mediation, age level, and the type of task on concept shift learning. He concluded that across tasks (e.g., shift learning and transposition) young children did not use verbal mediation to facilitate learning. The age at which this ability occurred varied as the function of the task format, stimuli, and concept to be learned. Reese also pointed out that mediation was not a necessary process for learning to respond consistently to all concepts (e.g., acquired equivalents of cues already required).

In summary, the ability to generate mediated responses increased with age, and varied as a function of developmental level (e.g., Kendler & Kendler, 1962; Tighe & Tighe, 1970). With respect to development, results showed that children below the age of 5 learned extradimensional shifts or nonreversal shifts faster than reversal shifts; children around the age of 7 learned reversal shifts faster than nonreversal shifts (Kendler & Kendler, 1962). Differences in the ability to mediate were suggested to explain these findings.

HYPOTHESIS-TESTING

An area of study that has received considerable research attention is that of hypothesis-testing. Levine (1970, 1975) initially proposed the Subset-Sampling Theory to describe the hypothesis-testing behaviors of adults. Gholson et al.

(1972) modified Levine's task and applied this theory to work with children (for a review, see Gholson, 1980; Gholson & Beilin, 1978; Levine, 1975). Briefly, the child is shown a pair of stimuli that differ on two cues on each of four dimensions (see "General Considerations," Fig. 2). The child's task is to identify the cue or hypothesis predetermined by the examiner as the solution. The child is provided with two kinds of trials (feedback and outcome trials) and a series of four blank-trial probes. On the feedback trials, the child is told whether or not the stimulus selected contains the correct cue. Interspersed between feedback trials are four non-outcome or blank trials referred to as the blank-trials probe. During the blank-trials probe, no feedback is given and the child's basis for selection is inferred from the response patterns, which either conform to the testing of a hypothesis or to a response set. Testing and evaluating hypotheses eventually leads to solution of the problems. Response sets indicate systematic responding and are used to describe perseveration on a hypothesis or position of a stimulus and do not lead to solutions of problems.

Levine's Subset-Sampling Theory is based on certain assumptions. First, competent problem solvers begin a problem with a plan. This plan dictates how hypotheses are sampled and evaluated. The subject samples hypotheses randomly from a universal set of hypotheses. Second, subjects respond on the basis of a single hypothesis. Third, if a hypothesis is confirmed, it is retained, and, if disconfirmed, it is eliminated. Finally, if feedback is not provided, the hypothesis is retained on those trials (Levine, 1970). The hypothesis-testing task, employing the blank-trials probe, allows determination of what is attended to, responses to feedback, and the strategy applied.

Gholson et al. (1972) identify three strategies used by children and adults to solve the hypothesis testing problems. These are the Focusing Strategy, Dimension Checking Strategy, and the Hypothesis Checking Strategy. The Focusing Strategy is the most efficient strategy, enabling the problem-solver to solve the problems in the fewest number of trials possible. Children and adults who use this strategy process all available information simultaneously and take into account feedback across trials. Children using the Dimension Checking Strategy do not process and evaluate all the available information. Instead, only those cues associated with a specific dimension (e.g., color) are processed and evaluated simultaneously. The Hypothesis Checking Strategy is the least efficient strategy. Children who use this strategy process and evaluate cues separately (e.g., red, then green). The efficiency of the strategy used increases with age.

In addition to strategies, children may respond with response sets. Response sets are orderly, but do not lead to solution of problems. Response sets indicate perseveration on the position of the stimulus, or on a specific hypothesis. This type of response pattern is observed with preschool children almost exclusively.

Hypothesis-Testing Behaviors

A number of explanations are offered to account for differences in the hypothesis-testing behaviors of children. These are mediation (Phillips & Levine, 1975); stimulus differentiation (Gholson & McConville, 1974); selective attention (Offenbach, 1974); memory (Eimas, 1969, 1970); and feedback (Gholson & McConville, 1974; Parrill-Burnstein, 1978a). The studies reviewed in this next section are organized according to these explanations.

STIMULUS DIFFERENTIATION

Gholson and McConville (1974) studied the effect of providing or not providing feedback on a stimulus differentiation task presented prior to the hypothesis-testing task. On the stimulus differentiation task, youngsters selected which of two stimuli were identical and which was the odd stimulus. Children in the experimental group were told whether they were right or wrong after each choice; children in the control group were not told anything following their choices. Following this, the hypothesis-testing task, employing the blank-trial procedure, was presented in an identical fashion to both groups. The results showed that on the stimulus differentiation task, the groups did not differ and solved almost all of the problems. However, when hypothesis-testing tasks data were analyzed, those in the experimental group tested significantly more hypotheses, made significantly more consistent responses to feedback, and solved significantly more problems.

Gholson and McConville (1974) reported that only about 18% of the protocols of each group could be categorized according to strategy. This was consistent with his earlier research (Gholson et al., 1972) and may suggest that the experimenter's and the subject's criteria for responding were different (Johnson, 1978). Of those that could be categorized, about 40% of the response patterns of the experimental group conformed to the Dimension Checking Strategy and another 10% to the Hypothesis Checking Strategy. Furthermore, children in the experimental group displayed more inconsistent or random responding than those in the control group. Rieber (1969) suggested that inconsistent or random responding indicated a transition between solution responses and nonsolution responses. The performance of the control group consisted of stimulus preferences and position perseveration and replicated earlier findings (Gholson et al., 1972).

SELECTIVE ATTENTION

Offenbach (1974) evaluated the effects of selective attention on the hypothesis-testing behaviors. First, third, and fifth graders, college students, and an older population were subjects used in this task. Offenbach's task required the subject to select, through pointing, one of the eight hypotheses that were decomposed and represented individually on a wheel (i.e., red component, green component). Subjects selected their choice on the wheel prior to selecting the stimulus that contained that cue on the hypothesis-testing task. The subjects were not required to verbalize their choice. Extensive pretraining was provided to teach the subjects how to use the wheel correctly.

Offenbach's (1974) wheel technique yielded similar results as when the blank-trial probe was used. A difference was that requiring the subject to select an hypothesis prior to stimulus selection eliminated most position perseveration. Offenbach also examined the type of shift after the first error and the first correct response. After the first error, first graders and aged populations performed more intradimensional shifts than those in the other grades. Extradimensional shifts were performed faster by those in the other grades. Extradimensional shifts were performed faster by those in grades three and five and college students. As Offenbach pointed out, extradimensional shifts were more similar to the Dimension Checking Strategy and intradimensional shifts were more similar to the Hypothesis Checking Strategy. After the first correct response, few systematic differences were observed. With respect to solution, about 45% of the problems were solved. College students solved the most and the aged the least.

To summarize, Offenbach's selective attention procedure required subjects to focus attention, through overt selection, on a specific hypothesis. This procedure proved effective in increasing selective attention to hypotheses and facilitating certain problem-solving behaviors.

MEDIATION

With respect to mediation and the hypothesis-testing task, two transfer conditions were studied: (1) labeling the hypothesis selected prior to the actual choice (introtacts); and (2) the effect of previous solutions on later problems. This latter type of transfer is discussed first.

Phillips, Levine, and O'Brien (1978) attempted to equate the concept of transfer associated with intradimensional shift behavior with that of hypothesis-testing behavior. Their subjects were second, sixth, eighth, and twelfth graders. Within this study, an intradimensional shift was defined as selection of a new cue, but within the same dimension as the reinforced cue from the preceding problem. Only the first response on the new problem was analyzed. For example, if yellow were the correct solution on the preceding problem, and when given the first trial of the next problem, the child responded with the color cue blue, this was interpreted as an intradimensional shift which required mediation.

Phillips et al. (1978) found that second and sixth graders made intradimensional shifts, which decreased over problems. In contrast, eighth and twelfth graders did not. Instead, they frequently selected cues associated with a new

Concept Organization

dimension. These results were interpreted as being inconsistent with those of the mediation explanation offered for shift behavior (e.g., Kendler & Kendler, 1962). However, four basic differences between Phillips et al.'s (1978) procedures and Kendler's procedure were worth noting. First, unlike the shift task, hypotheses were enumerated at the beginning of each problem. Second, during pretraining on the hypothesis testing task, the relationship between stimuli and the correct cue was indicated to the child. Third, the experimenter announced at the end of each hypothesis testing problem that a new problem was to be presented; and, fourth, during concept shift learning, the change in solution was abrupt, possibly encouraging a specific shift response.

Verbal mediation or verbal labeling similar to that described for shift behavior was also investigated using the hypothesis testing task. Phillips and Levine (1975) required children to verbalize their selected hypothesis prior to selection. The verbal label was referred to as an introtact and was used in place of the blank-trial probe described earlier. Both types of probes yielded almost identical results after the sixth grade. For second graders, however, the type of the probe used affected responding. With younger children, introtact yielded more consistent performance between choice and previous feedback, as well as increasing the number of hypotheses tested. Phillips and Levine suggested that introtacts decreased the memory requirement, directed the attention to the cues, and therefore facilitated hypothesis testing and problem-solving behaviors. They concluded that blank-trial probes exaggerated deficits or development differences, while the nonprobe conditions yielded results somewhere in between.

FEEDBACK

Parrill-Burnstein (1978a) investigated the effects of stimulus differentiation, memory, selective attention, and feedback on the hypothesis-testing behaviors of kindergarten children. She taught youngsters to use a strategy identical in product to the Dimension Checking Strategy (Gholson et al., 1972). The baseline data she initially obtained were similar to those obtained by other researchers (e.g., Gholson et al., 1972); kindergarten children tended to respond with response sets rather than with strategies. During training, the children were taught either a component or a sequence of components analyzed as necessary to solve the discrimination learning problems. There were four conditions: group 1 enumerated verbally the four cues associated with the first correct stimulus. In addition to the instruction given to those in group 1, children in group 2 were given visual representations of the four cues enumerated. Those in group 3, in addition to instructions provided to group 2, were taught to isolate and test one cue at a time. Children in the final condition were taught the complete sequence of problem-solving steps. In addition to the instructions given to group 3, the children in group 4 were given information about how to respond appropriately to feedback. They were taught to eliminate or remove an incorrect hypothesis and retest or leave a confirmed hypothesis. Children in this group solved 100% of the posttest problems.

In a later study, (Parrill-Burnstein, 1978a), kindergarten children were taught the focusing strategy. Using a similar design, Parrill-Burnstein found those children who were taught the complete sequence of steps, including the appropriate response to feedback, solved approximately 70 percent of the problems, which was significantly better than those in the other training conditions. The complexity of the focusing strategy was reflected in the fewer number of problems solved when compared to teaching the Dimension Checking Strategy. In other words, it was more difficult for kindergarten children to process the stimulus information simultaneously than when evaluated separately.

Parrill-Burnstein interpreted her results as indicating that the suggestion of a strategy did not elicit problem-solving behaviors. However, teaching the complete task analysis, including instructions about the appropriate responses to feedback, was successful in producing more sophisticated problem-solving behaviors in children who initially perseverated on an unsuccessful response.

Richman and Gholson (1978), with second- and sixth-grade children, studied the effects of observational learning on hypothesis testing behavior. Children were either shown a tape of a model demonstrating the Focusing Strategy, the Dimension Checking Strategy, or no explicit strategy. Results showed that children benefited the most when exposed to a strategy most consistent with their developmental level (e.g., second graders, Dimension Checking Strategy; sixth graders, Focusing Strategy). Second graders performed best after observing the Dimension Checking Strategy and poorest when exposed to the videotape of the Focusing Strategy. Children in the sixth grade performed similarly in all three conditions.

In summary, the use of the hypothesis-testing task, employing either the blank-trial probe(s) (e.g., Gholson et al., 1972), introtact(s) (Phillips & Levine, 1975), or the wheel technique (Offenbach, 1974), yielded consistent developmental findings. Findings obtained were in line with those reported for concept shift learning. Preshcool children tended to perseverate on a position or stimulus preference (Gholson et al., 1972). Older children used strategies and solved more of the problems. The efficiency of the strategy used increased with age. Children in the first grade frequently used the Hypothesis Checking Strategy; those in the second grade increased in their use of the Dimension Checking Strategy; and fourth and sixth graders frequently used the Dimension Checking Strategy. Some sixth graders, and about 50% of the adults, used the Focusing Strategy (Gholson et al., 1972).

Hypothesis-testing behaviors were facilitated by a number of different techniques: stimulus differentiation training (Gholson & McConville, 1974); teaching the complete task analysis, including the appropriate response to feedback (Parrill-Burnstein, 1978a); increasing attention through hypothesis selection prior to responding (Offenbach, 1974); modeling age-appropriate strategies (Richman

& Gholson, 1978); and asking children to verbalize a hypothesis prior to selection (Phillips & Levine, 1975).

Concept Formation

During concept formation, material is organized into groups or clusters based on a specific criterion, selected over other possible combinations or criteria (Bruner, 1973). Consistent developmental trends are observed. Around the age of 6 years, a child's groupings are based on spatial locations or relationships (i.e., orange and tree). Between the ages of 6 and 9 years, a shift is observed in that an increase in groupings by similarities occurs (e.g., both grow). After 9 years, and continuing into early adulthood, categories are formed predominantly on class inclusion (e.g., Annett, 1959). Older adults, like young children, group items on the basis of complementary characteristics (N. W. Denney, 1974). These general developmental trends are obtained regardless of the procedures employed and stimuli used.

Two procedures designed to assess concept formation and study developmental trends are the card sorting task and the Twenty Questions Game. Stimuli are words, nonsense figures or familiar or meaningful material.

Various reasons are proposed to describe the developmental changes observed in subjects' performances on the card sorting task and Twenty Questions Game. Some suggest that because the tasks are unstructured by design, younger children and older adults feel more comfortable and less pressured to form groups according to similarities, although they are capable of grouping the stimuli (N. W. Denney, 1974). Denney (N. W. 1974) suggests that groupings based on similarities are encouraged through school instruction. The interpretation is that environmental factors are responsible for changes in criteria (N. W. Denney, 1974). Others suggested that young children are less able to organize information (Mandler, 1967) and are functioning at a lower level of perceptual development.

TWENTY QUESTIONS GAME

One task used to study concept formation is Mosher and Hornsby's (1966) Twenty Questions Game. In this task, the child is presented with a series of items in various colors, different spatial locations, and from different categories (i.e., fruits, clothes). The child's task is to try to guess the item predetermined by the examiner as correct. The subject is allowed to ask up to 20 questions. The objective is to find the solution item in the fewest number of questions possible. If the child asks a question that eliminates two or more items, the question is referred to as a Constraint Seeking Question (e.g., "Is it a tool?"). Questions about individual items are referred to as Hypothesis Seeking Questions (e.g., "Is it the boat?"). Constraint Seeking Questions are more efficient, since more hypotheses can be eliminated than when Hypothesis Scanning Questions are used.

Using this procedure, Mosher and Hornsby (1966) found that certain types of questions were asked at specific ages. Six-year-olds asked more Hypothesis Seeking Questions, while 8 and 11-year-olds asked more Constraint Seeking Questions. The younger children recognized the value of Constraint Seeking Questions over Hypothesis Seeking Questions, although they did not spontaneously generate the former type of question. Van Horn and Bartz (1968) did not replicate this latter finding.

Van Horn and Bartz (1968) found that the array of the items affected performance. The array was either arranged by categories (ordered), or the items were placed at random (random). The performance of 7- and 8-year-olds was influenced less by ordering the array than that of the 6-year-olds. Removing the items eliminated by the questions asked did not influence performance.

When Denney and her colleagues (D. R. Denney, 1972; Denney, Denney, & Ziobrowski, 1975) studied the effects of eliminating items through modeling, they found that models who demonstrated both the strategy and the elimination of items were most effective in increasing Constraint Seeking Questions. Denney et al. (1975) exposed 6-year-olds to one of three modeling conditions or to a control condition. The adult model either verbalized a strategy, verbalized a strategy and removed eliminated items, verbalized and illustrated a strategy for asking specific types of questions, or did not demonstrate a strategy. Results showed that children in all three modeling conditions differed significantly from the control group by increasing the number of Constraint Seeking Questions asked. Also, children who removed items eliminated by the questions performed best.

In another study, Denney (1975) again studied the effects of modeling on the type of question asked. Children aged 6, 8, and 10 years were exposed to one of three models: a model who verbalized constraint seeking questions; a model who verbalized the constraint seeking strategy and then the appropriate question (e.g., "These are all animals"); or a model who required the child to rehearse or verbalize the strategy demonstrated (i.e., "Don't ask about one item"). Results indicated that only those exposed to the last modeling condition differed significantly from the control condition. However, all three modeling conditions produced a significant increase in the number of Constraint Seeking Questions asked. Further analysis indicated that only the six-year-olds responded differently as the function of the modeling condition. For these children, it was necessary for the model to both discuss and demonstrate Constraint Seeking Questions. This finding replicated an earlier finding that six-year-olds did not benefit from observing models alone (Denney, 1972).

To summarize, with respect to the Twenty Questions Game, six-year-olds asked Hypothesis Seeking Questions, i.e., questions about specific items. The 7- and 8-year-olds asked both Hypothesis Seeking Questions and Constraint Seeking Questions, indicating a possible transition period. Older children asked Constraint Seeking Questions almost exclusively (e.g., D. R. Denney, 1972, 1975; Mosher & Hornsby, 1966). These developmental trends were consistent with earlier reports. For example, when compared to the Hypothesis Testing Task,

Hypothesis Seeking Questions were similar in concept to the Hypothesis Checking Strategy, and Constraint Seeking Questions were similar in concept to the Dimension Checking Strategy. These equated strategies were observed at approximately the same ages.

CARD SORTING

As with the Twenty Questions Game, card sorting tasks allow inferences to be made about the categories formed by the subject. While the Twenty Questions Game requires verbalization of categories in question form, card sorting tasks may or may not require verbal justification for the groups sorted (Annett, 1959). During the free classification or card sorting task, the child's ability to spontaneously organize information is assessed. The child is asked to group together the items that go together. The common characteristic between items indicates the basis of the sort. Regardless of the type of card sorting task employed, the developmental findings are similar when compared to the Twenty Questions Game.

Annett (1959), using the standard card sorting task, investigated free classification. The subject was required to state verbally the reason for each group formed. Five types of verbalizations were differentiated: (1) no explanation; (2) enumeration (e.g., dog, cat, horse); (3) contiguity (e.g., apple, tree); (4) similarity (hat, cap); and (5) class names (e.g., animals). Annett (1959) found that both the actual types, and the verbalizations, varied as a function of age. The 5- and 6-year-olds did not sort on the basis of common characteristics and frequently did not explain their responses. "No explanation" responses decreased sharply with an increase in age. Before age 7, verbal enumerations of items predominated and then decreased. The 7- and 8-year-olds grouped items into pairs (i.e., screw and screwdriver). The use of contiguity criteria peaked at age 8 and then declined. By age 9, and through early adulthood, items were grouped on similar criteria into categories or classes. In addition to these developmental changes, an increase in the number of items within each category and a decrease in the number of categories formed was observed with an increase in age. Annett concluded that children had the "facts" or information about items, and that the difference reflected their use of such information.

D. R. Denney (1972) also investigated sorting with and without verbal labeling using nonsense figures of different shapes and colors. She suggested that the development of a concept was indicated in a change from noncategory sorts to category sorts that were based on complementary and then similar criteria. Complementary criteria were based on an interrelationship (i.e., boat/bird/water) and resulted from an increased awareness of temporal and spatial relationships. Similar criteria were based on perceptual or functional attributes.

Denney's (1972) subjects were 2-, 4-, 6-, 8-, and 12-year-old youngsters. The child's task was to either group objects into different categories, or to select examples of a given object. In the first condition the child was asked to synthesize categories; in the latter condition the child was asked to analyze categories.

Four types of categories were differentiated: (1) no similarity; (2) color; (3) form; and (4) building with similarities.

Using the card sorting task, Denney found that 2-year-olds formed groups based primarily on the location of objects. Categories based on similarity and building with similarity decreased with an increase in age. A significant increase in the use of form, and a significant decrease in the use of color, were observed after age 6. Fewer categories and more items within categories were observed to increase with age. These results were consistent with Annett's (1959) findings.

When the verbal label condition was compared to the free sort condition, interesting findings emerged. In the free sort condition, a greater frequency of form responses was observed, as well as a greater variety of responses. Denney concluded that the similar developmental changes, a decrease in variability with age and an increase in dominance of the form response, were observed using both tasks. Denney suggested that these changes were due to environmental pressures (i.e., school encourages categories based on concepts such as form), and that young children and older adults were capable of using similar criteria but chose not to.

To summarize, tasks such as card sorting and the Twenty Questions Game allowed study of concept formation. Development of concept formation progressed from concrete to abstract levels of classification. At the more concrete levels, spatial and temporal cues as well as perceptual and functional characteristics were the basis for such groupings. At the more abstract level, items were grouped on the basis of less observable characteristics, frequently involving symbols such as words. Consistent developmental changes were observed across tasks before the age of 6, between the ages of 7 and 8, and again between the ages of 9 and 12. These differences were interpreted as indicating changes in the ability to use available information about items (Annett, 1959; Mosher & Hornsby, 1966).

Simple Concept Selection

Simple Concept Selection tasks are presented to determine the effect of dimensional salience on cognitive development. Two types of Simple Concept Selection tasks are the Concept Identification Task and Dimension Preference Test.

CONCEPT IDENTIFICATION AND
DIMENSIONAL PREFERENCE

Concept Identification Task and Dimension Preference Test are discussed together, as they are usually studied within the same experiment. On a dimension preference task, the child is presented with a two-dimensional standard (e.g., red triangle). Then, the child is shown two stimuli, both of which contain one of the same attributes as the standard (e.g., red square and blue triangle). The child's task is to select the stimulus that is most like the standard. The child's preference for a dimension is inferred from his or her response choice (e.g., Wolff, 1966).

The Concept Identification Task, which frequently follows the Dimension Preference Test, allows inference of preference also. Two-dimensional stimuli are presented as pairs on each of the series of trials. The child's task is to respond consistently to the predetermined attribute. Feedback (correctness or incorrectness of the child's choice) is given on every trial. Preference is assessed by calculating the number of trials to criterion when either the preferred or nonpreferred dimension is dominant.

Preference for a dimension affected concept identification, but only during preschool and early school grades. Young children solved the concept identification problems faster when their preferred dimension was relevant (e.g., Suchman & Trabasso, 1966a, 1966b; Brian & Goodenough, 1929). For example, when the solution was form and was the preferred dimension, performance was similar for children in the first, fifth, seventh, tenth grades, and college students (Odom & Mumbauer, 1971), and for kindergarten, first, and third grade children (Mitler & Harris, 1969). With older children, performance was similar when their preferred dimension was either relevant or irrelevant (Odom & Mumbauer, 1971). Preferences associated with age were color, before age 5 years (Suchman & Trabasso, 1966b); size or brightness, around 6 years (Wolff, 1966); and form, after age 8 years (Mitler & Harris, 1969; Odum & Mumbauer, 1971).

When the performance of younger children was compared to the performance of older children and adults, significant differences were obtained. Mitler and Harris (1969) studied preference for form, color, and number. Their subjects were kindergarten children, first graders, and third graders. Both dimension preference and concept identification tasks were presented. On the preference task, only kindergarten children differed significantly from third graders when total errors were compared. A comparison of trials to the criterion on the concept identification task indicated an inverse relationship between age and number of trials to criterion.

Mitler and Harris also investigated the effect of order of task presentation on performance. They found that significantly more children who were given the preference test first failed to reach criterion on the Concept Identification Task. It was suggested that presenting tasks in this sequence encouraged the child to maintain attention to the preferred dimension, which was not always relevant. Mitler and Harris concluded that the form dimension was both available and relevant for children older than 5 years, and that color, though not the preferred dimension, was still available.

Using the same stimuli as Mitler and Harris (1969), Suchman and Trabasso (1966b) worked with nursery school and kindergarten children. Both the Dimension Preference Test and Concept Identification Task were presented. The dimension preference task was presented first. These authors found a significant relationship between dimension preference and performance on the concept identification task. When the preferred dimension was relevant, the concept was obtained faster than when the nonpreferred dimension was relevant.

To summarize, when presented with several concept organization tasks, consistent changes in behavior were obtained. During kindergarten and before the age of 5, fewer children attained solution. Part of this difference was related to selective attention. Children at this age were influenced by spatial location, specific attributes, and dimension preferences. Frequently, preference or bias for stimulus dimension resulted in more trials to criterion (e.g., Suchman & Trabasso, 1966b), perseveration (e.g., Gholson et al., 1972), or inconsistent responding (Rieber, 1969). Also, young children attended to cues individually rather than simultaneously, and grouped those cues on the basis of position, such as right or left (Gholson et al., 1972); or nearness (e.g., Annett, 1959).

Between the ages of 6 and 9 years, a transition period was observed. At approximately 9 years of age, the use of verbal mediators was spontaneous and facilitated concept identification (e.g., Kendler & Kendler, 1962). The ability to associate stimuli on the basis of dimensions was in transition. This shift in attention to dimension changed the type of strategies formulated and used (e.g., Gholson et al., 1972; Mosher & Hornsby, 1966). More specifically, the efficiency of the strategy used increased within this age range.

In summary, with respect to strategy formation and use, a number of systematic plans were identified (e.g., Bruner, 1956). Generally, kindergarten children and preschool children did not use plans that lead to solutions of problems. When children first began to use strategies, individual items rather than dimensions were evaluated (e.g., Mosher & Hornsby, 1966); this was also reflected in the questions these children asked (Mosher & Hornsby, 1966). By age 9, or around the sixth grade, categories were more inclusive and less diverse (Annett, 1967). Generally, cognitive shifts, either in terms of availability or usability (Mitler & Harris, 1969) of information processing, were observed after kindergarten age, at second grade, at sixth grade to early adulthood, and at later adulthood. Some reasons for these changes were differences in motivation (N. W. Denney, 1974), clustering criteria (Annett, 1959), attention (Offenbach, 1974), and feedback (Gholson & McConville, 1974; Parrill-Burnstein, 1978a).

CONCEPT ORGANIZATION AND LEARNING DISABILITIES

Studies of the concept organization skills of children with learning disabilities are also organized according to the three types of cognitive organization tasks: Complex Concept Selection; Concept Formation; and Simple Concept Selection. Implications for the levels of information processing (e.g., selective attention, response generation, and feedback) are discussed. Problems organizing concepts are stressed and findings with children with learning disabilities are

Complex Concept Selection

CONCEPT SHIFT LEARNING

Freibergs and Douglass (1969) studied concept shift learning of hyperactive children and children without learning problems. Hyperactive children with abnormal EEGs were excluded from their sample. Administration of drugs was discontinued prior to and during the study. Children in the hyperactive group were selected by two staff psychologists and were reported as overactive by both parents and teachers. Children in both the hyperactive group and the normal control group ranged in age from 6 to 12 years; mean IQ was within the average range.

The procedure was conducted over two sessions, the second session following the first session by 2 months. Two concept learning tasks were presented during each session: a concept identification task and a reversal shift task. Stimuli for the concept identification task were presented in pairs, one of which contained the exemplar of the concept predetermined by the experimenter as solution. After the child solved the concept identification problem, a reversal shift was instituted. In addition to two concept learning tasks, the rate of reinforcement was varied within both tasks and was either partial or intermittent, continuous-immediate, or continuous-delayed.

Freibergs and Douglass (1969) found that when the children were presented with the concept identification problems, significantly more children in the normal group reached criterion than in the hyperactive group. With this task, the rate of reinforcement had an interesting effect. Hyperactive children did not differ significantly from normal children under conditions of continuous reinforcement, either delayed or immediate. In fact, partial reinforcement was significantly more difficult than continuous reinforcement for children in all groups. Furthermore, hyperactive children performed significantly poorer than normal under the partial reinforcement condition. These results were interpreted as suggesting that with continuous reinforcement, the child's orienting response to the task was reinforced, resulting in better and more sustained attention. This was particularly the case for those in the hyperactive group.

With respect to the reversal shift data, Freibergs and Douglass (1969) did not obtain significant differences between groups. Also, the effects of reinforcement were not significant. These results were interpreted as indicating that hyperactive children were not more rigid in maintaining nonreinforced response choices than those without hyperactivity. These authors suggested that these findings supported an attentional rather than global cognitive deficit as an explanation of hyperactivity.

During the second session, Freibergs and Douglass (1969) used new stimuli and followed the same format described above for the concept identification and reversal shift tasks. Similar results were obtained when the concept identification task data were analyzed. Differences between groups under continuous reinforcement were not significant. All children continued to have greatest difficulty under the partial reinforcement schedule. The effect was even more pronounced with hyperactive children. Performance of the normal children was significantly better on session two; performance of the hyperactive children was significantly poorer on session two. These results were interpreted as indicating that positive transfer of learning from session one to session two occurred for normal children, but not for hyperactive children.

When reversal shift data were examined, hyperactive children took significantly more trials to reach criteria after the reversal shift was instituted than normal children. It was possible that for hyperactive children, an incorrect and never reinforced response took longer to extinguish and was not modified by feedback (i.e., Gholson et al., 1972). Significant effects as a function of the rate of reinforcement were also found. Similar to performance on the concept identification task, children did better under continuous rather than partial reinforcement conditions. This difference was greatest with hyperactive children.

In summary, Freibergs and Douglass (1969) suggested that during continuous reinforcement, the task-orienting response was reinforced. Alternate explanations were also feasible. First, partial reinforcement maintains higher rates of responding than continuous reinforcement (Reynolds, 1968). Irrelevant but inconsistently reinforced responses were maintained longer by normal children, but particularly by hyperactive children. Continuous feedback may have allowed the repeated evaluations of the concept tested. This may be necessary in order for responses to be maintained if correct, or eliminated if incorrect. Furthermore, the temporal continuity of reinforcement (delayed or immediate) was not as influential as the actual rate of reinforcement (continuous or partial). Two other effects were obtained. Hyperactive children did not transfer what was learned in one session to a second session. It was proposed that a learning set was not established for the hyperactive children after the initial session. Performance was also unreliable and more variable when the hyperactive children were considered. Variability in performance is a key characteristic of many hyperactive children.

HYPOTHESIS-TESTING TASK

Parrill-Burnstein and Baker-Ward (1979) used the hypothesis testing task and the blank trial procedure with children with and without learning disabilities. These authors worked with two learning disabled populations enrolled in two different private schools for children with learning disabilities. When equated on achievement, children in one school (LD I) were older than those in the other school (LD II). In addition, a comparison group of children without learning problems was included. Children were in grades one through five. The dependent measures were the number of problems solved, the number of hypotheses tested, and the number of responses consistent with the feedback information.

Parrill-Burnstein and Baker-Ward (1979) found that children with learning disabilities, regardless of the school, solved significantly fewer problems than those in the comparison group. A significant age effect was also obtained. Children in the first grade solved significantly fewer problems than children in the fifth grade. These developmental findings were similar to those obtained with children without learning problems (Gholson et al., 1972).

In order to solve this problem, hypotheses must be tested and appropriate responses to feedback must be made. Children with learning disabilities tested significantly fewer hypotheses and were less consistent following feedback than were children without learning problems. Further analysis indicated that children with learning disabilities in one school (LD I) tested significantly fewer hypotheses than those in the other school or the comparison group. When these children were not testing hypotheses, response sets (stimulus positions and preferences) were observed. This type of responding was similar to that observed with younger children without learning problems (e.g., Gholson & Beilin, 1978), and was interpreted as reflecting basic problems in selective attention.

When children with learning disabilities tested hypotheses, their responses were not always consistent with feedback. For a hypothesis to be consistent with feedback, it must be retained and repeated when feedback is correct and eliminated and changed when the feedback is negative. After negative feedback, a new hypothesis is selected that was not tested and disconfirmed previously. These three criteria must be met before responses were considered consistent with feedback.

Children with learning disabilities in different schools responded inconsistently to feedback, but for different reasons. Children in group LD II with verbal learning disabilities retained a hypothesis following positive feedback and eliminated a hypothesis following negative feedback. In this way, responses were consistent with feedback. However, when these children sampled another hypothesis following negative feedback, they selected an already disconfirmed hypothesis. This is referred to as sampling with replacement (Restle, 1962). Children in group LD I also responded consistently to feedback some of the time. Unlike children in group LD II, children in this group eliminated the response regardless of whether or not it was reinforced. This was only appropriate after negative feedback. Similar to those children with verbal learning disabilities, these youngsters also retested a disconfirmed hypothesis. In this way, reinforcement was intermittent for both groups of children with learning disabilities. Intermittent reinforcement maintains high levels of responding and responses are more resistant to extinction (Reynolds, 1968).

In summary, with respect to the hypothesis testing task, children with learning disabilities solved fewer problems than those children without learning problems. The locus of nonsolution was at the level of selective attention and appropriate response to feedback. Children with learning disabilities tested hypotheses less frequently than normal children, and did not always select responses consistent with the feedback they had received. Children from different schools for children with learning disabilities tested hypotheses with equal frequency but responded differently to feedback (Parrill-Burnstein & Baker-Ward, 1979).

In conclusion, hyperactive children and children with learning disabilities had problems solving the three concept learning tasks (concept identification, reversal shift, and hypothesis testing). The lack of solution reflected problems attending to relevant cues (Freibergs & Douglass, 1969; Parrill-Burnstein & Baker-Ward, 1979); generating and evaluating hypotheses (Parrill-Burnstein & Baker-Ward, 1979); responding appropriately to feedback (Parrill-Burnstein & Baker-Ward, 1979); and responding reliably across time (Freibergs & Douglass, 1969). Inconsistent responses were reinforced some of the time, took longer to extinguish (Freibergs & Douglass, 1969), and varied as a function of the type of learning disability (Parrill-Burnstein & Baker-Ward, 1979).

Concept Formation

To evaluate concept formation in children with learning disabilities, a card sorting task was used. Using this task, significant differences were obtained when the responses of children with learning disabilities were compared to those without learning problems.

Parrill-Burnstein (1978b) worked with three groups of children who were equated on achievement: group LD I consisted of children with learning disabilities; group LD II was a group of children with learning disabilities from a different school who were somewhat older than those in group LD I; and group 3 was a comparison group of children without learning problems. Children in groups LD I and LD II were of at least average intelligence. The WISC-R profiles of these two groups were similar. The children were in grades one through five and were worked with as part of a larger study. The experiment was conducted in two phases. During phase one, baseline data were collected. Each child was asked to group together the pictures that went together. During phase two, children were told that there were five main groups or categories and were again asked to group the items together that went together.

Parrill-Burnstein found no group differences in performance when the children were asked to group the items spontaneously. Consistent with other researchers (e.g., Annett, 1959), the number of categories formed decreased with age, and the number of items within each category increased as age increased. When the children were told there were five main categories or groups, children in the three groups improved significantly in the number of correct categories formed. However, after this instruction, significant differences were obtained. Children in group LD II performed poorest and differed significantly from those in the other two groups, who, in turn, did not differ from each other. Further examination of these data indicated that for the most part children in LD II group continued to group the items as they had during phase one, or formed groups with five items in each instead of five groups.

These data were interpreted as suggesting that not all children with learning disabilities benefited from the verbal instruction provided to facilitate concept organization. Those that did not, may have had problems with the comprehension of verbal language. The importance of differentiating within the learning disabilities population was supported. Also, similar grade trends were observed for children in all three groups. A difference in performance rather than a developmental delay was interpreted when a significant interaction between grade and age was not obtained.

Significant grade effects were also obtained under both conditions. Further analyses revealed that the first graders' performance differed from that of the children in the other four grades; the performance of children in grades two through five did not differ. Many of the categories the first graders formed were associations of two items (e.g., pig/corn). This was consistent with prior research with children without learning problems (e.g., Annett, 1959).

Simple Concept Selection

CONCEPT IDENTIFICATION

Browning (1967) studied concept identification in the presence or absence of visual distractors placed on the periphery of the apparatus. Subjects were children with or without the diagnosis of minimal brain dysfunction (MBD). Children in the MBD group were in classes for perceptually handicapped. Behavioral characteristics described by Strauss and Lehtinen (1947) were the basis for such placement. Children in the MBD group and the normal group were further subdivided into experimental and control groups. Children without learning problems were in grades one through four. The mean age for MBD children and normal children was approximately 8 years, 9 months and was not significantly different. Significant differences were found when IQ data were compared. The IQs of children in the control MBD group were significantly lower than those in the other three groups. This initial difference in IQs dramatically affected results.

As part of their larger study, Parrill-Burnstein and Baker-Ward (1979) investigated the responses of children with and without learning disabilities to a complex visual theme and to distractor items. Children were from different schools for children with learning disabilities. Children in group LD I were younger than those in group LD II, although they were matched on achievement level. The stimulus was a picture of a group activity (e.g., a birthday party), with separate items positioned in the four corners (e.g., bottle, shoe, comb, etc.). The distractors for this task were placed on the periphery but could be considered part of the stimulus by the subjects. The task was to tell a story about the picture. Children in the three groups did not differ when total words and syntax were considered. Significant differences as a function of content, the ability to abstract about the theme, and integration of the distractors were obtained.

With respect to the peripheral items, children in group LD I mentioned these items significantly less frequently than those from group LD II. Children in group LD II mentioned the items as frequently as children in group LD I. However, qualitative differences between group LD II and those without learning problems were obtained. Children in this learning disabilities group labeled or enumerated the objects, while normal children integrated them into their story, as, for example, presents.

In summary, differences in the selective attention and integration of cues were obtained when the responses of children with and without learning disabilities were compared. Differences in the performance of children with learning disabilities and in the presence and placement of distractor items (Parrill-Burnstein & Baker-Ward, 1979) were significant.

CONCLUSION

In order for children to solve the concept organization problems reviewed in this chapter, they must attend to relevant information; generate response options; and make appropriate responses to feedback. Among children with learning disabilities, differences in selective attention, response generation, and appropriate response to feedback hindered solution of the concept learning problems. This was evidenced when concept identification tasks were examined (Freibergs & Douglass, 1969), when reversal shift performance was evaluated (Freibergs & Douglass, 1969), and when the hypothesis testing task was used (Parrill-Burnstein & Baker-Ward, 1979).

Inconsistent and variable performance in terms of responses to relevant cues (Freibergs & Douglass, 1969), distractions (Parrill-Burnstein, 1978), or changes over specified time intervals (Freibergs & Douglass, 1969) characterized the response patterns of children with learning disabilities. It was suggested that those response patterns led to intermittent reinforcement schedules, which resulted in inappropriate behaviors that took longer to extinguish.

With respect to reinforcement schedules, the responses of hyperactive children were more appropriate when feedback was continuous rather than partial (Freibergs & Douglass, 1969). The implications were that hyperactive children (Freibergs & Douglass, 1969) with learning problems and children with learning disabilities (Parrill-Burnstein & Baker-Ward, 1979) needed consistent feedback in order to maintain correct responses and eliminate incorrect responses.

IMPLICATIONS

With respect to concept organization, children with learning disabilities solved problems faster and used more sophisticated strategies when reinforcement was continuous (Freibergs & Douglass, 1969); took more time to extinguish responses when reinforcement was intermittent (Freibergs & Douglass, 1969); identified and generated fewer acceptable hypotheses (Parrill-Burnstein & Baker-Ward, 1979); and responded appropriately to feedback some of the time (Parrill-Burnstein & Baker-Ward, 1979). Children from one learning disabilities group benefited and others were hindered by verbal cues (Parrill-Burnstein & Baker-Ward, 1979).

These research findings suggest the following guideline for clinicians: (1) instruct or assess strategies; (2) institute continuous reinforcement schedules; (3) differentiate within the learning disabilities categories; (4) determine the intact and deficit information processing levels (e.g., selective attention and response generation; (4) present verbal and nonverbal cues simultaneously, but not as competing cues; and (5) apply task analysis procedures when designing training procedures. Suggestions for remediation and research are organized according to three tasks: card sorting, the Twenty Questions Game, and the Hypothesis Testing Task.

REMEDIATION

Card Sorting

Card sorting encourages analysis and synthesis of categories. The suggestions reported here can be used with actual picture representations or three-dimensional objects.

Present the child with an object and ask that the object's characteristics (e.g., function, label, color, shape) be enumerated. If the child can read, write down the characteristics in the order enumerated. Then, ask the child to select the characteristics that provide the most information about the object. This is usually the label or function of the object. Proceed through the list of characteristics until all have been ordered according to their relevance, that is, how much information they provide.

A second task, which uses a similar procedure, is to have the child enumerate the characteristics of a series of objects, presented one at a time. If the child can read, write down what is enumerated. Then, ask the child to underline the characteristics that both objects have in common. If more than one characteristic is common to the two objects, ask the child to put them in order according to relevancy. This procedure can be expanded to include more objects and more pictures.

Sorting can also be used to encourage classification in more than one logical combination. For example, present the child with a group of geometric figures that vary from each other on the basis of only one dimension (e.g., color or shape). Ask the child to group those objects as well. In this way, the child is encouraged to synthesize categories.

To facilitate analysis of categories, present the child with a standard or reference stimulus (e.g., dog) and a group of items, and ask that the items that go with the standard be grouped together. The child should verbalize the relationship that is the basis for the choice.

Verbal stimuli can also be used. For example, present the child with a pair of words and ask that he or she state the relationship between the words. If the child has difficulty, present the visual representation of the words and ask the relationship to be verbalized. Work with words alone should be accomplished as soon as possible.

Question Games

Question games provide an interesting format, which children enjoy. Show the child a picture of a group activity. Tell the child you are thinking of something in the picture. The child can ask as many questions as necessary until the object is named. The child could be given various numbers of points depending on the kinds of questions that her or she asks. For example, the child could receive the same number of points as the percentage of the items eliminated by that particular question. You can also ask the child to state verbally how many items he or she is able to eliminate based on the question asked.

Data with children without learning problems suggest that these children benefit from the modeling of more sophisticated questions (D. B. Denney, 1972). The child can be asked to observe the teacher/clinician playing a question game using stimuli similar to that of the Twenty Questions Game. The object of the game is to guess the predetermined solution, object, or attribute as quickly as possible. The child observes two models; one models hypothesis seeking questions and another models constraint seeking questions. Transfer of the modeling procedure and the child's ability to identify the more sophisticated strategy should be evaluated. The child should also be asked to justify verbally his or her choice of a particular model.

Hypothesis-Testing

These next few tasks provide information using multidimensional stimuli and incorporating mediation and modeling techniques.

Present the child with a pair of stimuli constructed in a similar fashion to Gholson et al. (1972). The stimuli should vary on at least four dimensions. Ask the child to identify the predetermined attribute. First, ask that all possible attributes or hypotheses be verbalized. If help is needed, list attributes for the child. This may involve presenting the child with visual representation of the hypotheses enumerated (Offenbach, 1974; Parrill-Burnstein, 1978a). Then, ask that these eight hypotheses be sorted according to dimension. Again, the visual representation might help in terms of instruction.

To facilitate appropriate response to feedback, a continuation of both tasks might be to have the child point to and label each hypothesis to be tested and initially have the clinician model what the consequences of feedback means: "The red is wrong, move it away," versus "the red is right, try it again" (Parrill-Burnstein, 1978). This should be repeated until all problems are solved. Also, attention to what is resampled when a response is disconfirmed needs attention. It is suggested that the children be asked to remove cues that were disconfirmed so that this type of resampling error will not occur.

An even simpler task would be to use stimuli like those used with the hypothesis testing task and have all the confirmed hypotheses or positive stimuli remain present so that the child can infer the solution (Eimas, 1969, 1970).

Modeling of age appropriate strategies can also be used to facilitate hypothesis testing behavior (Richman & Gholson, 1978). Modeling and verbalizations (D. R. Denney, 1975) appear the most effective techniques. Have the teacher/ clinician model the strategy using visual presentation of the cues (Parrill-Burnstein, 1978a). While demonstrating, it is important that the model talk through each step, both in sequence as well as in terms of the rationale behind the step. As soon as possible, have the child perform while the model continues to verbalize; eventually, the child will verbalize as he or she works.

RESEARCH IMPLICATIONS

It is suggested that research efforts incorporate the following: a normal comparison group; differentiation within the learning disabilities population; collection of baseline data; evaluation of the effects of strategy training; and assessment of the effects of varying schedules of reinforcement.

Card Sorting

Children with learning disabilities performed similarly to children without learning problems when spontaneous sorts were observed. However, when told the number of logical categories, children with learning disabilities from a different school were not aided (Parrill-Burnstein & Baker-Ward, 1979). To follow up this effect, two simple experiments are suggested.

First, have the children group items spontaneously and then require verbal justifications for the groupings (Annett, 1959). Compare these findings to those obtained by such researchers as Annett (1959).

In another experiment, three conditions will be necessary. In condition one, have children group items spontaneously and require verbal justification for the sort. In condition two, tell the children the number of logical categories and ask the children to group the items again, requiring a verbal justification here also. In condition three, select a card from each of the main categories and ask the child to group items on the basis of that exemplar. Again, verbal justification of the grouping should be obtained.

Question Game

To date, no published data are available about the types of questions children with learning disabilities ask when presented with concept organization tasks. To study the content of the questions asked by children with learning disabilities, it is suggested that the Twenty Questions Game be used.

Similar to Van Horn and Bartz (1968), it is suggested that these youngsters be presented with an ordered array, as well as a random array, to see if this affects the types of questions asked.

Using the same task, expose children with learning disabilities to models of hypothesis seeking and constraint seeking questions, and ask the child to identify the most efficient (Mosher & Hornsby, 1966). Feedback about correctness or incorrectness of the choice should be immediate. Play the game again and evaluate the effects of observing the models.

Hypothesis-Testing

Children with learning disabilities tested fewer hypotheses, retested disconfirmed hypotheses, and responded inconsistently to feedback when presented with the hypothesis testing task (Parrill-Burnstein & Baker-Ward, 1979).

Research with children without learning problems suggests the probe technique affects the performance at younger ages (Phillips & Levine, 1975). Introtacts elicit more consistent hypothesis testing behaviors than the blank-trial probe with children less than 8 years of age (Phillips & Levine, 1975). It is suggested that children with learning disabilities be tested using introtacts as well as nonprobe techniques to determine if their performance is effective.

Children with learning disabilities can be taught to use strategies and solve hypothesis testing problems (Hoskins, 1979). Hoskins' procedure incorporated a task analysis of the hypothesis testing task (Parrill-Burnstein, 1978) with a modeling of a strategy (Richman & Gholson, 1978). However, it was not clear if teaching the complete task analysis or teaching the appropriate response to feedback was the locus of nonsolution. This next experiment is directed at that question.

Provide group one with the verbal strategy but without demonstration. Provide group two with the verbal strategy and demonstration. Provide group three with the same information as two but require the child to demonstrate as the clinician verbalizes. And, finally, provide group four with the same information as group three except that after training, the strategy should be verbalized. Compare blank-trial probes, introtacts, and continuous reinforcement as well as the condition under which concept organization is facilitated.

REFERENCES

Annett, M. The classification of instances of your common class concepts by children and adults. *British Journal of Educational Psychology,* 1959, *29,* 223–236.

Brian, C. R., & Goodenough, F. L. The relative potency of color and form perception at various ages. *Journal of Experimental Psychology,* 1929, *12,* 197–213.

Browning, R. M. Effects of irrelevant peripheral visual stimuli on discrimination learning in minimally brain-damaged children. *Journal of Consulting Psychology,* 1967, *31*(4), 371–376.

Bruner, J. S. *Beyond the information given.* New York: W. W. Norton & Company, 1973.

Bruner, J. S., Goodnow, J. J., & Austin, G. A. *A study of thinking.* New York: Wiley, 1956.

Bruner, J. S., Olver, K. R., & Greenfield, P. M. *Studies in cognitive growth.* New York: Wiley, 1966.

Caron, A. J. Discrimination shifts in three-year olds as a function of shift procedure. *Developmental Psychology,* 1970, *3*(2), 236–241.

Denney, D. R. The effects of exemplary and cognitive models and self-rehearsal on children's interrogative strategies. *Journal of Experimental Child Psychology,* 1975, *19,* 476–488.

Denney, D. R. Modeling and eliciting effects upon conceptual strategies. *Child Development,* 1972, *43,* 810–823.

Denney, N. W. A developmental study of free classification in children. *Child Development,* 1972, *43,* 221–232.

Denney, N. W. Evidence for developmental changes in categorization criteria for children and adults. *Human Development,* 1974, *17,* 41–53.

Dickerson, D. J. Performance of preschool children on three dimensional shifts. *Psychonomic Science,* 1966, *4*(12), 417–418.

Eimas, P. D. A developmental study of hypothesis behavior and focusing. *Journal of Experimental Child Psychology,* 1969, *8,* 160–172.

Eimas, P. D. Effects of memory aids on hypothesis behavior and focusing in young children and adults. *Journal of Experimental Psychology,* 1970, *10,* 319–336.

Freibergs, V., & Douglass, J. I. Concept learning in hyperactive and normal children. *Journal of Abnormal Psychology,* 1969, *74,* 388–395.

Gholson, B., & Beilin, H. A developmental model of human learning. In H. W. Reese &

L. P. Lipsitt (Eds.), *Advances in child development and behavior*, (Vol. 13). New York: Academic Press, 1978.

Gholson, B. *The cognitive developmental basis of human learning: Studies in hypothesis testing*. New York: Academic Press, 1980.

Gholson, B., Levine, M., & Phillips, S. Hypothesis strategies and stereotypes in discrimination learning. *Journal of Experimental Child Psychology*, 1972, *13*, 423–446.

Gholson, B., & McConville, K. Effects of stimulus differentiation training upon hypotheses, strategies, and stereotypes in discrimination learning among kindergarten children. *Journal of Experimental Child Psychology*, 1974, *18*, 81–97.

Hagen, J. W. The effects of distraction. *Child Development*, 1967, *38*, 685–694.

Hallahan, D. P., Kauffman, J. M., & Ball, D. W. Selective attention and cognitive tempo of low achieving and high achieving sixth grade males. *Perceptual and Motor Skills*, 1973, *36*, 579–583.

Hardwick, D. A., McIntyre, C. W., & Pick, H. L. The content and manipulation of cognitive maps in children and adults. *Monographs of the Society for Research in Child Development*, 1976, *4*(3), Serial No. 166.

Hoskins, B. B. *A study of hypothesis testing behavior in language disordered children*. Unpublished doctoral dissertation, Northwestern University, 1979.

Johnson, E. S. Two approaches to selection strategies: A reply to Laughlin's comments. *Journal of Experimental Psychology: General*, 1978, *107*(3), 273–275.

Johnson, E. S. Validation of concept-learning strategies. *Journal of Experimental Psychology: General*, 1978b, *107*(3), 237–266.

Kendler, H. H., & Kendler, T. S. Vertical and horizontal processes in problem solving. *Psychological Review*, 1962, *69*(1), 1–16.

Kendler, H. H., Kendler, T. S., & Ward, J. W. An ontogenetic analysis of optional intradimensional and extradimensional shifts. *Journal of Experimental Psychology*, 1972, *95*(1), 102–109.

Levine, M. Human discrimination learning: The subset-sampling assumption. *Psychological Bulletin*, 1970, *74*(6), 397–404.

Levine, M. *A cognitive theory of learning: Research on hypothesis testing*. Hillsdale, N.J.: Lawrence Erlbaum Associates, 1975.

Mitler, M. M., & Harris, L. Dimension preference and performance on a series of concept identification tasks in kindergarten, first-grade, and third-grade children. *Journal of Experimental Child Psychology*, 1969, *7*, 374–384.

Mosher, F. A., & Hornsby, J. R. On asking questions. In J. S. Bruner, R. R. Olver, & P.M. Greenfield (Eds.), *Studies in cognitive growth*. New York: Wiley, 1966.

Odom, R. D., & Mumbauer, C. C. Dimensional salience and identification of the relevant dimension in problem solving: A developmental study. *Developmental Psychology*, 1971, *4*(2), 135–140.

Offenbach, S. I. A developmental study of hypothesis testing and cue selection strategies. *Developmental Psychology*, 1974, *10*(4), 484–490.

Parrill-Burnstein, M. Teaching kindergarten children to solve problems: An information processing approach. *Child Development*, 1978a, *49*(3), 700–706.

Parrill-Burnstein, M. *Card sorting and learning disabilities: A developmental study*. Paper presented at the annual meeting of the Southeastern Psychological Association, Atlanta, May 1978b.

Parrill-Burnstein, M., & Baker-Ward, L. Learning disabilities: A social-cognitive difference. *Learning Disabilities: An Audio Journal for Continuing Education,* 1979, *3*, (10).

Phillips, S., & Levine, M. Probing for hypotheses with adults and children: Blank trials and introtracts. *Journal of Experimental Psychology: General,* 1975, *194*, 327–354.

Phillips, S., Levine, M., and O'Brien, J. T. Transfer in discrimination learning: Do children mediate more than adults. *Journal of Experimental Child Psychology,* 1978, *26*, 161–171.

Piaget, J., & Inhelder, B. *The psychology of the child.* New York: Basic Books, 1969.

Reese, H. W. Verbal mediation as a function of age level. *Psychological Bulletin,* 1962, *59*(6), 502–509.

Reese, H. W. *The perception of stimulus relations: Discrimination learning and transposition.* New York: Academic Press, 1968.

Restle, F. The selection of strategies in cue learning. *Psychological Review,* 1962, *69*(4), 329–343.

Reynolds, G. S. *A primer of operant conditioning.* Greenview, Illinois: Scott Foresman & Company, 1968.

Richman, S., & Gholson, B. Strategy modeling, age, and information-processing efficiency. *Journal of Experimental Child Psychology,* 1978, *26*(1), 58–70.

Rieber, M. Hypothesis testing in children as a function of age. *Developmental Psychology,* 1969, *1*(4), 389–395.

Shantz, C. U. The development of social cognition. In E. M. Hetherington (Ed.), *Review of child development research* (Vol. 5). Chicago: University of Chicago Press, 1975.

Suchman, R., & Trabasso, T. Color and form preference in young children. *Journal of Experimental Child Psychology,* 1966a, *3*, 177–187.

Suchman, R., & Trabasso, T. Stimulus preference and cue function in young children's concept attainment. *Journal of Experimental Child Psychology,* 1966b, *3*, 188–198.

Tighe, T. J. Subproblem analysis of discrimination learning. In G. H. Bower (Ed.), *The psychology of learning and motivation.* New York: Academic Press, 1973, pp. 183–225.

Tighe, T. J., Glick, J. & Cole, M. Subproblem analysis of discrimination shift learning. *Psychonomic Science,* 1971, *24*, 159–160.

Tighe, T. J., & Tighe, L. S. Optional shift behavior of children as a function of age, type of pretraining, and stimulus salience. *Journal of Experimental Child Psychology,* 1970, *9*, 272–285.

Tighe, T. J., & Tighe, L. S. Stimulus control in children's learning. *Minnesota Symposia on Child Psychology,* 1972, *6*.

Van Horn, K. R., & Bartz, W. H. Information seeking strategies in cognitive development. *Psychonomic Science,* 1968, *11*(10), 341–342.

Wolff, J. L. The role of dimensional preferences in discrimination learning. *Psychonomic Science,* 1966, *5*(12), 455–456.

Zeaman, D., & House, B. The role of attention in retardate discrimination learning. In N. R. Ellis (Ed.), *Handbook of mental deficiency.* New York: McGraw-Hill Book Company, 1963.

FURTHER READINGS

Anderson, R. C. Can first graders learn an advanced problem-solving skill? *Journal of Educational Psychology,* 1965, *56*(6), 283–294.

Anderson, R. C. Part-task versus whole-task procedures for teaching a problem-solving skill to first graders. *Journal of Educational Psychology,* 1968, *59*(3), 207–214.

Anderson, R. P., Halcomb, C. G., & Doyle, R. B. The measurement of attentional deficits. *Exceptional Children,* 1973, *39,* 534–539.

Beaty, W. E., & Weir, M. W. Children's performance on the intermediate-size transposition problem as a function of two different training procedures. *Journal of Experimental Child Psychology,* 1966, *4,* 332–340.

Bruner, J. S. *The relevance of education.* New York: Norton, 1971.

Bryan, T. The effect of forced mediation upon short-term memory of children with learning disabilities. *Journal of Learning Disabilities,* 1972, *5*(66), 25–29.

Buss, A. H. Reversal and nonreversal shifts in concept formation with partial reinforcement eliminated. *Journal of Experimental Psychology,* 1956, *52*(3), 162–166.

Campione, J. C. The generality of transfer: Effects of age and similarity of training and transfer tasks. *Journal of Experimental Child Psychology,* 1973, *15,* 407–418.

Campione, J. C., & Beaton, V. L. Transfer of training: Some boundary conditions and initial theory. *Journal of Experimental Child Psychology,* 1972, *13,* 94–114.

Fritz, J. J. Reversal-shift behavior in children with specific learning disabilities. *Perceptual and Motor Skills,* 1974, *38,* 431–438.

Gholson, B., & Schuepfer, T. Commentary on Kendler's paper: An alternative perspective. In H. W. Reese & L. P. Lipsitt (Eds.), *Advances in child development and behavior,* (Vol. 13). New York: Academic Press, 1978.

Goodnow, J. J. The role of modalities in perceptual and cognitive development. In J. P. Hill (Ed.), *Minnesota symposia on child psychology* (Vol. 5). Minneapolis: The University of Minnesota Press, 1972.

Goulet, L. R. Training transfer, and the development of complex behavior. *Human Development,* 1970, *13,* 213–240.

Hallahan, D. P. Distractability in the learning disabled child. In W. M. Cruickshank & D. P. Hallahan (Eds.), *Perceptual and learning disabilities in children, Vol. 2: Research and theory.* Syracuse: Syracuse University Press, 1975.

Honig, W. K. Prediction of preference, transposition, and transposition-reversal from the generalization gradient. *Journal of Experimental Psychology,* 1962, *64,* 239–248.

House, B. J., Brown, A. L., & Scott, M. S. Children's discrimination learning based on identity or difference. In H. Reese (Ed.), *Advances in child development and behavior,* (Vol. 11). New York: Academic Press, 1974.

Ingalls, R. P., & Dickerson, D. J. Development of hypothesis behavior in human concept identification. *Developmental Psychology,* 1969, *1,* 707–716.

Kendler, H. H., & Kendler, T. S. Reversal shift behavior: Two basic issues. *Psychological Bulletin,* 1969, *72*(3), 229–232.

Kendler, T. S. An ontogeny of mediational deficiency. *Child Development,* 1972, *43,* 1–17.

Kendler, T. S. The effect of training and stimulus variables on reversal-shift ontogeny. *Journal of Experimental Child Psychology,* 1974, *17,* 87–106.

Kuenne, M. R. Experimental investigation of the relation of language to transposition behavior in young children. *Journal of Experimental Psychology*, 1946, *36*, 471–490.

Laughlin, P. R. Selection strategies as normative and descriptive models: Comments on Johnson's "The validation of concept-learning strategies." *Journal of Experimental Psychology: General*, 1978, *107*(3), 267–272.

Mandler, G. Organization and memory. In R. W. Spence & J. T. Spence (Eds.), *The psychology of learning and motivation*, (Vol. 1). New York: Academic Press, 1967.

Porter, W. L. Absolute versus relational responding in children. *Journal of Experimental Child Psychology*, 1969, *7*, 485–491.

Reese, H. W. *Basic learning processes in childhood.* New York: Holt, Rinehart & Winston, 1976.

Rogers, C. J., & Johnson, P. J. Attribute identification in children as a function of stimulus dimensionality. *Journal of Experimental Child Psychology*, 1973, *15*, 216–221.

Schuepfer, T., & Gholson, B. Effects of I.Q. and mental age on hypothesis testing in normal and retarded children: A methodological analysis. *Developmental Psychology*, 1978, *14*(4), 423–424.

Shapson, S. M. Hypothesis testing and cognitive style in children. *Journal of Educational Psychology*, 1977, *69*(4), 452–463.

Silleroy, R. S., & Johnson P. J. The effects of perceptual pretraining on concept identification and preference. *Journal of Experimental Child Psychology*, 1973, *15*, 462–472.

Smiley, S. S. Optional shift behavior as a function of age and dimensional dominance. *Journal of Experimental Child Psychology*, 1973, *16*, 451–458.

Smiley, S., & Weir, M. The role of dimensional dominance in reversal shift behavior. *Journal of Experimental Child Psychology*, 1966, *4*, 296–307.

Spiker, C. C., & Cantor, J. H. Introtracts as predictors of discrimination performance in kindergarten children. *Journal of Experimental Child Psychology*, 1977, *23*, 520–538.

Stevens, D., Boydstun, J., Dykman, R., et al. Relationship of presumed minimal brain dysfunction to performance on selected behavioral tasks. *Archives of General Psychiatry*, 1967, *16*, 281–285.

Strauss, A., & Lehtinen, L. *Psychopathology and education of the brain-impaired child.* New York: Grune & Stratton, 1947.

Suchman, R. G. Color-form preferences, discriminative accuracy, and learning of deaf and hearing children. *Child Development*, 1966, *37*, 439–451.

Tarver, S. G., Hallahan, D. P., Kauffman, J. M., et al. Verbal rehearsal and selective attention in children. *Journal of Experimental Child Psychology*, 1976, 22(3), 379–385.

Tighe, T. Subproblem analysis of discrimination learning. In G. H. Bower (Ed.), *The psychology of learning and motivation.* New York: Academic Press, 1973.

Tighe, T. J., & Tighe, L. S. Perceptual learning in the discrimination process of children: An analysis of five variables in perceptual pretraining. *Journal of Experimental Psychology*, 1968, *77*, 125–134.

Toppino, T. C., & Johnson, P. J. Effects of category composition and response label on attribute identification concept performance. *Journal of Experimental Psychology*, 1973, *101*(2), 289–295.

Torgesen, J., & Goldman, T. Verbal rehearsal and short-term memory in reading-disabled children. *Child Development,* 1977, *48*(1), 56–60.

Trabasso, T., Deutsch, J. A., & Gilman, R. Attention in discrimination learning of young children. *Journal of Experimental Child Psychology,* 1966, *4,* 9–19.

Trabasso, T., & Gelman, R. Attention in discrimination learning of young children. *Journal of Experimental Child Psychology,* 1966, *4,* 9–19.

Wolff, J. L. Concept-shift and discrimination-reversal learning in humans. *Psychological Bulletin,* 1967, *68*(6), 369–408.

Zeaman, D., & House, B. J. Interpretations of developmental trends in discriminative transfer. In A. D. Pick (Ed.), *Minnesota symposia on child psychology.* Minneapolis: University of Minnesota Press, 1974.

Zeiler, M. D. solution of the two-stimulus transposition problem by four- and five-year-old children. *Journal of Experimental Psychology,* 1966, *71,* 576–579.

Zeiler, M. D. Stimulus definition and choice. In L. P. Kipsitt & C. C. Spiker (Eds.), *Advances in child development and behavior* (Vol. 3). New York: Academic Press, 1967.

Zeiler, M. D., & Friednicks, A. G. Absolute and relational discriminations involving three stimuli. *Journal of Experimental Psychology,* 1969, *82,* 448–452.

Zeiler, M. D., & Gardner, A. M. Intermediate size discrimination in seven- and eight-year-old children. *Journal of Experimental Psychology,* 1966, *71,* 203–207.

Zeiler, M. D., & Slaten, C. S. Individual gradients of transposition and absolute choice. *Journal of Experimental Psychology,* 1967, *5,* 172–185.

3
Memory

Memory allows progression through the various levels of the problem-solving process (Craik & Lockhart, 1972); it is essential for generating responses and responding appropriately following feedback. Memory assumes adequate selective attention and stimulus differentiation. The terms *memory* and *memory span* are used interchangeably in this discussion; both terms refer to the number of items recalled or recognized.

As a process, memory consists of three components: encoding, storage, and retrieval. Encoding refers to the acquisition of information. Storage refers to the length of time that the information is available, either immediately (short-term) or after a delay (long-term). Retrieval is of three types: recognition, cued recall, and free recall. Recognition occurs in the presence of the object or event; cued recall occurs in the presence of part, or an association of, the object or event; and free recall occurs in the absence of the object or event. Available research is organized according to two of these, recognition and recall, and the level of information processing required.

Although the ability to remember increases with age, the reasons for this increase are unclear. The major hypothesis is that children become proficient as they become older in using previously acquired knowledge to form task-appropriate strategies for handling incoming information (Zaporozhets & Elkonin, 1971). In contrast, memory storage capacity—the "hardware" of the information processing system—is not generally found to differ with age (Chi, 1976). Among the strategies postulated as increasing the memory span are the ability to rehearse (Flavell, 1970), and the ability to impose organization on encoded information (Miller, 1956).

Huttenlocher and Burke (1976) and Myers and Perlmutter (1979) take a different position regarding the increase of memory span with age. Huttenlocher and Burke offer evidence supporting the hypothesis that the development of span is related to an increase in an individual's ability to identify the items and encode information about their order. Similarly, Myers and Perlmutter (1978) suggest that memory improvement with age is related to increases in the child's knowledge base. As the child's knowledge about the world becomes more extensive, incoming information is more meaningful and more interrelated; consequently, it is more memorable. Theories of memory are an outgrowth of these hypotheses.

THEORIES

Four theoretical constructs reviewed here are depth of the processing model (Craik & Lockhart, 1972); the knowledge base model (Atkinson & Shiffrin, 1968); the metamemory model (Flavell & Wellman, 1977); and Piaget's memory schema.

Depth of Processing Model

Craik and Lockhart (1972) suggest that what is retained by adults is a function of the level or depth of processing required by the orienting task. These authors hypothesize that the stimulus is first encoded and analyzed at a perceptual level. A memory trace is a by-product of this perceptual analysis. The persistence of the trace is determined by the depth or level at which it is processed. Depth of processing refers to how elaborate or deep the analysis of the item is. The levels of analysis imply a hierarchy of stages that incoming information can progress through in order to be remembered. These stages may involve sensory, perceptual, and/or cognitive analysis.

Once past the perceptual analysis stage, information may be stored in either long-term or short-term memory. Acoustic or phonemic information (i.e., tones or sounds) is stored in short-term memory and requires continued processing at a constant depth. On a serial position curve, information remembered at this level is reflected in the recency effect. The recency effect is used to describe memory for items presented last in the series. For long-term storage, information is encoded semantically or cognitively and is processed at a greater depth than the items stored in short-term memory. Processing of this type produces a primary effect and reflects memory for those items presented first in the series. It is suggested that the primacy effect is the result of active rehearsal. Spontaneous rehearsal increases with age (Flavell, 1970).

Atkinson and Shiffrin (1968) also propose that to-be-remembered information is analyzed. Unlike Craik and Lockhart (1972), these authors hypothesize that this analysis is sequential rather than hierarchical, and involves moving information from one memory store to another. First, sensory information is registered, that is, perceived. If further analyzed, this sensory information takes on meaning, primarily verbal, and progresses to the short-term memory store. To enter the long-term memory store, the information in the short-term memory store is further analyzed, that is, organized (i.e., associated, chunked) or rehearsed. The emphasis in this model is on the development of strategies.

Knowledge Base Model

A knowledge-based model is not fully articulated (Myers & Perlmutter, 1978). The basic assumption of this framework is that newly acquired information is rendered more meaningful by existing knowledge or cognitive structure. Myers and Perlmutter (1978) relate the information processing models of Craik and Lockhart (1972) and Atkinson and Shiffrin (1968) to work with children. Similar to Craik and Lockhart, Myers and Perlmutter describe the child as an information processor limited by both the extent of knowledge and lack of information stored in long-term memory. Furthermore, Myers and Perlmutter present data suggesting that development of memory span improves between the ages of 2 and 5, but this increase is due to an increase in strategy formation and utilization. Although recall increases between these ages, Myers and Perlmutter studied the serial position curves of the children and did not find a primacy effect. A recency effect was obtained with all children. These authors attribute the increase in recall to an increase in the child's ability to assign meaning to acquired information.

Myers and Perlmutter (1978) summarized the child's memory development between the ages of 2 and 5. Children as young as 2½ recognized approximately 80% of the to-be-remembered items as seen previously. In fact, recognition was considered excellent for children as young as 4½ years of age. Also, the 4- and 5-year-old children recognized new items and old items (items shown previously) equally well, while the youngest children had greater difficulty recognizing items as old or new. These authors suggested that the age difference in recognition observed between children between the ages of 2 and 5 was the effect of retention rather than changes in decision strategies.

A recency effect was observed at all ages, and limited recall was related to limitations generating representations. Semantic processing was initially inferred from children's superior recall of closely related items, as compared to more loosely related material. Cues such as part/whole relationships, habitat, item associations, or spatial layouts benefited the older children more than the younger children. These results suggested that children as young as 2 or 3 years have some kind of knowledge about categorical relationships.

Metamemory Model

Flavell and Wellman (1977) discuss the development of metamemory. Metamemory is a term coined by Flavell to describe an individual's knowledge or awareness of memory processes (e.g., storage and retrieval). Metamemory increases with age and is helpful in preparing for future retrieval. Metamemory allows older children to benefit from both implicit and explicit instructions.

Flavell and his colleagues (Appel, Cooper, McCarrell, Sims-Knight, Yussen, & Flavell, 1972) found that 11-year-old children, when told to remember information, were aware that implicit in these instructions was to do something to the material presented so as to remember it better. These youngsters spontaneously rehearsed or categorized the items during presentation. The 7-year-olds recognized that something needed to be done but did not employ any techniques to improve memory. In contrast to the performance of the 7-year-olds, Appel et al. found that 4-year-old children neither realized that something needed to be done nor instituted some procedure to facilitate memory.

In an earlier series of studies, Flavell and his associates (e.g., Flavell, 1970) found that first-grade children could be trained to rehearse to-be-remembered material, although they did not spontaneously do so. This induced rehearsal facilitated the children's recall performance. However, these youngsters only rehearsed when told to do so. Performance returned to baseline when the children ceased rehearsing.

Flavell (Flavell & Wellman, 1977; Kreutzer, Leonard, & Flavell, 1975) further specified several classes of variables that children learn to consider when performing memory tasks. These variables were person variables, task variables, strategy variables, and the interaction between variables. The effect of these variables was summarized in a metamemory schema. Knowledge of personal attributes or strategies was described as affecting memory ability; whereas, knowledge of past demands and item characteristics was suggested as affecting memory difficulty. Again, the ability to recognize the role of these variables on memory performance increased with age.

Piaget's Memory Schema

Piaget & Inhelder (1973) discuss memory as it fits into cognitive developmental theory. Age differences in memory are consistent with general changes in cognitive structure. With respect to cognitive structure or schemata, memory involves assimilation and accommodation of information. The result of these actions is a memory trace or image. Changes in memory are not associated with changes in encoding or decoding, but rather, refer to changes in the code used to transform such information. Memory traces are a result of information being stored. During the short-term memory phase, traces are registered and organized; during the long-term memory phase, the traces are integrated and become stable. Traces are retrieved through recognition, reconstruction, or recall.

Recognition implies awareness that a present object or action has been experienced before. In order to recognize the complete object, not all physical information need be present. Rather, under certain conditions a sign, such as a part, an aspect, or a cause of the object can cue recognition of that object. Recognition originates during the sensorimotor stage and continues throughout development. Changes in recognition reflect the constant and simultaneous assimilation and accommodation of information. During recognition, perceptual or conceptual information is internalized through the matching, identification, and expansion of available information.

The second or intermediate level between recognition and recall is the ability to reconstruct or represent cognitively an action. This accomplishment marks entrance into what is referred to as the representational stages. Reconstruction is an outgrowth of imitation involving mental images or memory traces, which are sequenced internally to allow observable recreations of real actions to occur. Because real actions include information that is both assimilated and accommodated, the recreation is not a carbon copy of physical events. Reconstruction precedes recall, and what is reconstructed may be later recalled.

Recall takes place in the absence of an object or event and is associated with transformations of information through reconstruction. In recall, a memory image is generated. Like recognition and reconstruction, recall is the product of what is assimilated and accommodated.

DEVELOPMENT

Rehearsal Strategies

The purpose here is not to debate the issue of how memory span develops, but rather to document that development. One way of evaluating age-related changes is to study the development of rehearsal strategies by examining the shape of the serial position curve. The child is presented with a list of items to be recalled. The order in which he or she recalls the items is charted. It is hypothesized that the items presented early in the list are retained or remembered through active rehearsal. The recall of these items is referred to as a *primacy effect*. Items presented last in the list do not require rehearsal because their retention is not interfered with by the presentation of additional items. When these items are recalled, a *recency effect* is obtained.

In terms of general development, children under 5 years of age neither label stimulus items, nor rehearse labels. Simple verbal labeling strategies generally do not occur prior to about age 8 years. However, by age 10, efficient cumulative verbal rehearsal strategies are used (Hagen, 1971). Strategies such as labeling, cumulative rehearsal, and chunking are observed by about age 11 (McCarver, 1972).

Children below the age of 5 generally do not label or rehearse labels spontaneously. However, Keeney, Canizzo, and Flavell (1967) found that first-grade children who did not rehearse or label items spontaneously could be taught to do so. Under the "forced instruction" they recalled information as well as those youngsters who rehearsed without instruction. Flavell (1970) referred to the lack of spontaneous rehearsal as indicating either a mediation or production deficiency. A production deficiency is when the child has the capability of using strategies but does not do so spontaneously. These youngsters could be induced to do so, and therefore increase their recall. Children who, when taught to rehearse, did not recall more items, demonstrated a mediation deficiency, or an inability to use mnemonic strategies to enhance recall performance. Children as young as 4 displayed a mediation deficiency, while children between the ages of 6 and 8 display a production deficiency (e.g., Hagen, Jongeward, & Kail, 1975; Keeney et al., 1967).

Serial Recall

In addition to an increase in serial recall, children between the ages of 12 and 14 show an increase in central recall and a decrease in incidental recall. Central recall refers to those items to which the child's attention has been directed. This selective attention frequently occurs through instructions. Incidental recall refers to items recalled to which the child's attention was not directed. A developmental increase in selective attention is most pronounced during the fifth through seventh grades (Hallahan, Kauffman, & Ball, 1974). Hagen (1967) studied the effects of distraction on selective attention. He found that central recall increased with age. Although incidental learning occurred at all age levels, at approximately the seventh grade, a significant decrease was observed.

Developmental changes are reported when children are asked to recall information, but are not required to recall the stimulus items in the order in which they are presented. This free recall is of two types: single-trial and multi-trial. During single-trial free recall the list is presented and recall is tested; then another list is presented and recall is tested. During multi-trial free recall, a list is presented and recall is tested; next, the same list is presented again, followed by a recall test. During this latter type of free recall, learning as a function of the number of presentations is evaluated.

Free recall is facilitated if the information to be encoded is semantic, if the child is told that he or she will be tested later, and if the child is require to sort stimuli into categories. As early as age 2, items are clustered semantically and the recall of one item can cue recall of another (Flavell & Wellman, 1977). Between the ages of 3 and 5, items are organized on the basis of taxinomic clusters (e.g., apples and oranges are both fruit). Older children code information as it relates to serial order. Cole, Frankel, and Sharp (1971) studied the development of free recall in children. These authors found that recall improved when the items presented were visual, written, and grouped according to semantic categories.

Recognition

Hagen et al. (1975) studied recognition of verbal material. These authors concluded that children as young as 4 could benefit from materials that could be encoded semantically. These authors also found that 7-year-old children made more false recognition errors (recognizing new items as old; i.e., seen previously) to acoustically similar words (e.g., goat-boat) than to categorical (e.g., goat-sheep) associations. This trend was reversed for 12-year-olds. For 8-year-old children, false recognition occurred when both highly associated synonyms and acoustically similar words were used as stimuli.

Another way of studying memory is recognition of faces. For faces to be distinguished, and subsequently remembered, both nonverbal and verbal cues must be associated and integrated. It has been found that the ability to recognize faces increases with age (Diamond & Carey, 1977). Recognition of faces improves between the ages of 6 and 10 years with little change after that. In addition, distractions such as changing clothing, facial pose, and lighting are successful in diverting attention from facial features with younger children (Diamond & Carey, 1977). When paraphernalia (e.g., scarf) is changed and the faces are unfamiliar, 6- and 8-year-olds have greatest difficulty. At age 10, less susceptibility to manipulations of paraphernalia is observed. Furthermore, children below the age of 10 tend to code faces in terms of isolated features. It is not until age 12 that reliance upon paraphernalia disappears altogether and that the configuration of features is encoded. Furthermore, recognition of faces increases when a judgment about the disposition of the face (e.g., mean or nice) is made over a judgment regarding physical features (e.g., big or little nose) (Blaney & Winograd, 1978).

Summary

Memory ability increases with age. Consistent with this age increase is the change in the encoding, organization, and retrieval of information. Memory is a part of the more general problem-solving process. Recalling the problem-solving sequence proposed in the introductory chapter, problem solving as a task requires selective attention, response generation, response execution, and appropriate responses to feedback. Applying this to memory, a child is asked to look at a series of pictures and is told that he or she will be asked later to recognize that picture. The child discriminates facial expression (selective attention). Then, the child is presented with three pictures, two distractors and one to-be-remembered item (response generation) and asked to identify one picture as seen previously. The child makes a selection (response execution) and, if correct (feedback), the child repeats this approach to remembering the information. If fewer faces are recognized, the child needs to devise a new memory plan (negative feedback).

According to the above analysis, the child must perform two types of memory activities. First, the hypotheses or responses that are generated are recalled. Second, correct responses are resampled while incorrect responses are excluded from the response pool and are not resampled. The number of responses or hypotheses that are evaluated after feedback and the number of trials to solution are a function of the strategy employed and the memory requirements of the task.

Problems in recall may indicate problems in response generation, and/or selective attention. Problems in recognition may indicate problems in selective attention. During recognition, limited response generation occurs and responses may be cued by the presence of the stimulus. Problems in recall may indicate problems in generating responses or cues as well as problems at the more basic level of selective attention, which is a prerequisite to response generation. If children with learning disabilities only have problems generating responses, recognition should be better than recall and similar to that of children without learning problems. In the next section, the studies investigating the memory abilities of children with learning disabilities are organized according to the two types of retrieval (recognition and recall) and the appropriate level of processing (e.g., selective attention).

STUDIES OF CHILDREN WITH LEARNING DISABILITIES

Recall

Studies evaluating the recall of children with learning disabilities focus on selective attention, serial position curves, and retrieval. Generally, children with learning disabilities retain less central information and recall similar amounts of incidental information when compared to those without learning problems. With respect to serial order and recall, unlike children without learning problems, young children with learning disabilities do not recall information presented first in the list. This lack of primacy effect is frequently noted with children younger than about 8 years of age. The lack of primacy effect was interpreted as indicating that children with learning disabilities at approximately the age of 8 do not rehearse items spontaneously. (With children without learning problems, spontaneous rehearsal is only emerging at this age.) Both primacy and recency effects were observed with older children with learning disabilities. Furthermore, under certain conditions, induced rehearsal facilitated recall, while under other conditions it did not.

SELECTIVE ATTENTION

Hallahan, Kaufman, and Ball, 1974 conducted a number of experiments evaluating the memory skills of children with learning disabilities. Frequently, Hagen's Central-Incidental Learning Task was employed (Hagen & Hale, 1973). In this task, the child is shown a series of cards on which two figures, an animal and a common tool, are drawn. The child is told only to remember one of the objects (animal) on each presentation. After each presentation, the cards are presented face down in rows and columns. The child's task is to turn over the card that is the same as a probe item (animal) presented by the experimenter. This measures central-incidental learning of the object is assessed by presenting the child with all of the animals and object cards and asking the child to put together the ones that were originally presented together. Although the two tasks were equated during discussion, each evaluates a different aspect of memory. Central recall, recall of the animal, evaluates associations of an animal with a spatial location; the incidental recall task evaluates recognition or the association of two items, both present and one possibly acting as a cue for the other.

Tarver, Hallahan, Kaufman et al. (1976) conducted two experiments to study selective attention and serial recall with two different age groups of children with learning disabilities. In the first experiment, the subjects were 33 white, middle-class boys, 18 with learning disabilities and 15 without learning problems. The approximate age range of the children was 8 years, 6 months. The children with learning disabilities were of at least average intelligence and were a minimum of 6 months below grade level in reading achievement. The two groups were matched on chronological age, mental age, and IQ. All children were first presented with Hagen's Central-Incidental Learning Task.

The results showed that central recall was significantly greater for children without learning problems when compared to those with learning disabilities. However, incidental memory was similar for both groups. These results were interpreted as indicating that 8-year-old children without learning problems tune out incidental information and attend selectively to central information while children with learning disabilities do not. Furthermore, when the serial position curve was examined, a primacy effect was obtained for children without learning problems but not for those with learning disabilities, the implications being that children with learning disabilities did not rehearse the items presented initially; as a result, these items were not stored in long-term memory. Children in both groups showed recency effects.

In a second experiment, Tarver et al. (1976) worked with two older groups of children with learning disabilities. The mean ages for these two groups were 10 years, 2 months and 13 years, 5 months. There were 18 subjects in each age group. A normal comparison group was not included, which severely limits the interpretation of these findings. Hagen's task was again administered. One half of the children in each group were told to rehearse, by verbally labeling the items as they were presented. Rehearsal was cumulative, that is, preceding items were rehearsed each time later presented items were rehearsed. Results showed that under both conditions, older children with learning disabilities rehearsed spontaneously and that induced rehearsal had a facilitating effect on selective attention at both age levels.

Tarver et al. concluded that central recall of children with learning disabilities increased with age and that the lag observed with the youngest group was evidence of a developmental delay. Also, the lack of a primacy effect observed with 8-year-old children with learning disabilities was interpreted as indicating a delay using a verbal strategy to encode information (8-year-old children without learning disabilities began to use verbal strategies spontaneously around this age). Lastly, performance was improved by provision of appropriate strategies.

Heins et al. (1976) also used Hagen's task with children with learning disabilities who were classified as either impulsive or reflective. (For a discussion of reflective and impulsive children, see Chapter 2.) These authors found that reflective children recalled more central information than impulsive children. However, the two groups did not differ significantly when memory for incidental information was evaluated.

Mercer et al. (1975) used Hagen's task in conjunction with high and low modelers. Their subjects were 20 boys between the ages of 9 years, 6 months and 14 years, 4 months (mean age: 12 years, 4 months; standard deviation of approximately 1 year) from a residential school for children with learning disabilities. These children were first presented Hagen's task and then shown a 13-minute video tape. The video tape involved in adult model performing 20 demonstrations (e.g., selecting a dart gun, aiming it at a target, and shooting). The child was told to observe carefully the models' activities and that a prize would be given if he or she could imitate correctly the models' movements. The children were separated into low and high modeling conditions based on how well they imitated the models' movements (median split); this was the basis for comparison on Hagen's task. The results showed that high modelers recalled more central information than low modelers. Children's memory for incidental information was similar.

More recently, Hallahan et al. (1978) administered a modification of Hagen's task to 48 children from a private, residential school for children with learning disabilities. These children ranged in age from about 7½ to 14½ years. Sixteen subjects were randomly assigned to one of three conditions: a reinforcement condition, a response cost condition, or a controlled condition. In the response cost condition, the youngest children were 2 years younger than those in the other two groups. In the reinforcement condition, the child received money for correct responses, 3 cents for the first card and 1 cent for the second card. In the response cost condition, money was taken away from the child when an error was made. In thecontrol condition, the child was given 2 cents for both correct responses to the cards. No control conditions to assess the effects of receiving only verbal feedback or of receiving no feedback were included.

The results showed that giving money improved performance; taking away money did not. Although results were discussed as though they were significant (e.g., alpha level .10), no significant main effects or interactions were obtained when an analysis of variance was performed on condition and type of stimuli. Examination of the serial position curve data indicated that only children in the reinforcement condition showed a primacy effect and recency effect. Children in the other two conditions showed recency but not primacy effects. These differences were significant. Hence, only children in the reinforcement condition were assumed to be using encoding strategies.

Suiter and Potter (1978) also evaluated verbal recall but used visual stimuli. Their subjects were 20 children between the ages of 8 years and 13 years, 8 months (mean age: 10 years, 4 months) in classes for children with language/learning disabilities. Prior screening ruled out those children with visual memory deficits. The 20 children were assigned to one of two conditions, ten in each condition. For group one, 40 pictures of concrete nouns were presented by categories. For group two, the pictures were presented randomly. The results indicated that the children shown the grouped pictures recalled significantly more pictures. These results were interpreted as indicating that language/learning disabilities children used internal paradigmatic organization through visual processing on a verbal recall task.

Swanson (1977a, 1977b) also used visual stimuli to evaluate recall. Attention was assessed by presenting different dimensional stimuli. In neither study was a normal comparison group employed. Instead, comparisons were made with either past reports of normal development or with the retarded population. In the first experiment (Swanson, 1977a), the effects of age and stimulus dimension were investigated. Twenty-two children with learning disabilities in two different age groups were tested. The mean age of the children in the youngest group was 8 years, 5 months and in the oldest group 10 years, 6 months. Children in both groups were from learning disabilities classes. The stimuli were six nonsense random shapes presented as three-dimensional, concrete objects, or the same shapes drawn on white cards. Initially, all of these items were presented for 2 seconds. Then, each child was presented with either the real objects or their two-dimensional representations. The child was allowed to examine each of six such stimuli for 2 seconds. After presentation, the card was either turned over or the three-dimensional object was covered. The child's task was to point to the position of the object or card that was the same as the probe item. This task was similar to Hagen's task in that spatial locations were associated with the probe items.

The findings were that older children performed significantly better than younger children, and that performance improved with age over most serial positions. A recency effect was obtained while a primacy effect was not. However, children in the older group who were shown three-dimensional objects did recall items presented first better than those in the other three groups.

Bauer (1977) used verbal stimuli when evaluating recall. Attention was manipulated by introducing or not introducing an interference task. Bauer conducted two experiments. In experiment one, 10-year-old children, 12 with learning disabilities and 12 without learning problems, were worked with. These children were matched for age, sex, IQ, and race. The children with learning disabilities were performing at least 2 years below academic expectancy, did not receive an IQ score below 80, and were not retarded or known to be suffering from any physical handicap. Both long-term and short-term memory were evaluated by comparing single-trial immediate and delayed free recall. The children were presented with lists of frequently used monosyllabic nouns. Each word was read only once by the examiner. After reading the total list, either a delay period was imposed or recall was immediate. During the delay period, the children either waited quietly or were required to repeat numbers after the examiner. Research conducted with children without learning problems suggested that the recency portion of the serial position curve was affected by interference of this type. The primacy portion of the curve is not. Implications were that the most recently presented items were stored in short-term memory and were more susceptible to this type of decay.

The results showed that overall recall of words was significantly better for children without learning problems when compared to those with learning disabilities. Furthermore, children with and without learning disabilities recalled significantly fewer words when the delay periods were filled. However, recall by children without learning problems was still significantly better under this condition. As expected, the delay had greatest impact on the recency effects were similar for both groups after immediate recall, while the primacy effects were significantly different after both recall conditions. Children with learning disabilities showed only a slight primacy effect under both conditions. These results were interpreted as indicating that children with learning disabilities were rehearsing at least some of the time.

Bauer's second experiment was an extension of the first and provided information about the effects of word lengths on recall. Thirteen children with learning disabilities and 13 children without learning disabilities were matched for age (mean age: 9 years, 7 months), sex (all males), IQ, and race. The procedure for presentation was essentially the same as that described for experiment one except that a fill delay condition was eliminated. The results showed that when three words were presented and recall was immediate, children with and without learning disabilities performed similarly. With longer lists and immediate recall, the primacy effect of children with learning disabilities was lower than those without learning problems. Recency effects were similar with delays; both the recency and primacy effects obtained were lower for children with learning disabilities. As the number of words increased, the primacy effect of children with learning disabilities decreased. When recall was delayed, children with learning disabilities recalled significantly fewer words.

The results of both experiments were interpreted as indicating that children with learning disabilities did not use rehearsal strategies as frequently as those without learning problems. Because recall was similar after three words were presented, short-term memory in terms of attention and retrieval was considered intact.

In a recent series of studies, Bauer (1979) studied serial recall of children with and without learning disabilities. Children were matched on age, sex, and race, but not IQ. Three experiments were conducted. In experiment one, auditory digits were used. There were two types of trials. The trials consisted of presenting digits not previously presented to the child (nonrepeated sequence) or presenting digits that had been exposed before (repeated sequence). Results indicated that children with learning disabilities recalled fewer items correctly

Memory

than those without learning problems. Furthermore, children without learning problems recalled significantly more digits in the repeated sequence condition than in the nonrepeated sequence condition. Children with learning disabilities performed similarly in both conditions.

In experiment two, color sequences were used and presentations were either visual or acoustic. Similar results were obtained to those in experiment one. Lower recall scores after a short delay as well as slower acquisition rates were obtained with children with learning disabilities.

In experiment three, number of digits and the sequence presented was manipulated. Children began with a specific series of digits and the sequence was increased by one on each trial. Children with learning disabilities recalled significantly shorter sequences than children without learning problems. Furthermore, children without learning problems improved more on later trials than children with learning disabilities. Acquisition was similar for both groups.

Results from the three experiments were interpreted as indicating differences in mnemonic strategies and attention employed by children with learning disabilities.

Torgesen, Murphy, and Ivey (1979) studied the influence of an orienting task on the memory performance of children with reading disabilities. The subjects were fourth-grade children identified by teachers as average and poor readers. The procedure was conducted in two phases and involved presenting the child with 24 pictures of common objects in a circular array. During phase 1, the child was asked to name and study the stimuli for 3 minutes, after which recall was tested. During phase 2, the child was shown the cards and asked to put together the ones that went together. Recall was tested both immediately after the sorting instructions, as well as after a 10-minute interim period.

Results indicated that during phase 1, the children with reading problems recalled fewer items than average readers. After phase 2, the orienting task, items recalled were similar. Results were interpreted as indicating problems employing efficient information processing strategies for children with reading problems.

Torgesen (1979), in an attempt to better understand the difficulty children with reading disabilities had in applying efficient strategies to facilitate recall, asked the children questions about remembering information. The children were approximately 9-years-old. The results indicated that children with reading problems described verbal rehearsal as a technique for remembering less frequently than other readers. These same children generated fewer solutions to remembering problems than children in the other group. These results were interpreted as indicating that children with reading problems experienced difficulty managing intact capabilities.

Summary. Work with learning-disabled children and Hagen's memory task provided evidence that these children did not recall as much relevant information when compared to those without learning problems. Incidental recall was similar for both groups. Before the age of 8 years, children with learning disabilities did not rehearse spontaneously; however, they could be induced to do so, with the result of enhancing recall performance (e.g., Hallahan et al., 1974). Children with learning disabilities rehearsed at least some of the time when presented with visual stimuli (Bauer, 1977); and did not improve recall with practice (Bauer, 1979). Presenting the items grouped by category (Suiter & Potter, 1978); providing instructions to improve using three-dimensional objects (Swanson, 1977a, 1977b); and directing attention (Torgesen et al., 1979) to the to-be-remembered stimuli increased the recall of learning-disabled children.

RESPONSE GENERATION

Ring (1976) used auditory and visual stimuli when evaluating recall. The effects of organizing the stimuli were evaluated by either presenting the stimuli in related groups or presenting the stimuli randomly. The child's task was to recall items presented previously. Ring studied the effects of linguistic content (tones versus words) and temporal groupings (pauses at regular intervals) on recall. Her subjects were children diagnosed as having learning disabilities and children without learning problems. These children were matched on age and sex. Mean age of the children with learning disabilities was 7 year, 7 months with a standard deviation of 3.26 years. This standard deviation suggested a great deal of variability with respect to age and should be taken into account when interpreting the results.

Criteria for identification as learning disabled were scores below the 50th percentile on either the expressive or receptive language subtest of the Northwestern Syntax Screening Test (Lee, 1969); a minimum IQ of 70; and failure to achieve at grade level. These criteria excluded children with learning disabilities who would be expected to achieve above or well below grade level and included children with learning problems whose IQ was below 90 (the suggested cutoff by many for learning disabilities). Furthermore, the inadequate reliability, validity, and standardization of the Northwestern Syntax Screening Test posed problems in using this test as a diagnostic rather than screening test (Salvia & Ysseldyke, 1978).

The auditory stimuli were of two types, grouped or ungrouped, and were of two kinds, tones or words. The linguistic stimuli consisted of either pure tones or one-syllable, high-frequency, English words. The children were tested individually on all combinations of the kinds and types of stimuli. The results showed that children with learning disabilities performed significantly poorer than the normal children under both grouped and ungrouped presentations. The learning-disabled children's decrement in performance was greater when the stimuli were auditory. Grouping the stimuli had no effect, but linguistic items were better recalled than auditory tones by both groups of children.

Bryan (1972) used both auditory and visual stimuli to evaluate long-term memory and forced mediation. Her subjects were 37 children, 22 with learning disabilities and 15 without learning problems. The age range was 8 years to 11 years with IQs ranging from 85 to 115. The task was a multi-trial free recall task. The list of 15 words or pictures of the words to be learned was presented over and over again with a test of recall after each presentation. Children were either told to pay close attention to what was presented, to say the information aloud, or that saying the information might help them remember better.

Results showed that, in general, children with learning disabilities performed poorer than those without learning problems when presented with both verbal and visual items. In addition, visual stimuli were better recalled than auditory stimuli. No significant effect was obtained for the type of instruction. Bryan concluded that rehearsal, or directing attention, did not facilitate recall of the children in the learning disabilities group. The wide age range of Bryan's subjects makes it hard to evaluate these results. This factor could account for the general lack of a facilitating effect of rehearsal with both children with and without learning disabilities.

With respect to response generation, the children with learning disabilities recalled fewer items than those without learning problems, particularly when the items were verbal (Bryan, 1972) or auditory (Ring, 1976).

FEEDBACK

Parrill-Burnstein and Baker-Ward (1979), in the context of the hypothesis-testing paradigm, studied appropriate responses to feedback. This experiment is mentioned only briefly here since it is discussed in greater detail in the Concept Organization chapter. The subjects were 138 children. There were three groups. Children in Groups I and II were from different private schools for children with learning disabilities. The 45 children in Group I were younger (by approximately 1–1½ years) than the 44 children in Group II. Group III consisted of 49 children without learning problems. Children from Groups I and II were of average intelligence but were performing academically below expectancy. Children in the three groups were equated on achievement. All of these youngsters were in grades one through five and were participating in a series of experiments.

The procedure involved presenting each child individually with two multidimensional stimuli. The child was asked to select one of the two stimuli. Following selection, feedback was provided and was either *correct* or *incorrect*. At this level, the appropriate response was to repeat a response if told it was correct and, if told it was incorrect, the child was to eliminate that choice and sample from other possible responses. Studying feedback allowed memory to be evaluated in two ways. First, memory for the number of possible correct responses was assessed; second, memory in terms of resampling was investigated.

Parrill-Burnstein and Baker-Ward found that children with learning disabilities did not respond to feedback as expected and that they differed significantly from those without learning problems. Children in Group II changed responses after both positive and negative feedback. Children in Group I retained responses appropriately after positive feedback, and changed responses as appropriate after negative feedback. Furthermore, children from both learning disabilities groups resampled from the set of disconfirmed or incorrect responses when feedback was negative. These results were interpreted as indicating that children with learning disabilities recalled or generated fewer hypotheses than those without learning problems; that responses to feedback were reinforced some of the time; and that children with learning disabilities still differed from children without learning problems when equated on achievement. In other words, a developmental delay solely accounted for by achievement was not substantiated.

Recognition

Recognition memory has been evaluated using pictures of faces and Hagen's Central-Incidental Learning Task. The findings when employing Hagen's tasks were reviewed under the *Recall* section headed *Selective Attention*. The child's ability to discriminate cues and integrate cues is summarized here. Generally, it was found that children with learning disabilities had difficulty encoding relevant features, but could be induced to do so with proper instruction.

SELECTIVE ATTENTION

To investigate whether or not children with learning disabilities had problems discriminating or attending selectively to facial features, two experiments were conducted (Parrill-Burnstein & Hazan-Ginzburg, 1980). The subjects in both experiments were 169 children in first through fifth grades. One hundred and twenty-four children were diagnosed as having learning disabilities and were in two private schools for children with learning disabilities. Group I included 50 children from the school; Group II included 74 children from the other school. Children in Group I were younger (by approximately 1–1½ years) than those in Group II. Group III included 45 children without learning disabilities. Children were equated on SES and achievement. Children in the learning disabilities class had a mean IQ of approximately 100c. IQ data for children without learning problems were not collected. These children were participating in a larger series of experiments.

In the first experiment, the stimuli were 168 photographs of faces presented in booklet form (Benton et al, 1975). There were 24 pages. On each page, a target item was placed immediately above six or nine other items. The 24 pages were divided into three sets. The types of items placed among the distractors differentiated the sets. Set A consisted of six pages with one target and six other faces. One face among the six was identical to the target. Set B consisted of nine pages with a target and six other faces. Among the six items, three were of the same face as the target item with the lighting changed. The format for set C was identical to that described for set A. However, within set C, the orientation of the faces placed among the distractors was changed.

The child's task on all three sets was to look at the target item as the examiner pointed to it and find the same face or faces among the distractors. The target item remained present throughout. The results showed that children with learning disabilities identified fewer faces than those without learning problems.

Further analysis indicated that children with learning disabilities from both groups performed significantly poorer than those without learning problems in the control group. A significant grade effect was also obtained. The trend was linear, though only those in the first two grades differed significantly from those in grades four and five. A significant interaction between grade and school was also found. This was due to the performance of those children with learning disabilities in Group I. Children in this group in grades one and two performed poorest. With respect to grade, performance of those in Group II was less systematic. Differences in performance were observed with those with learning disabilities in Group II—the implication being that within the heterogeneous category of learning disabilities, some children demonstrate delays and other differences in performance. The relationship between age and achievement and/or the extent of the discrepancy may be influential variables.

These results were interpreted as indicating that children with learning disabilities did not attend to subtle facial cues, which may have affected the development of visual constancy and, of course, memory. Furthermore, with respect to grade and learning disabilities, a general delay in performance was obtained with children in Group I who were in grades one and two.

In the second experiment, selective attention was further evaluated. The stimuli were photographs of faces organized into two sets. Set A consisted of 48 faces. There were 12 pages and four faces on each page. Included in these four faces was a target item (standard), an item identical to the target, and two distractor items. The target was placed above the other three items. Set B consisted of 72 pictures of faces. There were 24 pages with three pictures to a page. One of the 12 targets and 12 distractor items presented in set A was placed among the two other items on each page. The 48 distractors used in this set had never been shown before.

The procedure involved presenting set A to the child. The examiner pointed to the target item and to the other six items and instructed the child to find the one that was the same. These instructions were repeated for all 24 pages. Set B was presented 10 seconds after set A. The child was shown set B and instructed to find the photograph that was shown previously, which was a member of set A.

The results showed that although all children matched the same faces without difficulty, the three groups did not recognize the faces with equal frequency when retested with set B. Children with verbal learning disabilities performed poorest, followed by those from the heterogeneous group. Children in this latter group did not differ significantly from those in the other two groups. Only children with verbal learning disabilities differed significantly from those without learning problems. Significant grade and type of item effects were also obtained. Children in the first three grades recalled fewer items than those in grades four and five. Furthermore, targets were recalled more frequently than distractor items by children in both groups. A significant interaction between item and learning condition indicated that children with learning disabilities recognized fewer distractor items and fewer central items than those without learning problems.

The implications were that this type of memory changed as did other problem-solving activities, some time at or after the second grade. Children with learning disabilities demonstrated a similar grade trend as those without learning problems. A delay in development was not substantiated. Finally, the target items were recalled more frequently than the distractor items. This was expected. Attention was directed to those faces by pointing to them and requiring the child to match.

Parrill-Burnstein and Baker-Ward (1979) evaluated the effects of providing instructions to direct attention and integrate facial features. There were 140 children who were participants in a larger study: 90 with learning disabilities, and 50 without learning problems. The children with learning disabilities were from two private educational centers, 45 from each center, while those without learning problems were from regular classes in public schools. Children with learning disabilities in Group I were approximately 1–1½ years younger than those with learning disabilities in Group II. The children were equated on achievement.

The experiment was conducted in two phases, a pretest phase and an experimental phase. During the pretest, the child was shown a series of black and white pictures of the head and shoulders of male and female adults at various ages. The children were instructed to look at the faces carefully and told that their memory would be tested after the series had been presented. During the experimental phase, the children were told to make a judgment of *mean* or *nice* as each picture was presented.

The results showed that during pretest, children in Group II with learning disabilities recognized significantly fewer faces than those with learning disabilities in Group I and those without learning problems. Similar grade trends were observed for all three groups. After making a judgment of *mean* or *nice,* the groups did not differ in the number of faces recognized. Nonsystematic but significant grade differences were obtained. Again, children in all three groups performed similarly with respect to grade. The implications of these findings were interpreted as indicating that instructions to direct attention facilitated the use of strategies by the most impaired group, those from Group II. Differences discriminating or attending selectively were indicated and differences rather than delays in performance were found. With respect to this latter finding and the results reported previously (Parrill-Burnstein and Hagan-Ginzberg, 1980), the variability in performance may be influenced by task format and requirements.

Torgesen and Goldman (1977) studied rehearsal and short-term memory of reading disabled children. The subjects were 32 late second-grade children who were identified as either poor readers or good readers. The method involved presenting the child with a series of achromatic line drawings of common objects. The experimenter pointed to the picture of an object in a specific order and the child's task was to point to the picture in the sequence the examiner indicated. A 15-minute delay period was instituted between presentation and test of recall. During the delay period, the child was observed closely for evidence of rehearsal or verbalization. Each child was also asked how they remembered the information. Results indicated that good readers rehearsed and recalled more items than poor readers. Next the children were instructed to say aloud the picture names during both presentation and recall phases of the task. After this instruction, significant differences were not obtained.

Summary. Children with learning disabilities recalled and recognized fewer items when compared to those without learning problems when auditory or verbal stimuli were employed. Problems discriminating and attending selectively to relevant stimulus features impaired performance. In addition, these children generated fewer correct responses, resampled disconfirmed responses following negative feedback, and used fewer rehearsal strategies spontaneously. This latter finding was interpreted from the lack of primacy effects obtained with 8-year-old children with learning disabilities. Directing the children to use strategies produced differing results, which were interpreted as due to differences in methodology and experimental design of available research.

IMPLICATIONS FOR RESEARCH AND REMEDIATION

The data available regarding memory and children with learning disabilities could be grouped according to studies (1) employing Hagen's Central-Incidental Learning Task; (2) assessing the effects of rehearsal; (3) requiring spatial recognition and association; and (4) using both visual and auditory stimuli. In general, it was concluded that younger children with learning disabilities rehearsed at least some of the time while older children rehearsed as much as did children without learning problems (Tarver et al., 1976). Further, research showed that the type of stimulus presented to the child affected recall. Visual rather than auditory information was remembered best, and three-dimensional objects were better recognized than two-dimensional cues (Swanson, 1977a, 1977b).

Several general implications were drawn from this research: (1) learning-disabled children could benefit from the simultaneous presentation of auditory and visual information; (2) children with learning disabilities who did not use strategies spontaneously could be induced to do so; (3) such strategy induction (e.g., rehearsal) sometimes improved recall; and (4) it was suggested that further research better distinguish between attention, recognition, and recall. In Hagen's task, for example, attention was evaluated through a memory task; one for spatial-visual symbol association and a second for visual-visual recognition and association.

The suggestions for both remediation and research are organized according to memory components *encoding* and *storage*. Techniques classified as encoding are structured with emphasis on the cues available during presentation of the techniques. The two types of retrieval, recognition and recall, are distinguished under the separate subjects of encoding and storage.

Remediation

ENCODING

Four tasks are suggested to improve encoding. The emphasis is on organizing items into categories, associating pairs, and selecting auditory or visual correspondents.

To encourage a child to learn and remember visual or pictured information better, ask the child to sort a series of items into categories. Those not sorted, or those sorted incorrectly, should be corrected by the clinician. Then, the stimuli are removed and the child is asked to recall items *(free recall)*. No instruction to use categories is provided. If the child has difficulty, the clinician provides the categories as cues to recalling the individual items *(cued recall)*. If the child still has difficulty, present the words and ask again that they be grouped into the initial correct categories *(recognition)*.

A second task deals with the use of semantic cues to facilitate encoding. Children with learning disabilities may not use semantic cues to aid recall. Ask the children to use a sentence to describe the relationship between new vocabulary words, such as *cowboy* and *horse*—"the cowboy rides a horse." Then, ask the child to recall that word pair without cues *(total recall)*. If the child has difficulty, the clinician may give one member of the pair and finally both members of the pair randomly for the child to associate *(recognition)*.

It is also suggested that simultaneous processing of different representations of the same information encourages better encoding. Ask the child to select the picture of a word presented auditorily. Then ask the child to recall those words once the representation of the word has been removed *(recall)*. If the child has difficulty, present the previously presented words and new words and ask the child to identify those words as seen before ("old"), or not seen before ("new") *(recognition)*.

This final task is designed to encourage children to integrate and associate social cues that provide information about the beliefs, attitudes, and feelings of others. As the child learns to use such cues, memory performance should increase. Present the child with a series of faces and ask that he or she discuss how the person feels and the cues associated with that feeling (e.g., the expressions of the eyes and mouth). Then, show the child a series of the same faces with different expressions and ask that those shown earlier be identified. Initially present facial expressions that are very different. If the child has difficulty differentiating the same face with only the change in expression, present different faces as distractor items when evaluating recognition.

STORAGE

For purposes here, the storage of items is associated with rehearsal and other strategies to induce better retention. Two tasks are suggested.

Children with learning disabilities have difficulty remembering the spatial arrangements of items (e.g., Hagen's Central-Incidental Task). Show the child a series of words written on cards. As each card is presented, ask the child to say aloud the word. Then place the card face down and in order. On successive trials, the child is asked to continue repeating the words already exposed. In this way, rehearsal is cumulative. To assess memory, a probe is presented and the child is asked to place the specific picture on top of the correct picture placed face down *(matching)*. If the child has difficulty, the clinician can give the child a choice of three, and ask the child to pick the one that is correct *(recognition)*.

To aid memory for scenes using integration of cues, it is suggested that the child be presented with the picture of a complex activity. Ask that he or she tell a story about what is depicted. Remove the picture and ask the child again to relate the story. Replace the picture and compare accuracy of the two stories.

Research

For all the research described, it was suggested that a normal comparison group of children without learning problems be used, even if the performance of the learning disabilities child is compared to children with other problems (e.g., behavior disorders). In this way, how children with learning disabilities differ and are similar to expected performance is evaluated. It is also suggested that children of many ages or grades be worked with to provide information about a delay or deficit in performance. Longitudinal studies provide another and essential type of developmental information. Frequently, a mixed design is suggested. In this way, the children may act as their own controls.

ENCODING

To evaluate encoding of information, the stimuli are varied to include both meaningful and nonmeaningful items, social stimuli are employed, and emphasis is on the stimulus features of the receptive task. Five tasks are suggested.

It was shown that children with learning disabilities benefit from instruction to integrate facial features (e.g., label of faces *mean* or *nice*). Although children without learning problems do better when asked to make a judgment about the disposition of the face instead of labeling a physical feature such as the nose, this has not been studied with respect to children with learning disabilities. Present the child with 40 faces. On half of the presentations, ask the child to make a judgment of a disposition and on the remaining half, a judgment based on a physical feature such as the eyes or nose. Compare performance during the recognition task where these faces and new faces are presented.

On a matching task, children with learning disabilities correctly identify similar faces as frequently as those without learning problems. However, when tested later for recognition of both the faces matched and the distractor items, children with learning disabilities performed significantly poorer. After matching identical faces, ask the child to state verbally the disposition of each face (targets and distractors). Test for recognition of these faces and new faces.

Grouping to-be-remembered items by categories increases retrieval for children without learning problems. Present the child with 20 pictured items, which can be grouped into four categories with five items within each category. Remove the items and ask the child to name all the items he or she can. Then, present 20 new words, which can be grouped into four categories and require the child to sort the items into the appropriate categories. Again, evaluate *recall* and compare the two conditions.

Encoding of relevant stimuli, but this time a pictured situation, is measured. First, present the child with a series of pictured scenes and later ask that he or she recognize those scenes as presented before when shown among three distractors. Record recognition scores. Then, present the child with a similar but new stimulus and ask that a single word judgment of either warm or cold atmosphere be made. Require recognition of that scene when placed among three similar scenes. Again, recognition is recorded and the two conditions compared.

It is suggested that children with learning disabilities recognize as much incidental information as those without learning problems. It is also suggested that children with learning disabilities may benefit from verbal rehearsal. Present a card with two figures, such as an item or a tool (similar to Hagen's Central-Incidental Learning Task) and an animal. Tell the child that he or she is to remember the animal. Test for recognition of both the animal and tool. Similar to Hagen's task, it is suggested that to test recognition the child be presented with both animals and tools and be required to match up the items. Next, the child is presented with a series of pairs. Again, the child is told to remember the animals but asked to verbalize the labels of both the objects and the animals pictured. Again, the pictures are presented and the child is asked to pair together those that go together. The two conditions are then compared.

STORAGE

To evaluate storage and the different procedures used to facilitate storage, two tasks are suggested.

Children with learning disabilities correctly matched fewer pairs when tested with Hagen's Central-Incidental Learning Task. This task is suggested as a means of better assessing what facilitates encoding and therefore storage. Children are either assigned to one of the three conditions suggested below or are exposed to all conditions. (This latter is an example of a repeated measure.) The child is presented with two items such as a tool and an object. He or she is asked to either state a relationship between the two items (semantic encoding), name the function of each item of the pair (functional encoding), or simply repeat the names of the objects as presented. In this way, the effects of the type of encoding cue can be evaluated.

It has also been shown that under certain conditions verbal rehearsal facilitated recall, while under other conditions it did not. Present the child with a list of words and ask that they be recalled immediately after presentation. This allows gathering of baseline data. Then, require the child to repeat each word as presented. With one half of the subjects, rehearsal is cumulative, while with the remaining half it is not. Children in this latter condition simply say the name of each item as presented. This allows evaluation of what types of verbal rehearsal may benefit children with learning disabilities.

Summary. It has been documented that children at approximately 5 years of age can be induced to use rehearsal, with the effect of enhancing recall. However, when these children are not required to use rehearsal techniques, they cease doing so; consequently, performance decreases back to baseline. Evidence regarding children with learning disabilities is less clear. What has been suggested is that children less than 8 years of age with learning disabilities do not rehearse spontaneously. Within this study, require children who do not rehearse spontaneously to do so. Evaluate recall when they are required to continue rehearsing and when they are not required to continue. Compare the two conditions.

Data regarding the memory of children without learning problems is quite expansive. In the field of learning disabilities, this area has received greatest attention. However, the relationship between memory, concept learning, and attention with children with learning disabilities is not yet understood. What has been documented is that children with learning disabilities have problems at the prerequisite levels of processing.

REFERENCES

Appel, L. F., Cooper, R. G., McCarrell, N., et al. The development of the distinction between perceiving and memorizing. *Child Development,* 1972, *43,* 1365–1381.

Atkinson, R. C., & Shiffrin, R. M. Human memory: A proposed system and its control processes. In K. W. Spence & J. T. Spence (Eds.), *The psychology of learning and motivation* (Vol. 2). New York: Academic Press, 1968.

Bauer, R. H. Memory processes in children with learning disabilities: Evidence for deficient rehearsal. *Journal of Experimental Child Psychology,* 1977, *24,* 415–430.

Bauer, H. B. Recall after a short delay and acquisition in learning disabled and nondisabled children. *Journal of Learning Disabilities,* 1979, *12*(9), 596–607.

Benton, A. L., Van Allen, M. W., de Hamser, et al. Test of facial recognition, form 56: Stimulus and multiple choice pictures. Iowa City: Department of Neurology, University of Iowa Hospitals, 1975.

Blaney, R. L., & Winograd, E. Developmental differences in children's recognition memory for faces. *Developmental Psychology,* 1978, *14*(4), 441–442.

Bryan, T. The effect of forced mediation upon short-term memory of children with learning disabilities. *Journal of Learning Disabilities,* 1972, *5*(66), 25–29.

Chi, M. T. H. Short-term memory limitations in children: Capacity or processing deficits? *Memory and Cognition,* 1976, *4,* 559–572.

Cole, M., Frankel, F., & Sharp, D. Development of free recall learning in children. *Developmental Psychology,* 1971, *4,* 109–123.

Craik, F. I. M., & Lockhart, R. S. Levels of processing: A framework for memory research. *Journal of Verbal Learning and Verbal Behavior,* 1972, *11,* 671–684.

Diamond, R., & Carey, S. Developmental changes in the representation of faces. *Journal of Experimental Child Psychology,* 1977, *23*(1), 1-22.

Flavell, J. H. Developmental studies of mediated memory. In H. W. Reese & L. P. Lipsitt (Eds.), *Advances in child development and behavior* (Vol. 5). New York: Academic Press, 1970.

Flavell, J. H., & Wellman, H. M. Metamemory. In R. V. Kail & J. W. Hagen (Eds.), *Memory in cognitive development.* Hillsdale, N.J.: Lawrence Erlbaum Associates, 1977.

Hagen, J. W. Some thoughts on how children learn to remember. *Human Development,* 1971, *14,* 262-271.

Hagen, J. W., & Hale, G. A. The development of attention in children. In A. Pick (Ed.), *Minnesota symposia on child psychology,* (Vol. 7). Minneapolis: University of Minnesota Press, 1973.

Hagen, J. W., Jongeward, R. H., & Kail, R. V. Cognitive perspectives on the development of memory. In H. Reese (Ed.), *Advances in child development and behavior* (Vol. 10). New York: Academic Press, 1975.

Hallahan, D. P., Kaufman, J. M., & Ball, D. W. Effects of stimulus attenuation on selective attention performance of children. *Journal of Genetic Psychology,* 1974, *125,* 71-77.

Hallahan, D. P., Tarver, S. G., Kauffman, J. M., et al. The effect of reinforcement and response cost on selective attention. *Journal of Learning Disabilities,* 1978, *11*(7), 430-438.

Heins, E. D., Hallahan, D. P., Tarver S. G., et al. Relationship between cognitive tempo and selective attention in learning disabled children. *Perceptual and Motor Skills,* 1976, *42,* 233-234.

Huttenlocher, J., & Burke, D. Why does memory span increase with age? *Cognitive Psychology,* 1976, *8,* 1-31.

Keeney, T. J., Canizzo, S. R., & Flavell, J. H. Spontaneous and induced verbal rehearsal in a recall task. *Child Development,* 1967, *38,* 953-966.

Kreutzer, M. A., Leonard, C., & Flavell, J. H. An interview study of children's knowledge about memory. *Monographs of the Society for Research in Child Development,* 1975, *49*(1, Serial No. 159).

Lee, L. *Northwestern syntax screening test.* Evanston: Northwestern University Press, 1969.

McCarver, R. B. A developmental study of the effects of organizational cues on short-term memory. *Child Development,* 1972, *43,* 1317-1325.

Mercer, D. C., Cullinan, D., Hallahan, D. P., et al. Modeling and attention in learning disabled children. *Journal of Learning Disabilities,* 1975, *8,* 444-450.

Miller, G. A. The magical number seven, plus or minus two: Some limits on our capacity for processing information. *Psychological Review,* 1956, *63,* 81-97.

Myers, N. A., & Perlmutter, M. Memory in the years from two to five. In P. A. Ornstein (Ed.), *Memory development in children.* Hillsdale, N.J.: Lawrence Erlbaum Associates, 1979.

Parrill-Burnstein, M., & Baker-Ward, L. Learning disabilities: A social cognitive difference. *Learning Disabilities: An Audio Journal for Continuing Education,* Vol. III(10), 1979.

Parrill-Burnstein, M., & Hazan-Ginzburg E. *Social cognition and cognitive mapping: Understanding the impact of the learning disability.* Unpublished manuscript, Emory University, 1980.

Piaget, J., & Inhelder, B. *Memory and intelligence.* New York: Basic Books, 1973.
Ring, B. C. Effects of input organization on auditory short-term memory. *Journal of Learning Disabilities,* 1976, 9(9), 591–595.
Salvin, J., & Ysseldyke, J. E. *Assessment in special and remedial education.* Boston: Houghton Mifflin Co., 1978.
Suiter, M. L., & Potter, R. E. The effects of paradigmatic organization on verbal recall. *Journal of Learning Disabilities,* 1978, 11(4), 247–250.
Swanson, H. L. Nonverbal visual short-term memory as a function of age and dimensionality in learning-disabled children. *Child Development,* 977a, 48, 51–55.
Swanson, H. L. Response strategies and stimulus salience with learning disabled and mentally retarded children on a short-term memory task. *Journal of Learning Disabilities,* 1977b, 10(10), 635–642.
Tarver, S. G., Hallahan, D. P., Kaufman, J. M., et al. Verbal rehearsal and selective attention in children. *JEC4,* 1976, 22 (3), 375–385.
Torgesen, J. K. Factors related to poor performance on memory tasks in reading disabled children. *Learning Disabilities Quarterly,* 1979, 2(3), 17–23.
Torgesen, J., & Goldman, T. Verbal rehearsal and short-term memory in reading-disabled children. *Child Development,* 1977, 48(1), 56–60.
Torgesen, J. K., Murphy, H. A., & Ivey, C. Influence of an orienting task on memory performance. Journal of *Learning Disabilities,* 1979, 12(6), 396–401.
Zaporozhets, A. V., & Elkonin, D. B. *The psychology of preschool children.* Cambridge, Mass: MIT Press, 1971.

FURTHER READINGS

Belmont, J. M., & Butterfield, E. C. What the development of short-term memory is the development of. *Human Development,* 1971, 14, 236–249.
Bower, G. H. A multi-component theory of the memory trace. In H. W. Spence & J. T. Spence (Eds.), *The psychology of learning and motivation* (Vol. 1). New York: Academic Press, 1967.
Bower, G. H. Analysis of a mnemonic device. *American Scientist,* 1970, 55, 496–510.
Broadbent, D. E. *Perception and communication.* New York: Pergamon Press, 1958.
Brown, A. L. The development of memory: Knowing, knowing about knowing, and knowing how to know. In H. W. Reese (Ed.), *Advances in child development and behavior* (Vol. 10). New York: Academic Press, 1975.
Corsini, D. A. Developmental changes in the effect of nonverbal cues on retention. *Developmental Psychology,* 1969, 1, 425–435.
Davis, M. S., & Bray, N. W. Bisensory memory in normal and reading disability children. Bulletin of the *Psychonomic Society,* 1975, 6, 572–574.
Ebbinghaus, H. *Memory.* New York: Dover Publishers, 1964.
Flavell, J. H., Friedrichs, A. G., & Hoyt, J. D. Developmental changes in memorization processes. *Cognitive Psychology,* 1970, 1, 324–340.
Flavell, J. H. First discussant's comments: What is memory development the development of? *Human Development,* 1971, 14, 272–278.
Goyen, J. D., & Lyle, J. G. Short-term memory and visual discrimination in retarded readers. *Perceptual and Motor Skills,* 1973, 36, 403–408.

Guthrie, J. T., & Goldberg, H. K. Visual sequential memory in reading disability. *Journal of Learning Disabilities*, 1972, 5, 41–46.

Hagen, J. W. The effect of distraction. *Child Development*, 1967, 38, 685–694.

Kaess, W. A., & Witroyal, S. L. Memory for names and faces: A characteristic of social intelligence? *The Journal of Applied Psychology*, 1955, 39(6), 457–462.

Kail, R. V., Jr., & Hagen, J. W. *Perspectives on the development of memory and cognition*. Hillsdale, N.J.: Lawrence Erlbaum Associates, Publishers, 1977.

Kintsch, W. *Learning, memory and conceptual processes*. New York: Wiley & Sons, 1970.

Kobasigawa, A., & Middleton, D. B. Free recall of categorized items by children at three grade levels. *Child Development*, 1972, 43, 1067–1072.

Mandler, G. Organization and memory. In K. W. Spence & J. T. Spence (Eds.), *The psychology of learning and motivation* (Vol. 1). New York: Academic Press, 1967.

Massaro, D. W. Perceptual processes and forgetting in memory tasks. *Psychological Review*, 1970, 77, 557–567.

Murdock, B. B., Jr. Methodology in the study of human memory. In W. K. Estes, *Handbook of learning and cognitive processes: Attention and memory* (Vol. 4). New York: John Wiley & Sons, 1976.

Neisser, U. *Cognition and reality*. San Francisco: W. H. Freeman & Company, 1976.

Owings, R. D., & Baumeister, A. A. Levels of processing, encoding strategies, and memory development. *Journal of Experimental Child Psychology*, 1979, 28(1), 100–118.

Paivio, A. *Imagery and verbal processes*. New York: Holt, 1971.

Postman, L. Short-term memory and incidental learning. In A. W. Melton (Ed.), *Categories of human learning*. New York: Academic Press, 1964.

Reese, H. W. Verbal mediation as a function of age level. *Psychological Bulletin*, 1962, 59, 502–509.

Reese, H. W. The development of memory: Life-span perspectives. In H. W. Reese (Ed.), *Advances in child development and research* (Vol. 11). New York: Academic Press, 1976.

Ross, B. M., & Kerst, S. M. Developmental memory theories: Baldwin and Piaget. In H. W. Reese (Ed.), *Advances in child development and behavior* (Vol. 12). New York: Academic Press, 1978.

Samuels, S. J., & Anderson, R. H. Visual recognition memory, paired-associate learning, and reading achievement. *Journal of Educational Psychology*, 1973, 65, 160–167.

Senf, G. M. Development of immediate memory for bisensory stimuli in normal children and children with learning disorders. *Developmental Psychology*, 1969, 1, 1–28.

Senf, G. M., & Freudl, P. C. Memory and attention factors in specific learning disabilities. *Journal of Learning Disabilities*, 1971, 4, 94–106.

Wagner, D. A. The development of short-term and incidental memory: A cross-cultural study. *Child Development*, 1974, 45, 389–396.

Waugh, N. C., & Norman, D. A. Primary memory. *Psychological Review*, 1965, 72, 89–104.

Winograd, E. Recognition memory for faces following nine different judgments. *Bulletin of the Psychonomic Society*, 1976, 8(6), 419–421.

# 4
Language

Much language learning is a problem-solving activity of hypothesis testing (e.g., Bloom, 1973; Dale, 1976; Haskins, 1979). Language refers to the symbol systems used in communication; most often here, the terms language learning and language acquisition are used interchangeably. Language learning requires, in sequence: stimulus differentiation of regularities in verbal behavior; generation of hypotheses about regularities or rules; testing and evaluating those hypotheses; and retaining or modifying hypotheses based on feedback. In this chapter, four aspects of language are discussed: phonology, syntax, semantics, and pragmatics (Kretschmer & Kretschmer, 1978). Phonology refers to the actual speech sounds; syntax refers to the relationship of words within sentences; semantics refers to word meaning; and pragmatics refers to language use that occurs within context. Topics are organized according to these four aspects. Each aspect is discussed as it relates to hypothesis testing behaviors.

DEVELOPMENT OF LANGUAGE

Language development is predictable. Some researchers suggest that innate structures facilitate language learning (e.g., Chomsky, 1957; McNeill, 1970); others suggest that learning occurs in response to environmental contingencies (Mowrer, 1960; Skinner, 1957). Those who take an innatist or nativist position suggest that humans are born with a predisposition in the capacity and ability to acquire language (Chomsky, 1965; Lenneberg, 1964; McNeill, 197;). In other words, at birth the infant possesses a capability, a language acquisition device (McNeill, 1970), which enables language learning. Findings such as the follow-

117

ing are used in support of this position: (1) the universality of language and the predictable sequence of language development in divergent cultures (these are referred to as language universals); (2) the predictable relationship between language emergence and physical maturation; (3) difficulty in suppressing language; and (4) lack of success in teaching language to nonhumans (Lenneberg, 1964). It should be noted, however, that primates can learn to use language (Gardner & Gardner, 1969; Premack, 1971), but whether or not they use language creatively by producing novel utterances is in question.

Prelinguistic development is summarized by Dale (1976) as passing through four stages (Kaplan & Kaplan, 1971). These are: crying, cooing, babbling, and patterned speech. Stage 1, crying, begins at birth and is often interpreted by parents as indicating displeasure, discomfort, or hunger. Stage 2 begins at the end of the second month and is labeled cooing. During this period, infants often articulate sounds. Stage 3 begins with the onset of babbling. Babbling occurs by 6 months and may extend into the first year of life as jargon. Babbling is different from cooing in that more consonants and consonant-vowel combinations occur and vocalizations are more syllable-like. Stage 4 is described as the beginning of speech and begins during the end of the first year. During this period, the number of sounds vocalized decreases and consonant-vowel or consonant-vowel-consonants in various arrangements occur with increased frequency. It is during the second 6 months that the child's first words are spoken. By the end of the first year, children are usually labeling objects and events. Around 18 months, the construction of two-word utterances is observed. For the most part, nouns occur with greatest frequency. Some verbs, adverbs, and adjectives occur less frequently (Dale, 1976). Dale suggests that the formulation of sentences and the proper organization of words reflect the use of strategies.

Between the ages of 2 and 2½ years, extraction and generalization of syntactic rules occurs to a limited extent. A rule is a consistent approach to a problem. Rules function to help organize and make sense of information. Application of rules is not always appropriate. These may occur as overextensions or underextensions (Clark, 1973b). An overextension is to use a word that generalizes its meaning, to include an inappropriate referent. Underextension is to exclude a referent when it should be included. For example, a child refers to his or her dog as a dog but not the neighbor's different-breed dog. During 2½ to 3 years, the child uses two to three prepositions, demonstrative pronouns, and question forms. At approximately 36 months of age, the child produces simple sentences up to 10 or 11 words in length.

Later language development is discussed primarily in terms of changes in speech content, cognitive processing, and further development of inner language. Speech content refers to the knowledge verbalized; cognitive processing refers to the levels of analysis and synthesis of information. Inner language refers to symbolic representation. Around 3½ to 4 years of age, the child uses adjectives, adverbs, and auxiliaries. Sentence structures develop rapidly. Complex and compound sentences up to six to eight words in length are used. "How" and "why" questions are used. Between the ages of 4 and 4½ years, grammar is similar to adult speech; egocentric speech, that is, thinking aloud, declines (Vygotsky, 1962), and inner speech increases. At this point, the child engages in rather complex discourse.

By age 5 or 6 years, the child attempts such complex tasks as verbalizing cause-and-effect relationships, using pronouns correctly, and defining words according to perceptual and functional attributes. By the end of the sixth year, the child's language is accurate and essentially complete in structure and content. Events are verbalized in sequence, conclusions are drawn, and inferences made. Between 7 and 8 years, ideas are shared verbally, egocentric speech occurs less frequently, and inner speech continues to improve. By 12 years of age, parallel changes in language content and cognitive development occur. Changes in language are linked to changes in cognition, which are discussed in detail in the next section.

LANGUAGE AND COGNITION

Language and cognition are intricately related (e.g., Anglin, 1977; Bowerman, 1976; Piaget & Inhelder, 1969; Vygotsky, 1962). How language and cognition are related is a point of theoretical difference. Cognitive development is described as the development of thought (Vygotsky, 1962); concept attainment (Bruner, Goodnow, & Austin, 1956); and intelligence (Piaget & Inhelder, 1969). Language is proposed to determine thought (Whorf, 1957); influence thought (Vygotsky, 1962); interact with environmental consequences (Nelson, 1973); express cognitions (Bloom, 1973); and be shaped by reinforcement (Mowrer, 1960; Skinner, 1957). The most complete and influential theory of cognitive development that is applied to language learning is that of Piaget (Piaget & Inhelder, 1969).

In a Piagetian context, language is described as one of five symbolic processes: deferred imitation, play, drawing, mental imagery, and language. These processes are part of an active and ongoing process of construction that develops systematically; they are altered and built upon by means of reorganizing, reconstructing, and constructing knowledge. Processes involved in development are assimilation, accommodation, and equilibrium. Assimilation is a process by which new information is taken into an already existing structure of knowledge, referred to as schema. Accommodation is a process by which new information changes schema. Assimilation and accommodation occur simultaneously and in this way are interrelated. Together, they manage an equilibrium or cognitive balance. This balance becomes more stable with development.

According to Piaget, the periods or stages the child passes through are age-related but not age-determined. They are, in sequence, sensorimotor (approximately birth to 2 years); preoperational (2 to 7 years); concrete operations (7 to approximately 11 years); and formal operations (12 to 16 years). With respect to language learning, the sensorimotor period has received the most attention and is described in greatest detail below.

The sensorimotor period occurs from birth to 2 years and is marked by such developments as goal-directed behaviors (approximately 4 to 8 months), object permanence (6 to 12 months), and symbolic representations (18 months to 2 years). Symbolic representations are representations of information in the absence of the actual object. There are five patterns of representation behavior (Piaget & Inhelder, 1969), which appear simultaneously. These are, in order of complexity, deferred imitation, play, drawing, mental imagery, and language. Deferred limitation is imitation that starts after the model has disappeared. Play involves pretending. Drawing is graphic imitation. Mental imitations are internalized imagery. These four are all based on imitation. Language, the fifth, is acquired in the context of imitation and is the instrument of social adaptation (Piaget & Inhelder, 1969).

During the sensorimotor period, egocentric speech develops. According to Piaget, egocentric speech disappears (Piaget & Inhelder, 1969). Vygotsky (1962) and Luria (1961) suggest that egocentric speech "goes underground," that is, becomes covert. It is then referred to as inner speech.

Luria (1961) suggests that inner speech is used to regulate behavior. Using a simple motor action in response to verbal instruction, Luria suggests that egocentric speech first regulates overt behavior. The motor act involved squeezing a rubber ball in response to various visual stimuli. The dependent measure is the frequency of correct squeezes. This motor act is mediated by verbal instruction. Luria suggests that this format allows assessment of voluntary behavior regulated by speech. Verbal instructions are initially provided by the experimenter and later maintained by the child's own speech.

Luria describes four phases necessary for the eventual development of the child's ability to subordinate actions to the connections formed in his or her own speech. Phase 1, occurring at about 18 months or at the beginning of the child's second year, is the ability to initiate an action in response to adult speech. At this stage of development, the child can initiate a proper motor response, but cannot stop, let alone switch actions when additional verbal directions are provided. In other words, the child cannot inhibit an action once started. Instead the action initiated may intensify. The motor reaction system is dominant. The inhibitory functions of speech have not yet developed. In other words, the child uses speech to direct behavior only to a limited extent.

During phase 2, occurring generally between the ages of 3 and 4 years, substantial changes take place in the speech behavior of the child. At this stage of development, the child has the ability to initiate and inhibit a motor response in reaction to his or her own commands to "go" and "stop." When "don't press" is spoken by the child, disinhibition of the motor response occurs; that is, the child repeatedly presses the bulb in response to negative stimuli.

Phase 3 occurs between the ages of 4½ and 5½ and ends around 6 years. Here, the child's ability to internalize the verbal rule "Press to red, not to green," is established. The child responds without impulsivity. By age 6, speech is internalized, and the child correctly responds to more complicated instructions.

At phase 4, the final phase, verbal analysis of the situation becomes an important part of the child's thoughts. The child is able to orient to given signals based on verbal rules that he or she has formulated.

Recent reviews of Luria's work (Jarvis, 1968; Miller, Shelton, & Flavell, 1970) suggest problems in methodology and experimental design. Neither Jarvis (1968) nor Miller et al. (1970) was successful in replicating Luria's results. However, Wozniak (1972) suggests that in non-Soviet attempts to replicate Luria's findings, authors may have misinterpreted Luria's methodology, psychological assumptions, and theoretical postulations.

During Piaget's (Piaget & Inhelder, 1969) preoperational period (approximately 2 to 7 years), language symbolic functions develop rapidly. Between 2 and 4 years, preconceptual thinking occurs. Between 4 and 7 years, intuition develops.

During the concrete operational period, which occurs between approximately 7 and 11 years, the child internalizes such principles as reversibility. The child is limited to logic that relates concrete objects and events. During this stage, seriation is learned; terms denoting relationships are understood (although the child does not yet understand cause and effect); and rules are used to regulate cooperative activities. Here, the child deals with only one relationship at a time.

Formal operations commence at 12 to about 16 years, and characterize adult thinking. During this period, the individual reasons using symbols almost exclusively. Sophisticated hypothesis testing behaviors are observed. Language is used to hypothesize, mediate, and reconstruct knowledge. The individual evaluates hypotheses with feedback from internal (cognitive) and external (environmental) structures.

To summarize, Piaget's stages of cognitive development are transitional periods involving increases in logic and thinking. The child actively integrates and constructs knowledge about his or her world. Language, as a symbolic function, is considered by Piaget as the tool for social adaptation. Language develops after certain cognitive structures are developed, and thus, is dependent upon cognition.

In contrast, Vygotsky (1962) suggests that speech and thought have different roots. Initially, speech and thought develop along different lines and merge into word meaning to become verbal thoughts. Early speech development is preintellectual in content; early thought development is prelinguistic in content. Speech has three roots: expressive, social, and intentional. The primary function of speech is social intercourse, which is influenced by experience and logic. Social intercourse reflects conceptual development. Words are available when concepts are established. Words also direct or regulate our mental operations.

Vygotsky (1962) suggests that there are three developmental phases in concept formation, each of which is divided into several components. During the first phase, information is not organized but is grouped into heaps. In the second phase, the child thinks in what is referred to as complexes. Complexes are concrete groups of objects linked by factual relationships, which are discovered through experience. There are five successive stages in the development of verbal thinking at this phase: (1) associations—relationships based on single elements; (2) collections—complementary groupings; (3) chains—relationships between single elements that are linked to other relationships; (4) concepts—which lead to other concepts; and (5) pseudoconcepts—which appear adult-like but are formed on the basis of associations rather than other conceptual categories.

The third phase is the formation of true types of concepts. These concepts are based on determination of similarities between objects. In concept formation, when abstracted traits are synthesized, traits become the main instrument of thought. Association between words and thoughts is a structured process, circulatory in nature—from thought to word; from word to thought. As thoughts become more differentiated, they are less likely to be expressed in single words. The child masters syntax of speech before syntax of thought. Word meanings represent thoughts and change as the child develops. Speech changes from external to internal speech as a result of changes in functioning.

In summary, Vygotsky (1962) suggests that the initial development of speech is preintellectual and the initial development of thought is prelinguistic. The development of thinking proceeds from social to egocentric to inner speech. The social meaning of thought is represented through language. Thoughts pass first through meaning and then to words. A word acquires its sense from the context in which it appears. Social interactions with adults facilitate the child's development of concepts.

A more moderate position regarding language learning and concept acquisition is proposed by Anglin (1977). A brief overview of Anglin's position follows. In language acquisition, the child expresses existing concepts. Through the process of categorization, concepts develop. Categories are stimuli that are grouped into a class or category and are treated as equivalent. Categories allow us to organize the world into meaningful units. Concepts enable the formation of internal representation and guide in the classification of new instances.

Similarly, Nelson (1973) suggests that the child forms concepts prior to language learning. Nelson elaborates four steps in forming concepts: (1) identification of an object as an object; (2) identification of important relationships (usually based on function); (3) identification of new concepts by noting similar stable and salient characteristics; and (4) attaching a name or word to a concept. A word has meaning in the concept that it represents.

Briefly, authors suggest that language expresses cognition (Bloom, 1973); the child learns cultural concepts through language, that is, language determines or shapes thought (Whorf, 1957); cognitive structures formulate a base for language acquisition (Bowerman, 1976); and language influences thought rather than determines it (Cole & Schribner, 1971).

FOUR ASPECTS OF LANGUAGE

In this section, the four aspects or components of language acquisition are discussed. In phonology, the basic unit is the sound; in syntax, the basic unit is the sentence; in semantics, the basic unit is the proposition; and in pragmatics, the basic unit is the context in which the language occurs. Pragmatics ties phonology, semantics, and syntax together. Each of the components are viewed in relation to the problem-solving analysis of selective attention, response generation, response execution or testing, and response to feedback.

Phonology

A basic component of language is the phoneme or sound. Phonemes make up our production or articulation of speech. Phonemes are combined to form syllables and words, which are combined to form sentences.

Descriptions of the development of the phonologic system first reflect an attempt at emphasizing almost exclusively the motor functions of sound (Jakobson, 1968). Later descriptions are concerned with distinctive features of sounds. Distinctive features of sounds are a set of characteristics that differentiate sounds and sound categories (Kretschmer & Kretschmer, 1978). Distinctive features are defined as having phonemic, acoustic, and physiologic features. For example, the feature of a sound may be a "stop sound," requiring closing of the lips and stopping of air flow, and can be transcribed with a particular symbol. The most recent approach has been to take into account both motor and auditory components of sounds.

Jakobson was the first to formulate a description of the order of phonologic development. Jakobson's major focus was on the development of phonemic universals. Regardless of individual differences, phonemes developed in sequence. Ervin-Tripp (1966) reviews available data regarding phonologic development. The child first learns to differentiate vowels and consonants, which are referred to as vowel-consonant contrasts. What the child learns after differentiation is various combinations of sounds.

Dale (1976) summarizes phonological developments. Prevocalizations, between birth and 1 to 6 months, are marked by crying, cooing, and babbling. These prevocalizations occur first. Concomitantly, perception is present and developing. Near the end of this period, at about 1 to 1½ years, the child begins to combine phonemes and form words. After this is accomplished, vocalizations increase, and by 1½ years, the child's vocabulary consists of approximately 50 words (Nelson, 1973). Between 1½ and 2 years, dialogue emerges and one- to two-word utterances become commonplace. In addition, vocabulary increases rapidly. At this point in development, consonant-vowel-consonants and consonant-vowel combinations are used. Soon after this, the child attains production of vowels and consonant clusters. By age 4, utterances are well-formulated and most consonants are achieved. Between 4 and 7 years, the phonemic inventory is completed, and possibly so is phonologic development (Dale, 1976). Phonologic development is both systematic and rule-governed.

The phonemic system is a system of rules that determines how stress, intonation, and pitch are expressed (Dale, 1976). The child hypothesizes rules about the use of phonemic contrasts. The child generates and tests hypotheses about a sound with respect to a rule. The rule is applied across a series of examples. The Distinctive Features Model is amenable to our problem-solving analysis. For example, a child may substitute *t* for *s* in the word seen. In this way, the placement for production of the sound is retained. In this model, distinctive features include such characteristics as placement (e.g., labial), manner (e.g., plosive), sibilance (e.g., hissing sounds), and voicing. A child is more inclined to substitute sounds that share common features. It is proposed that distinctive features may be learned by the processes of selective attention, response generation, response testing, and appropriate response to feedback.

Syntax

Syntax, like phonology, is displayed in surface structure, that is, part of the actual verbal utterance. Similar to phonology, syntax is dependent on context. Chomsky (1957) has suggested that the structure of a sentence has both underlying or deep structure as well as surface structure. Deep structure is semantic and surface structure is phonetic (Morehead & Ingram, 1973). Dale (1976) summarizes this line of presentation. Dale suggests that the phonologic system is a set of rules that determines sound usage, stress, and intonation within a sentence. The semantic system is a set of rules for allowing word meanings to be linked together to form the meaning of a sentence. Case grammar deals with the meaning relationship between nouns and verbs within a sentence (Fillmore, 1966). For example, although "Horses talk sadly about their homelands" is proper surface structure, case structure indicates the context and appropriate sentence structure. This sentence is not semantically correct because the verb case requires a human animate noun; the noun "horse," of course, does not meet this requirement.

Syntax deals with the ordering of words within a sentence. Syntactic development is predictable and rule-governed (Chomsky, 1957). However, how it is acquired is a point of controversy. Chomsky uses a mathematical model to describe the internal or underlying process that focuses or syntax. Generally, according to Chomsky, the child generates language based on a rule. For example, the child says, "Baby goes" for "Baby went." The rule of "ed" or regular past tense is generalized and a novel sentence generated. The sentence is novel in that it has not been heard before.

Leonard (1972) suggests that transformational grammar exists at three levels. Level 1 consists of generation of the kernel sentence (i.e., "the boy goes home") where phrase-structure rules are applied. A phrase-structure rule is a rule that describes the grammatical relationship between words in sentences. Level 2 consists of generation of more complex sentences by modifying the kernel sentence (i.e., "the boy goes home" and "the boy is hungry" to form the sentence, "The hungry boy goes home"). Level 3 consists of generation of such rules as noun-verb agreement.

Brown (1973) describes stages of development associated with syntax. For the most part, these descriptions are based on the morpheme count or mean length of an utterance (MLU). The morpheme is the smallest meaningful component in a sentence of words. For example, cats contains two morphemes, *cat* and *s*. As more morphemes are added with development, language structures become more complex. Stated another way, a sentence is a collection of morphemes which indicate the complexity of the actual structure. How these morphemes are collected is the structure of the sentence (Dale, 1976).

Bellugi and Brown (1964) discuss three processes involved in the acquisition of syntax. These processes are *imitation and reduction, imitation with expansion,* and *induction of latent structures.* Imitation and reduction occur when a child repeats back, with modification, what he or she has heard. For example, when presented with "That is a big, blue ball," the child might respond, "Big, blue ball." In that way, the imitation is a reduction of what is heard. What is retained in imitation with reduction are nouns, verbs, and adjectives. These are often called "contentives" or content words. Words omitted are will, -ing forms, prepositions, articles, and can (Bellugi & Brown, 1964). These words or word-parts are referred to as "functors" or function words. Telegraphic speech is the term frequently used to describe this type of language behavior. Speech is telegraphic in that the words low in conveying information (e.g., function words) are excluded, as in a telegram.

During imitation with expansion, the adult expands the child's speech by adding functors (e.g., auxiliary prepositions and pronouns). Through this process, the child learns to identify through induction mature speech structures. The child uses many syntactical forms and expands phrases into subject-predicate combinations.

Syntactical development may be viewed as hypothesis testing behavior. The child formulates rules about regularities of syntax that he or she hears. For example, the child may determine the rule that nouns occur first in a sentence followed by an object. The child uses appropriate utterances with this construction rule. The parent expands or modifies these sentences and corrects the syntax. The child, on receiving feedback, makes his or her sentences more like the adult's.

Semantics

Semantic development affects the acquisition of word meaning, rules for sentence construction (Bowerman, 1976), and general intent (Kretschmer & Kretschmer, 1978). A proposition is the basic unit of meaning and conveys the speaker's intent (Kretschmer & Kretschmer, 1978). For example, the word "up" may indicate "pick the baby up" or may indicate lifting up of a toy. In the sentence, "Barbara is the small girl who hit the ball," there are three propositions: "Barbara is a girl," "Barbara is small," and "Barbara hit the ball." To date, most of the research regarding semantics has focused on the development of word meanings (Anglin, 1977; Bloom, 1973; Clark, 1973a, b). It is this aspect of semantics that is addressed here.

Not all researchers agree on how the meanings (semantics) of words develop. Anglin (1977) points out that word meanings develop both from specific to general and from general to specific. He provides as an example the development of the verbalized concept "dog." Dog can refer to specific breeds, which is more specific than the class, animals, of which dog is one. This latter category, animal, is more general than the category breed. What the child learns are word relationships, such as those characterized by synonomy (mother/mom), antonymy (mother-dad), and taxonomy (dog-animal). This type of development is related to conceptual development. For example, when a child acquires a word, he or she accumulates more knowledge about that word, which is incorporated into a hierarchical system of concepts. This system of concepts is sometimes referred to as a "conceptual field" (Lyons, 1977). When these concepts or "nodes" embedded in this field are labeled or "lexicalized," they are said to characterize a semantic field or "semantic network." The links established between the labeled concepts (words) are called "semantic relations"; the attributes defining labeled concepts are called "semantic features." Thus, semantics includes theories of "fields," "features," and "relations" (Evens et al., 1980).

Developmental accomplishments are associated with different ages. At about 1 year of age, single-word utterances evolve, which reflect cognitive categories of experience (Bloom, 1973). Categories become more general and specific. Midway into the second year, the child generalizes words learned to encompass new instances. This develops into the last half of the second year (Bloom, 1973). In the second half of the second year, vocabulary increases and the child learns to encode experiences linguistically. Functional conceptual notions such as existence, nonexistence, and recurrence organize the child's experiences (Bloom, 1973).

Nelson (1973) approaches semantics from a different angle. She makes the following assumptions regarding the developing of context and syntax: (1) preverbal development presupposes linguistic development; (2) the child is an active processor of information who encodes sets of features about the perceptual world; (3) the infant's environment is organized into concepts or schemata; (4)

Language

the infant tests hypotheses about the organization of the environment and gradually builds on that information; and (5) cognitive development interacts with linguistic development.

Clark (1973b) suggests three stages in the acquisition of word meanings: (1) nonlinguistic strategies based on perceptual features, overextensions, and partial semantic knowledge; (2) a transitional stage between stages 1 and 3; and (3) full semantic knowledge; that is, the child forms categories that are similar to adult categories. Clark (1973a, b) offers a slightly different perspective from Anglin and suggests that development proceeds from general to specific. Young children initially overgeneralize or overextend meanings before using words to indicate specific meanings. These attributes are associated with words or features. Initially, features are perceptual attributes, such as shape and color, which are learned and used. To describe this process, Clark (1973a) suggests the Semantic Features Hypothesis and notes observations of overextensions in the child's language to support this hypothesis.

The Semantic Features Hypothesis assumes that the child first identifies words on the basis of partial meaning; these partial meanings are based on an incomplete accumulation of features (Clark, 1973a). Features are the defining characteristics of words. For example, the word *dog* can be defined in terms of the following features: four legs, black, barks, etc. The child learns which hypotheses define the concept represented by the word. There is also an interaction between the child's individual knowledge about the world and his or her cultural knowledge, or what is considered culturally appropriate (Cole & Scribner, 1971). The child's incomplete accumulation of features is in part similar to the adult category of features associated with word meanings, but total synthesis is lacking. In acquiring features, more features are added until the group of features corresponds to the adult category. The child selects from these features those which apply to specific words. Words can be broken down and described as consisting of features.

Bloom (1973) differentiates between semantic knowledge and conceptual knowledge. Semantic knowledge is the meaning of relationships among words. Conceptual knowledge is knowledge of the underlying relationship recognized to exist among persons, objects, and events. Conceptual representation does not depend on knowledge of a linguistic code.

Bloom focuses on words and suggests that one- and two-word utterances reflect knowledge about the world of objects, events, and relationships rather than knowledge of sentence structures. Bloom elaborates her notions of two types of word forms: substantive and relational. Substantive words are nouns that are based on perceptual features. Relational words are based on function.

Nelson (1973) studied the acquisition of the first 50 words children utter between the ages of 4 and 2 years. Nelson proposes an interaction model of semantic development, which is presented in Figure 4-1. Nelson suggests that children first acquire words to match pre-existing concepts. Initially, these are

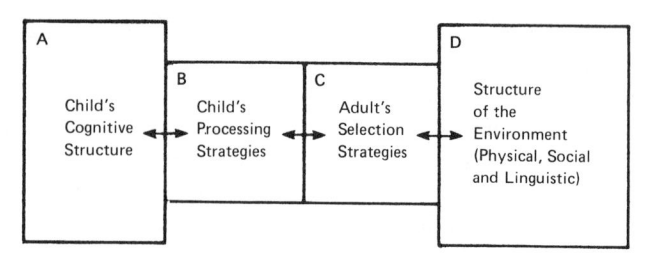

```
┌─────────────┬─────────────┬─────────────┬──────────────────┐
│ A           │ B           │ C           │ D                │
│             │             │             │                  │
│ Child's     │ Child's     │ Adult's     │ Structure        │
│ Cognitive   │ Processing  │ Selection   │ of the           │
│ Structure   │ Strategies  │ Strategies  │ Environment      │
│             │             │             │ (Physical, Social│
│             │             │             │ and Linguistic)  │
└─────────────┴─────────────┴─────────────┴──────────────────┘
```

Fig. 4-1. Nelson's components of the interaction system. (From Nelson, K. Structure and strategy in learning to talk. *Monographs of the Society for Research in Child Development,* 1973, *38* Reprinted by permission.)

based on perceptual features such as shape, movement, and noise. After initially acquiring a word, the child refines a concept to match a word. Children make hypotheses about the way the language of their community is used. Parents provide feedback about the correctness or incorrectness of the hypotheses formed. Finally, the child develops additional strategies based on the present stage of problem-solving, feedback information given, and parents' selection strategies. The process model shown in Figure 4-1 is based on the assumptions. A brief description of Nelson's model follows: (1) the child's prelinguistic organization, based on perception and representation, determines how and what the child learns; (2) the child develops and uses strategies to acquire new information and to match pre-existing knowledge; (3) parents determine, to a large extent, the content of the child's cognitive construction; and (4) the environment is the source for the information the child learns and understands.

In summary, Bloom (1973), Nelson (1973), and Clark (1973a) all may be seen to suggest that semantic learning is hypothesis testing. One criticism of the semantic features model, which is elaborated here, is its inability to account for other aspects of word meanings (i.e., the meaning relations or "links" existing among words in a semantic network of words). A complete account of semantic knowledge must describe not only what "features" define words, but also the meaning relationships established among them (e.g., part-whole relationships, taxonomic relationships; Evens et al., 1980).

The Semantic Features Model, however, does lend itself nicely to a hypothesis testing paradigm. For example, a child sees an animal—a dog—and calls it Buffy, black, or big. The child differentiates these features and selects one as the object of the word, such as black (the child may not entertain all three). Whenever the child sees that feature, black, he or she verbalizes the word dog. If the child sees a black cat and says dog, the word is incorrect. If an adult says "no" or provides negative feedback, that response is changed or altered. If the child sees a dog that is black and calls it a dog, he or she would be reinforced, that is, given positive feedback and would be expected to retain that response. In this latter example, if the child is correct, he or she should generalize or use that response in similar or same situations.

In summary, semantic learning is reflected in the words and sentences children utter. Semantic learning is also dependent on the context in which the language is occurring. Semantic learning, like phonology and syntax, may be viewed as hypothesis testing behavior.

Pragmatics

Pragmatics is the study of language use in a social context and begins before speech during the first year (Bates, 1976). Bates suggests that semantics emerges from pragmatics and that syntax emerges from semantics. In this way, pragmatics is involved in both the learning of syntax and semantics. As discussed above, pragmatics or language use in context is also an important component in phonology. Context ties phonology, semantics, and syntactic development together. Without context, language communication could not take place (Kretschmer & Kretschmer, 1978). The context of an utterance determines what is said, what is interpreted, and what is inferred (Kretschmer & Kretschmer, 1978). Furthermore, context is an important part in the structure of language in general. Pragmatics is defined by Bates (1976) as the rules governing the use of language in context.

Kretschmer and Kretschmer (1978) suggest five major concepts when dealing with pragmatics. These are speech acts, sentence utilization, presupposition, information organization, and conversational constraints. Speech acts represent the speaker's underlying communicative intent, which is referred to as illocutionary force of the sentence. Speech acts facilitate ongoing communication and social interactions. The intention of speech acts may be either implicit or explicit. The most common speech acts of English are declarative (tell), interrogative (question), request (order), expression (feel), and commission (promise).

Sentence utilization refers to the intended purpose of the sentence produced (Kretschmer & Kretschmer, 1978). Where speech acts convey intent, sentence utilization conveys intended action for the listener. Kretschmer and Kretschmer use an example the question format: "Who took the ball?" is different from "Did Tom take the ball?" In the second question, the intent of action for listener is to verify. In the first question, the intent of action is to elicit new information. Other examples are provided by Kretschmer and Kretschmer (1978).

Presuppositions refer to assumptions the speaker makes about both the listener and communication situations. During interchange, assumptions (presuppositions) are made. If these assumptions are incorrect, they are modified during the verbal exchange. Kretschmer and Kretschmer (1978) differentiate between three presuppositions. These are pragmatic presuppositions, semantic presuppositions, and psychological presuppositions. Psychological presuppositions are assumptions made about the level of information possessed by the listener; pragmatic presuppositions are assumptions the speaker makes about the communication needs of the situation; and semantic presuppositions are assumptions about the meaning conveyed.

Common informational organization entails beginning a sentence with a known and concluding with new or unknown information. In this way, new or old information is integrated with the existing information. Organization of information within a sentence influences the interpretation and retention of that information. In this way, language is controlled by discourse rather than by sentence structure. Conversational constraints of discourse are the rules of social convention that dictate conversations. For example, one rule is not to interrupt the speaker while he or she is speaking.

Bates (1976) discusses four types of pragmatic structures: performatives, presuppositions, conversational postulates, and propositions. Performatives are speech acts. Conversational postulates are conversational constraints. Presupposition is defined by use: as an object or property of a sentence or presupposing an activity of speakers. This definition is similar to that formulated by Kretschmer and Kretschmer (1978).

Bates, like Kretschmer and Kretschmer, distinguishes three types of presuppositions: semantic, psychological, and pragmatic. Generally, semantic presuppositions are of three types: assertive meaning, entailed meaning, and presupposed meaning. Assertive meaning refers to whether or not meaning is asserted by a sentence in terms of its being either true or false. Entailed meaning refers to truth, which may not be asserted by the sentence. For example: "John has a cat" asserts and if it is false, still "John has an animal" may be true. Pragmatic presupposition refers to the relationship between the sentence and the context. This information is implied by the context rather than the actual sentence structure. For example, "Mrs. Jones ate bread." Pragmatic presupposition is that Mrs. Jones is an adult. Psychological presupposition is presumed by the speaker using the sentence, though not necessarily presupposed by the actual sentence.

The study of pragmatics is not yet discussed in terms of hypothesis-testing behavior. However, future research may show that pragmatics, like phonology, semantics, and syntax, is rule-governed and requires stimulus differentiation, hypothesis formulation and testing, and modifying the response after feedback. In this way, one learns to apply the rules associated with context.

In summary, the acquisition of language is systematic, rule-governed, and predictable. Much language learning is acquired by means of hypothesis-testing. The child differentiates linguistic regularities and subsequently formulates hypotheses based on that differentiation; next, the child tests hypotheses; and, finally, the child evaluates their correctness and retains or changes the applica-

Language

tion of a rule. Not all children develop language normally. This is the topic of our next section.

LANGUAGE DISORDERS

Work with children with learning disorders and learning disabilities adds new information to our knowledge of normal language development. Behaviors regarded as unimportant in the normal child take on importance when they do not develop properly in children with deviant language. Understanding deviant language enables a more specific understanding of the deficit and this, in turn, facilitates remedial planning. Research reported here is organized according to the topics phonology, syntax, semantics, and pragmatics.

Phonology

In the disordered child, phonologic rules may take on different forms and may not necessarily have an obvious relationship to the language environment to which the child is exposed. Compton (1976) performed a distinctive features analysis of children's deviant speech to demonstrate how phonemes were related. He observed regularities in abnormal speech and concluded that deviant speech was systematic and rule-governed. Characteristics of deviant speech were inappropriate or inadequate omissions, substitutions, and generalizations. In other words, children developed another phonologic system.

Compton concludes that children with language disorders display a certain type of rigidity in that they carry on certain phonologic patterns (e.g., omissions and substitutions) that generally drop out when children move from one stage of development to another. Analysis of the child's deviant speech reveals specific systematic patterns. Again, this is used to support evidence for the child's acquisition of a different phonologic system.

Syntax

Various hypotheses have been offered to explain the syntax deficits observed in children with language disorders (Lee, 1966; Leonard, 1972; Menyuk, 1964). Lee (1966) suggests that language-disordered children do not simply show a delay in the acquisition of syntax, but rather a difference in the ability to generalize linguistic rules. Syntactical development, as discussed above, depends upon this ability. Other researchers have shown that normal and language-disordered children differ on their mean length of utterance at the same chronological age (Menyuk, 1964; Morehead & Ingram, 1973). In other words, language-disordered children produce less than children without language problems. This difference in output may reflect problems (e.g., discrimination) receiving, understanding, organizing, generating, and/or retrieving linguistic information. Furthermore, the most specific type of error made in syntactical formation is the omission of specific words and morphological structures (Leonard, 1972; Menyuk, 1964).

Menyuk (1964) compared 10 normal and 10 language-impaired children between the ages of 3 years and 5 years, 10 months. The 10 children diagnosed as language-impaired were identified by teachers and speech clinicians as using infantile speech. These children were matched on the basis of age, IQ, and SES with normal controls. Language samples were elicited using projective tests, during conversation with an adult, and during conversation with peers while role-playing a family situation. In addition, three children in each group were required to repeat sentences provided by a model. These sentences consisted of various grammatical transformations. Four other children in each group were required to repeat sentences with exemplars of various restricted forms.

Results of Menyuk's (1964) study indicated that many of the normal children used grammatical transformations more frequently than language-impaired children. Furthermore, children with infantile language made omissions more frequently and produced more ungrammatical sentences than children without learning problems. Increased use of correct sentences and grammatic transformations occurred with an increase in age for normal comparison groups but not language-impaired children. Data regarding repetitions indicated more accurate performance with normal children. The infantile language group omitted more grammatical structures than children without learning problems and differed in their use of phrase structure rules.

Menyuk interprets these results as indicating qualitative differences in language performance rather than reflecting delays in language development. Suggested qualitative differences were in both the coding of the syntax of language and in production of syntactically appropriate utterances.

Leonard (1972) studied the syntactical and morphological structures used by nine language-impaired and nine normal children. All children were enrolled in a kindergarten program, and the mean age for both groups was 5 years, 3 months. A 50-word utterance language sample was obtained using the Children's Apperception Test. Verbal probes were used by the examiner to encourage the children to discuss the various stimuli. Syntactic and morphological structures were analyzed in terms of phrase structure, transformations, and morphological grammar. The analysis suggested by Lee and Canter (1971) was also performed. No difference between children on structures used was found. However, frequency data did indicate significant differences in the number of transformations used.

Children without learning problems used more transformations than the language-disordered group.

Morehead and Ingram (1973) worked with 15 normal and 15 linguistically deviant children. The children were matched on the basis of mean length of utterance. Children in the normal group ranged in age from 1 year, 7 months to 3 years, 1 month with a mean age of 2 years, 4 months. Children in the language-disordered group ranged in age from 3 years, 6 months to 9 years, 6 months, with a mean age of 6 years, 7 months. Within these two groups, the five following linguistic level were represented: (1) base structure; (2) transformations; (3) construction type; (4) inflectional morphology; and (5) selected lexical items representing minor syntactical categories.

Language samples were collected under three conditions: (1) spontaneous language during free play; (2) elicited language during free play; and (3) elicited language while viewing a children's book. Results indicated that: (1) phrase structure was similar between the two groups; (2) more difficult transformations were observed only with the normal group; (3) the language-disordered group produced more inflected speech at the first three linguistic levels than the normal group; and (4) no significant differences were found in the frequency or type of transformational rules used by the two groups.

These results were interpreted as indicating a marked delay in onset time from one level to the next and in the acquisition period for acquiring transformations. Differences appeared to be in the ability to select and develop grammatical and semantic features.

Authors have also investigated the facilitating effects of various kinds of language intervention (Courtright & Courtright, 1976; Leonard, 1975b). Leonard worked with eight children ranging in age from 5 to 9 years who were diagnosed by a speech pathologist as demonstrating deficiencies in grammatical expression. Each child's mean utterance length was at least three words. No child prior to training used either the auxiliary (is) or the negative (don't) at the beginning of the study.

Baseline data were gathered during the first phase of the study; during the second phase, teaching procedures were instituted. During testing, or the gathering of baseline data, each child was presented with a picture and asked to talk about it. The words "is" and "do-don't" were logical words to be used in the descriptions. During teaching, the child observed the model's utterances using "don't" and "is," which was reinforced, or observed the model uttering sentences omitting the words "is" and "don't" which was not reinforced. The responses taught either paralleled the normal development of that structure (e.g., Daddy sleep; Daddy sleeping; Daddy is sleeping) or were additive (e.g., is; is sleeping; Daddy is sleeping).

Results indicated that children reached criteria faster and received a higher percentage of correct responses during training with developmental rather than additive sequences. Further, children taught either the developmental or additive sequence performed better than controls. Leonard suggested differences in perception and used the relevant features in language acquisition to explain some of these results.

Courtright and Courtright (1976) worked with eight children between the ages of 5 years and 10 years who were judged by speech clinicians to be disordered in the production of the personal pronoun "they." Comprehension of "they" was intact. The procedure consisted of three phases: (1) mimicry phase, during which the child was provided with the correct, complete sentence and then asked to imitate it (without reinforcement); (2) a modeling condition, which was identical to condition 1 except that the correct structure was repeated 20 times before the child was asked to respond; and (3) the presentation of 20 new pictures where the child was asked, as during baseline, to produce the correct sentence.

Results indicated that children in both mimicry and modeling conditions increased in the correct use of "they" after training. Significant differences in the effectiveness of the two methods were not obtained. These results were interpreted with caution, because the children differed at the baseline. Once this initial difference was satisfactorily adjusted, however, significant differences between the mimicry and modeling conditions were obtained; modeling was the more effective technique.

Morehead and Ingram (1973) differentiated between normal and linguistically deviant children on the basis of their base syntax. They found differences in the efficiency of the system used. Along these same lines, Johnston and Schery (1976) found that language-deviant children differed in a progression from the use of morphological rules to consistent generalization or generalized applicability.

In summary, with respect to syntax, many utterances of language-disordered children were similar to normal children (Morehead & Ingram, 1973). When differences were observed, they were primarily omissions (Leonard, 1972; Menyuk, 1964), and differences in use of grammatic expression (Leonard, 1972). Training techniques using modeling were effective in facilitating changes (Courtright & Courtright, 1976; Leonard, 1975). It was hypothesized that these differences reflected qualitative differences (Lee, 1966; Menyuk, 1964); encoding problems (Menyuk, 1964); lack of attention to relevant features (Leonard, 1972); and delays in the acquisition of transformations (Morehead & Ingram, 1973).

Semantics

Studies examining the semantic development of children with language disorders reported many similarities in their profiles and those of normal children (Friedman & Carpenter, 1976; Leonard, Boulders, & Miller, 1976). One study

(Hoskins, 1979) reported differences in the use of hypothesis testing to determine a semantic category between normal children and language-disordered children. Children with language disorders did not demonstrate as much flexibility in using strategies to learn new semantic categories as children without language disorders do; differences in hypothesis testing behaviors were observed with regard to responding to feedback when attempting to acquire a semantic category (Hoskins, 1979).

Friedman and Carpenter (1976) studied eight children, four diagnosed as having infantile language, and four without learning problems. The children were matched on mean length of utterances, sex, and SES. Mean length of utterance was based on Brown's (1973) criteria. At stage 1, the mean length of utterance according to Brown was between 1.4 and 2.2 level. The language infantile group ranged in age from 3 years, 5 months to 4 years, 10 months (mean age: 4 years, 1 month). Children in this group had normal hearing, normal general IQ, and significant delays in either receptive or expressive language functioning as determined by speech pathologists. Children in the group without learning problems ranged in age from 1 year, 10 months to 2 years, 3 months with a mean age of 2 years, 1 month.

Three hundred nonimitative two-word utterances were collected either at home (seven children) or at school (one child). The utterances were classified into ten semantic categories. The context in which each utterance occurred was taken into account when making this assignment.

Results indicated that the only significant difference between groups was for category designated "introducer plus entity." This category referred to using the names of the referent (i.e., "this ball" or "it baby" while pointing).

Friedman and Carpenter (1976) concluded that children at the stage 1 level of development, regardless of the impairment, showed as much flexibility in the use of semantic relations as children without language problems. This was interpreted as supporting a qualitative rather than quantitative difference reflecting differences in symbolizing and organizing concepts among children with language disorders. It should be noted that the "semantic relations" used in this study are similar to the case relations proposed by Fillmore (1966) and should not be confused with the "semantic relations" discussed by others (Evens et al., 1980).

Leonard et al. (1976) examined the semantic relations reflected in language usage. Their subjects were 40 children, 20 evaluated by a speech pathologist as demonstrating defective language usage, and 20 without language problems. Ten children with defective language and ten children without learning problems ranged in age from 2 years, 11 months to 4 years, 2 months (mean age: 3 years, 7 months). This group was referred to as the younger group with and without language problems. The ten remaining children in each group ranged in age from 4 years, 8 months to 5 years, 8 months with a mean age of 5 years, 2 months.

These groups were referred to as the older groups with and without language disorders. The children were matched on chronological age, not mean length of utterance.

A 50-utterance corpus was collected for each child by asking him or her to tell a story about pictures of a projective test *(Children's Apperception Test)*. Five questions were directed at each of ten pictures in order to facilitate collection of this corpus. Analysis was based on Fillmore's (1968) case relations analysis as modified for use with children. Results indicated a great deal of similarity in performance. Differences in the frequency of specific semantic relations were obtained. When the two groups were matched on mean length of utterance, no significant differences were found in their performance with respect to semantic relations.

In a particularly provocative study, Hoskins (1979) examined semantic development as reflected in hypothesis testing behavior. Subjects were 40 children between the ages of 8 and 9 years. Twenty were language disordered and 20 were without learning or language problems. Children with language disorders were enrolled in self-contained classes for children with language disorders and demonstrated average IQ performance.

Hoskins used a hypothesis testing task employing a blank trials procedure (Gholson, Levine, & Phillips, 1972) and a training technique combining Parrill-Burnstein's (1978) task analysis and Richman and Gholson's (1978) modeling procedure. This allowed assessment of the hypotheses tested by the children, and their response to feedback. The children were presented with a set of stimuli (two pictures) differing on one of four dimensions. The child's task was to associate a nonsense word with one of the eight features. The experiment was conducted in five phases: practice, pretest, training, posttest, and generalization. One half of the children in each group received either continued practice (control group) or training (experimental group). Training involved providing the children with visual representations of the cues or features and teaching them to manipulate those cues appropriately. During posttest, the visual cues remained present without instruction about how to use them. During generalization, no visual cues were available.

The results showed that the most striking difference in the performance of the language-disordered children was their response to feedback. Children in this group continued to test the hypothesis following negative feedback rather than to select a new hypothesis. Language-disordered children required more trials to solve the problems and, in addition, solved fewer problems. Language/learning-disordered children receiving training were taught to use age-appropriate strategies, which eliminated differences between their performance and that of normal controls.

In summary, many children with language disorders demonstrated knowledge of semantic categories similar to normal controls when the groups were equated on mean length of utterance (Friedman & Carpenter, 1976; Leonard et al., 1976). When matched on chronological age, differences were observed in the frequencies of the semantic categories used (Leonard et al., 1976). These findings can be interpreted as suggesting a delay in the performance of the language disordered group.

Pragmatics

Unlike studies of syntax and semantics, studies regarding pragmatics in learning-disordered children are few. For the most part, children with language disorders respond to situational context in many of the same ways as children without language disorders (Gallagher & Darnton, 1978).

Gallagher and Darnton (1978) worked with 12 children at Brown's three stages of development: stage 1, mean length of utterance 1.6, age 42 months; stage 2, mean length of utterance 2.4, age 49 months; and, stage 3, mean length of utterance 3.1, age 64 months. These children had normal intelligence, were sensorially intact and without organic deficits. These children were also identified by speech and language pathologists as having language disorders. A language disorder was defined as either receptive or expressive performance at least 1 year below age level.

A 1-hour spontaneous language sample was elicited from each child. Twenty times during the hour, the examiner pretended not to understand the child and responded with "What?" Results indicated that when the examiner responded with "What?", language-disordered children revised their utterances. This occurred at all three levels of development. The changing in the message differed and was less systematic than those observed with children without learning problems.

Gallagher and Darnton (1978) concluded that language-disordered children are as sensitive to contextual cues as normal children. They respond appropriately in changing their verbal command, but inappropriately in terms of the types of revisions that they make.

In summary, with respect to phonology, syntax, and semantics, the finding of differences in each language area depended on the criteria for selecting comparison groups. When the language-disordered children and the normal children were matched for mean length of utterance, their performances were similar. When matched on chronological age, deficits in performance were observed and were considered more severe than those obtained when matched on mean length of utterance.

With respect to pragmatics, language-disordered children were as sensitive to contextual cues as children without language problems and revised their language when appropriate but did not alter their language appropriately (Gallagher & Darnton, 1978). In terms of hypothesis testing behaviors, deficits generating appropriate verbal responses (Menyuk, 1964) and in responding appropriately to verbal feedback (Gallagher & Darnton, 1978; Hoskins, 1979) were noted.

RESEARCH AND REMEDIATION IMPLICATIONS

The major research finding discussed earlier in this chapter was that the language systems that language-disordered children employ are usually systematic and rule-governed. Primarily, substitutions and omissions characterize the child with language-disordered speech. Given that the language-disordered child can acquire rules but may have difficulty with rule application, it is first necessary to analyze current language. After doing such an analysis, it is suggested that remedial programs be designed based on findings from both abnormal and normal development.

The remediation suggested in this discussion begins with a task analysis (Johnson & Myklebust, 1967). It considers the level of complexity of the stimulus, and the expected outcome of the task (Gagne & Briggs, 1979). The following techniques are incorporated: modeling (Bandura, 1969); simultaneous processing of information (Johnson & Myklebust, 1967); and presenting stimuli that consistently elicit responses that are rewarded. The problem-solving analysis of selective attention, response generation, response execution, and feedback is incorporated. Remedial implications are presented first.

Remediation Implications

PHONOLOGY

Children with language disorders may acquire their phonologic system by testing hypotheses (Hoskins, 1980, personal communication). The first two tasks suggested are based on the problem-solving sequence associated with hypothesis-testing.

First, the child is required to associate and expand associations based on a single phoneme or a combination of phonemes. Find a sound that the child consistently uses to ask for something. Present the child first with the actual object that represents that sound and elicit that sound consistently. This can be expanded to include action sounds such as "ah" for up, indicating "baby up" or "lift the toy up." This expands the child's concepts for that phoneme.

Using this same procedure, expand the verbal response to include consonant-vowel combinations approaching actual words. Follow the same sequence: first, elicit it consistently with the figure; then, use it to present other items within that same category. In this way, phonetics and semantics are related.

Another activity might involve requiring the child to imitate the clinician's sound. Once the child can imitate the sound with ease, he or she can use that sound consistently to represent a characteristic of three-dimensional objects, such as /ne/ with the body part knee. This can be expanded to include pictures rather than a three-dimensional object. Again, imitation of a specific sound associated with a picture is suggested. Following this, it is suggested that whenever the picture is presented, the child emit the sound. That sound can be used to include other items that belong to the same category.

SYNTAX

The child may be seen to acquire a syntactical system by testing hypotheses. Therefore, the activities described here are based on hypothesis-testing behaviors. The child is directed to move through space, combine information, and complete information when provided with most of the parts.

It is suggested that imitation be used to help the child develop the initial base sentence, such as, "This is a _____." Presenting the child with objects that he or she already knows is suggested. Whatever word is used to label that object is used in the context of the following sentence: "This is a ball," in response to "What is this?" or in holding up a ball. Then, it is suggested that the child be required to repeat or model the clinician's sentence structure, incorporating the word ball within the syntactical context.

In learning verb tenses, it is suggested that many children would benefit from actually moving through space as an indication of time. Therefore, it is suggested that when teaching present, past, and future tense, the following sequence be employed. First, ask the child to get up and say that you want him or her to eventually do an activity such as walk to the door and to be ready to use the words, "I will walk to the door," indicating the preparatory movement. Then, requiring the same child to actually start moving from the seat to the door, repeating as he or she moves, "I am walking to the door," is suggested. Once he or she is at the door, or has completed the action, it is suggested that the past tense be modeled for the child.

It is also possible to combine sentences or incorporate parts of a sentence into another. To encourage a child to do this, it is suggested that first a structure be provided if it is not elicited describing, for example, an object using many different characteristics (i.e., "This is a ball." "This is a red ball." "This is a big ball."). The child, after studying all the different sentences used to describe the characteristics, is given a model sentence by the clinician that incorporates two thoughts (i.e., "This is a red ball."). This should be encouraged until the child has included such words as adjectives and, later, more complex noun and verb phrases.

SEMANTICS

The child has been described as acquiring a semantic system by testing hypotheses. This is particularly clear when viewed from the perspective of Clark's Semantic Features Hypothesis. Further, having the child express relationships in words is another useful way of looking at semantic processing. The types of suggestions that follow are based on increasing and clarifying relationships that are expressed in words.

For example, asking the child to pick out the most relevant verbal statement that he or she can about an object is suggested. Other characteristics of that object are elaborated and enumerated. It is suggested that they be listed if the child can read and spoken if the child cannot. The word descriptions should include such characteristics as size, function, label, and similar features to other items that would fall within the same category. Again, asking the child to identify the word that provides the most information about the object is suggested.

After the child has completed an activity such as that described above, it is suggested that he or she be presented with two objects that are related and asked to describe how the objects are related. Again, the child is to select the most relevant statement relating the two objects. If the child has difficulty, it is suggested that each object be taken in isolation and broken down into the specified characteristics associated with the first suggestion. After the child has done this for both objects, it is suggested that both objects be presented, the list read, and the child asked to identify which are common between the two objects. After the child has identified such statements, it is suggested that he or she pick the one that provides the most information. If the child does not select the statement that provides the most information, the clinician verbalizes each statement and discusses the attributes represented by the statement.

A third suggestion would be to increase the child's understanding of more abstract words such as analogies, synonyms, antonyms, etc. In terms of helping a child acquire multiple word meanings, the following is suggested. First, present the word and ask the child to elaborate as many meanings as he or she can associate with that word; then, provide the child with a new vocabulary word that is similar in meaning to the word just defined; next, show the child how that word can be used interchangeably with the first word; and finally, ask the child again to elaborate various word meanings and encourage the use of the new vocabulary word in the listing. It is also possible to look at word analogies and indicate a relationship between the first two words and the other words or between the first words in each part of the analogy.

PRAGMATICS

It is suggested that future research may indicate that acquisition of pragmatics occurs via the testing of hypotheses. Generally, what has been found is that children with language disorders do use context. What they attend to and how they use that information differentiates these children from children without language disorders. The following remedial suggestions emphasize (1) how to interact appropriately with others; and (2) how to interpret the intent of others.

It is common knowledge that both children that you have selected in the class have been invited to a specific party. The first child begins looking at the other child and says, "Come here" (stimulus differentiation). A specific child will move toward the first child interpreting the intent of the sentence as being for him to move and come forward. The children are asked how that particular child knew that he was the one being talked to and not any other child in the class. Such cues as at whom the child was looking when the command was spoken should be discussed.

After the child comes, the first child responds with, "Who's coming?" (presuppose that Saturday is the party date, which generates questions like the one just asked; response generation). The second child answers with the names of four other children (sentence utilization). The child is given feedback, that is, an answer to his question, and continues with additional information such as "I am going Saturday" (information organization). Information organization is used to refer to this last example in that it is assumed that the child is going Saturday night, which is a given, and you presume knowledge about the party by asking questions such as "Who is going?" You use sentence utilization by asking if the second child is going. Then you behave, in doing the interaction, in accordance with specific cultural expectations (conversational constraint).

Other remedial techniques that would be helpful are presented in the chapter, Social Cognition. It is because context implies a social cognitive setting that the two are interrelated. Hence, remedial techniques used in one area would benefit performance in the other area.

Research Implications

Research designed here evaluates the effects of remediation after collection of baseline data. Practical links between research and remediation are established. It is suggested in all experiments that a normal comparison group be included. It is also suggested that children be matched on SES, IQ, and either achievement level or age. If the children are matched on age, they may differ on achievement; if matched on achievement, they may differ with respect to age.

PHONOLOGY

Children with language disorders acquire phonology systematically but in a different way than do normal children. More specific information is severely lacking about this development. Research suggestions here are designed to ascertain the following: the frequency of consistent object or event sound associations; the part of speech the sound corresponds to; and the sound concepts identified.

The child's expressive language is evaluated under two conditions: first, when it is spontaneous; second, when it is elicited by an experimenter. During the first condition, the child is with the examiner. The examiner presents the child with a toy that makes noise. The child's spontaneous verbalizations are taped and later transcribed with particular attention paid to the contjxt in which the utterance occurs. The experimenter should not engage in any discussion with the child if at all possible. In the second condition, the examiner shows the child a series of familiar objects. The examiner uses either a label, function, or adjective to describe the object and requires the child to imitate this verbalization. Utterances are again recorded and later transcribed.

To analyze these data for each condition, frequency counts (chi square) of sounds consistent with the particular part of speech are tabulated. Frequency counts of the type of referent discussed such as an object or event are also calculated. In addition, it is important to evaluate whether or not the child increases significantly in the number of appropriate utterances during the second condition when speech is elicited. The study can also be tabulated to compare one sound-object (i.e., ba/ball) versus sound event associations (i.e., ma–to go home).

SYNTAX

In syntax, as with phonology, the performance of language-disordered children is seen as systematic and rule-governed. The following two suggestions provide children with instruction about how to use these rules. There are data to suggest that movement may facilitate such learning; this is incorporated into the first procedure. Emphasis is placed on evaluating the effects of remediation using tense markings.

Show the child a series of pictures depicting tense changes (e.g., boy walking, present tense; boy across the yard, past tense; boy preparing to walk across the yard, future tense). Ask the child to point to the picture of each example of the sound structure provided by the examiner. The examiner uses present, past, and future tense sentences. After baseline data are obtained, ask the child to stand up, get ready, and give the structure "Will walk." Next, have the child walk from the table to the door, repeating, "_____ is walking." Once the child has reached the door, "John walked" is stated, and so on. Number of correct responses is the dependent measure. The independent measure is the type of structure taught (e.g., present tense).

A second remedial technique evaluates effectiveness of a remediation technique using complete sentence elicitation. The experiment is conducted in two phases and is a repeated measures design. Present each child with 25 pictures or actual three-dimensional objects and ask the child to answer questions such as, "What is this?" The fact of whether or not the child uses complete sentences, a phrase, or a single word to answer the question is later recorded and transcribed. In this way, baseline data are gathered prior to implementing intervention or remediation.

During phase two, the child is presented with an object. The clinician asks the question and answers it by modeling the complete, appropriate sentence structure (e.g., "This is a _____."). The child repeats these complete sentences. After 25 problems are solved, the child is presented with 10 new objects or pictures and is asked the question, "What is this?" Responses are recorded and are compared with baseline performance with an analysis of variants to see if the child increases in the use of complete sentence structures following remediation.

SEMANTICS

Semantic acquisition is the focus of two suggested experiments. In the first experiment, spontaneous ordering is investigated through language descriptions. In the second experiment, the effect of teaching order of meanings is evaluated. What is stressed is that cerain verbal labels provide more information about concrete objects than others.

In the first experiment, the child is presented with a series of objects and asked simply to describe each. These verbal descriptions are recorded and later transcribed. Frequency of occurrence for the following characteristics are tabulated: name, size, color, function, etc. Also, the order of elaboration is rated from most to least in terms of how much information is contained in each description word.

The second experiment is a repeated measures design with pretest, intervention, and posttest. The child is presented with two objects and asked to verbalize how they are alike. If the child does not respond with the most relevant relationship, which is defined as the most inclusive statement (e.g., four legs versus animal), the following sequence is suggested.

1. The child is asked to describe each object individually. The child is given the structure of name, function, size, color, and other features, either written or verbalized by the experimenter.
2. The child is asked to look at the description of both objects and mark similarities and descriptions.
3. The child is asked to evaluate (state verbally) which word provides the most information about the relationship. To evaluate generalization, the child is presented with two new objects and asked to tell how they are alike.

PRAGMATICS

Two experiments are designed to study pragmatics. In the first, whether or not the child can use the context surrounding written language is investigated. In the second, who well the child interprets social information given nonverbal cues is evaluated.

To encourage the child to deal with context using written material, it is suggested that he or she be provided with a picture that accompanies a written page. Then, the child is asked to look at the picture and to describe what about the picture might give cues as to what the rest of the written paragraph is about. Next, the child is asked to generate some hypotheses about what he or she thinks the story is about. These are written down or verbalized by the experimenter. Then, the child is asked to read the paragraph and to identify which of his or her hypotheses were consistent with what the paragraph was actually about. These data can be summarized in terms of either correct or incorrect hypotheses. Then, in condition two, the child is given such questions as, "What do you see?"; "What are the people doing?"; "How are they working together?"; "What are the people doing?"; "How are they working together?"; and so forth. Then, a new story is presented and the child is asked to describe what he or she thinks the story might be about based on the picture. Again, the number of hypotheses generated as well as the number of correct hypotheses are tabulated and evaluated using an analysis of variants technique.

In the second experiment, the child is asked to look at a picture and to describe or tell a story about the picture. The story is recorded and later transcribed. Then, the child is asked to look at the picture and to discuss such issues as, "How close are the figures?"; "What do the facial expressions imply?"; "What do the figures seem to be doing together?" After this, the child is again asked to look at a picture and to describe again what is going on. This latter performance assessment is compared with earlier performance assessment.

REFERENCES

Anglin, J. M. *Word, object, and conceptual development*. New York: Norton, 1977.
Bandura, A. *Principles of behavior modification*. New York: Holt, Rinehart and Winston, 1969.
Bates, E. *Language and context: The acquisition of pragmatics*. New York: Academic Press, 1976.
Bellugi, U., & Brown, R. (Eds.). *The acquisition of language*. Chicago: The University of Chicago Press, 1964.
Bloom, L. *One word at a time: The use of single-word utterances before syntax*. The Hague: Mouton, 1973.
Bowerman, M. Semantic factors in the acquisition of rules for word use and sentence construction. In D. Morehead & A. Morehead (Eds.), *Normal and deficient child language*. Baltimore: University Park Press, 1976.
Brown, R. A. *First language: The early stages*. Cambridge: Harvard University Press, 1973.
Bruner, J. S., Goodnow, J., & Austin, C. A. *A study of thinking*. New York: Wiley, 1956.
Chomsky, N. *Aspects of the theory of syntax*. Cambridge: MIT Press, 1965.
Chomsky, N. *Syntactic Structures*. The Hague: Mouton, 1957.
Clark, E. What's in a word? On the child's acquisition of semantics in his first language.

In T. Moore (Ed.), *Cognitive development and the acquisition of language*. New York: Academic Press, 1973a.

Clark, E. V. Non-linguistic strategies and the acquisition of word meanings. *Cognition*, 1973b, *2*(2), 161–182.

Cole, M., & Scribner, S. *Culture and thought: A psychological introduction*. New York: John Wiley & Sons, Inc., 1971.

Compton, A. Generative studies of children's phonological disorders: Clinical ramifications. In D. Morehead & A. Morehead (Eds.), *Normal and deficient child language*. Baltimore: Baltimore University Press, 1976.

Courtright, J. A., & Courtright, I. C. Imitative modeling as a theoretical base for instructing language-disordered children. *Journal of Speech and Hearing Research*, 1976, *19*, 651–654.

Dale, P. S. *Language development structure and function* (2nd ed.). New York: Holt, Rinehart & Winston, 1976.

Evens, M., Litowitz, B., Markowitz, J., et al. *Lexical-semantic relations: A comparative survey*. Edmonton: Linguistic Research, Inc. 1980.

Ervin-Tripp, S. Language development. In L. W. Hoffman & M. C. Hoffman (Eds.), *Review of child development research* (Vol. 2). New York: Russell Sage Foundation, 1966.

Fillmore, C. J. The case for case. In E. Boch and R. T. Harns (Eds.), *Universals in linguistic theory*. New York: Holt, Rhinehart, and Winston, 1968.

Friedman, P. P., & Carpenter, R. L. Semantic relations used by normal and language-impaired children at stage I. *Journal of Speech and Hearing Research*, 1976, *19*, 784–795.

Gagné, R. M., & Briggs, L. J. *Principles of instructional design* (2nd ed.). New York: Holt, Rinehart and Winston, 1979.

Gallagher, T. M., & Darnton, B. A. Conversational aspects of the speech of language-disordered children: Revision behaviors. *Journal of Speech and Hearing Research*, 1978, *21*, 118–135.

Gardner, A., & Gardner, B. Teaching sign language to a chimpanzee. *Science*, 1969, *165*, 664–672.

Gholson, B., Levine, M., & Phillips, S. Hypotheses, strategies, and stereotypes in discrimination learning. *Journal of Experimental Child Psychology*, 1972, *13*, 423–446.

Hoskins, B. B. *A study of hypothesis testing behavior in language disordered children*. Unpublished doctoral dissertation, Northwestern University, 1979.

Hoskins, B. B. Personal Communication, July 16, 1979.

Jakobson, R. *Child language aphasia and phonological universals*. A. Keiter (trans). The Hague: Mouton, 1968.

Jarvis, P. E. Verbal control of sensory-motor performance: A test of Luria's hypothesis. *Human Development*, 1968, *11*, 172–183.

Johnson, D. J., & Myklebust, H. R. *Learning disabilities: Educational principles and practices*. New York: Grune & Stratton, 1967.

Johnston, J. R., & Schery, T. K. The use of grammatical morphemes by children with communication disorders. In D. M. Morehead and A. E. Morehead (Eds.). *Normal and deficient child language*. Baltimore: University Park, 1976.

Kaplan, E., & Kaplan, G. The prelinguistic child. In J. Elliot (Ed.), *Human development and cognitive processes*. New York: Holt, Rinehart and Winston, 1971, pp. 359–381.

Kretschmer, R. R., & Kretschmer, L. W. *Language development and intervention with the hearing impaired.* Baltimore: University Park Press, 1978.

Lee, L. L. Developmental sentence types: A method for comparing normal and deviant syntactic development in children's language. *Journal of Speech and Hearing Disorders,* 1966, *31*(4), 311–330.

Lee, L. L., & Canter, S. M. Developmental sentence scoring: A clinical procedure for estimating syntactic development in children's spontaneous speech. *Journal of Speech and Hearing Disorders,* 1971, *36*(3), 315–340.

Lenneberg, E. H. A biological perspective of language. In E. Lenneberg (Ed.), *New directions in the study of language.* Cambridge: MIT Press, 1964.

Leonard, L. B. What is deviant language? *Journal of Speech and Hearing Disorders,* 1972, *37*(4), 427–446.

Leonard, L. B. Developmental, considerations in the management of language disabled children. *Journal of Learning Disabilities,* 1975a, *8*(4), 232–237.

Leonard, L. B. Relational meaning and the facilitation of slow learning children's language. *American Journal of Mental Deficiencies,* 1975b, *80,* 180–185.

Leonard, L. B., Boulders, J. G., & Miller, J. A. An examination of the semantic relations reflected in the language usage of normal and language-disordered children. *Journal of Speech and Hearing Research,* 1976, *19,* 357–370.

Luria, A. *The role of speech in the regulation of normal and abnormal behavior.* New York: Liveright Publishing Corporation, 1961.

Lyons, John. *Semantics.* New York: Cambridge University Press, 1977.

McNeill, D. *The acquisition of language: The study of developmental psycholinguistics.* New York: Harper & Row, 1970.

Menyuk, P. Comparison of grammar of children with functionally deviant and normal speech. *Journal of Speech and Hearing Research,* 1964, *7,* 109–121.

Miller, S. A., Shelton, J., & Flavell, J. H. A test of Luria's hypothesis concerning the development of verbal self-regulation. *Child Development,* 1970, *41,* 651–665.

Morehead, D. M., & Ingram, D. The development of base syntax in normal and linguistically deviant children. *Journal of Speech and Hearing Research,* 1973, *16,* 330–352.

Mowrer, O. H. *Learning theory and the symbolic processes.* New York: John Wiley & Sons, 1960.

Nelson, K. Structure and strategy in learning to talk. *Monographs of the Society for Research in Child Development,* 1973, *38,* 1–135.

Parrill-Burnstein, M. Teaching kindergarten children to solve problems: An information-processing approach. *Child Development,* 1978, *49,* 700–706.

Piaget, J., & Inhelder, B. *The psychology of the child.* New York: Basic Books, Inc., 1969.

Premack, D. Language in chimpanzee? *Science,* 1971, *172,* 808–822.

Richman, S., & Gholson, B. Strategy modeling, age, and information-processing efficiency. *Journal of Experimental Child Psychology,* 1978, *26,* 58–70.

Skinner, B. *Verbal behavior.* New York: Appleton-Century-Crofts, 1957.

Vygotsky, L. S. [*Thought and language.*] (E. Hanfmann an Gertrude Vakar, Eds. and transl.) Cambridge: MIT Press, 1962.

Whorf, B. L. Benjamin Lee Whorf and linguistic field theory. *Southwestern Journal of Anthropology,* 1957, *13,* 201–211.

Wozniak, R. H. Verbal regulation of motor behavior: Soviet research and non-Soviet replications. *Human Development,* 1972, *15,* 13–57.

FURTHER READINGS

Baron, J. Semantic components and conceptual development. *Cognition,* 1973, *2*(3), 299–317.

Bates, E. Pragmatics and sociolinguistics in child language. In D. Morehead & A. Morehead (Eds.), *Normal and deficient child language.* Baltimore: University Park Press, 1976.

Beilin, H. Constructing cognitive operations linguistically. In H. Reese (Ed.), *Advances in child development and behavior* (Vol. 11). New York: Academic Press, 1976.

Berko, J. The child's learning of English morphology. *Word,* 1958, *14,* 150–177.

Bernstein, B. Social class and linguistic development: A theory of social learning. In A. H. Halsey, J. Floud, & A. Anderson (Eds.), *Economy, education and society.* New York: Harcourt, Brace & World, 1961.

Berry, M. F. *Language disorders of children: The bases of diagnoses.* Englewood Cliffs, N.J.: Prentice-Hall, Inc., 1969.

Bloom, L. Talking, understanding and thinking. In R. L. Schiefelbusch & F. L. Lloyd (Eds.), *Language perspectives: Acquisition, retardation and intervention.* Baltimore: University Park Press, 1974.

Bloom, L., Hood, L., & Lightbrown, P. Imitation in language development: If, when and why. *Cognitive Psychology, 1974, 6,* 370–420.

Bloom, L., & Lahey, M. *Language development and language disorders.* New York: John Wiley & Sons, 1978.

Bowerman, M. F. Discussion summary: Development of concepts underlying language. In R. L. Schiefelbusch & F. L. Lloyd (Eds.), *Language perspectives: Acquisition, retardation and intervention.* Baltimore: University Park Press, 1974.

Bowerman, M. Semantic and syntactic development. In R. L. Schiefelbusch (Ed.), *Bases of language intervention.* Baltimore: University Park Press, 1978.

Brown, R. Language and categories. In J. S. Bruner et al. (Eds.), *A study of thinking.* New York: Wiley & Sons, 1956.

Brown, R. The development of why questions in child speech. *Journal of Verbal Learning and Verbal Behavior,* 1968, *7,* 279–290.

Bruner, J. S. From communication to language: A psychological perspective. *Cognition,* 1974/1975, *3*(3), 255–287.

Carrow, E. A test using elicited imitations in assessing grammatical structure in children. *Journal of Speech and Hearing Disorders,* 1974, *39*(4), 437–444.

Chafe, W. *Meaning and the structure of language.* Chicago: University of Chicago Press, 1970.

Chafe, W. L. Discourse structure and human knowledge. In J. B. Caroll & R. O. Freedle (Eds.), *Language comprehension and the acquisition of knowledge.* Washington, D.C.: V. H. Winston & Sons, Inc., 1972.

Chomsky, N. *Syntactic structures.* The Hague: Mouton, 1969.

Chomsky, N. Deep structure, surface structure, and semantic representation. In D. Steinberg & L. Jakobovits (Eds.), *Semantics: An interdisciplinary reader in philosophy, linguistics, and psychology.* Cambridge: Cambridge University Press, 1971.

Chomsky, N. *Language and mind* (2nd ed.). New York: Harcourt Brace Jovanovich, 1972.

Clark, E. On the acquisition of the meaning of before and after. *Journal of Verbal Learning and Verbal Behavior,* 1971, *10,* 266–275.

Clark, E. V. Some aspects of the conceptual basis for first language acquisition. In R. L. Schiefelbusch & F. L. Lloyd (Eds.), *Language perspectives: Acquisition, retardation and intervention.* Baltimore: University Park Press, 1974.

Cole, M., Gay, J., Glick, J. A., et al. *The cultural context of learning and thinking.* New York: Basic Books, 1971.

Ervin-Tripp, S. An overview of theories of grammatical development. In D. I. Slobin (Ed.), *The antogenesis of grammar: A theoretical symposium.* New York: Academic Press, 1971, pp. 189–212.

Harris, P. Inferences and semantic development. *Journal of Child Language,* 1975, *2*(1), 143–152.

Holland, A. L. Language therapy for children: Some thoughts on context and content. *Journal of Speech and Hearing Disorders,* 1975, *40,* 514–523.

McNeill, D. The development of language. In P. H. Mussen (Ed.), *Carmichael's manual of child psychology* (Vol. 1, 3rd ed.). New York: Wiley & Sons, 1970.

Menyuk, P. Syntactic structures in the language of children. *Child Development,* 1963, *34,* 407–422.

Menyuk, P. *Sentences children use.* Cambridge: MIT Press, 1969.

Menyuk, P. *The acquisition and development of language.* Englewood Cliffs, N.J.: Prentice-Hall, Inc., 1971.

Menyuk, P. Early development of receptive language: From babbling to words. In R. Schiefelbusch & L. Loyd (Eds.), *Language perspectives: Acquisition, retardation and intervention.* Baltimore: University Park Press, 1974.

Miller, G. A. *The psychology of communication.* New York: Basic Books, 1967.

Moore, T. E. (Ed.). *Cognitive development and the acquisition of language.* New York: Academic Press, 1973.

Morehead, D., & Morehead, D. (Eds.). *Normal and deficient child language.* Baltimore: Baltimore University Press, 1976.

Mowrer, O. H. The psychologist looks at language. *American Journal of Psychology,* 1954, *9,* 660–694.

Nelson, K. (Ed.). *Children's language* (Vol. 1). New York: Gardner Press, Inc., 1978.

Nelson, K. Concept, word, and sentence: Interrelations in acquisition and development. *Psychological Review,* 1974, *81,* 267–285.

Weller, C. The effect of two language training approaches on syntactical skills of language deviant children. *Journal of Learning Disabilities,* 1979, *12*(7), 470–479.

Wiig, E. H., & Semel, E. M. Comprehension of linguistic concepts requiring logical operations by learning-disabled children. *Journal of Speech and Hearing Research,* 1973, *16,* 616–626.

Wilcox, M. J., & Leonard, L. B. Experimental acquisition of wh-- questions in language-disordered children. *Journal of Speech and Hearing Research,* 1978, *21,* 220–239.

Zaporozhets, A. V., & Elkonin, D. B. (Eds.). *The psychology of preschool children.* Cambridge: The MIT Press, 1971.

5
Cognitive Mapping

Cognitive maps underlie much problem-solving activity (Neisser, 1976). Cognitive maps have been defined as mental pictures of our environment (Boulding, 1961); orienting schema (Neisser, 1976); and as spatial images organized into environmental strategies (Downs & Stea, 1973). It is implied in each definition that cognitive maps are constructed prior to actual movement, and that they allow anticipation and organization of responses to the environment. Cognitive maps are products of the cognitive mapping process (Downs & Stea, 1973). Cognitive mapping as a process is involved in the development of motor proficiency, revisualization, mental rotations, and perspective-taking skills.

Motor proficiency is the ability to physically move through space with ease. Revisualization is the ability to represent mentally visual stimuli that have been removed from the visual fields. Mental rotations are the imagined movements of objects or an object array to another location. Perspective taking is imagining that an object is moved to another position, and that the corresponding perspective or view is taken of that situation (Hardwick, McIntyre, & Pick, 1976). This chapter is organized according to the topics of motor proficiency, revisualization, mental rotations, and perspective taking. The order of presentation is from simple to complex skills.

DEVELOPMENT

Cognitive mapping skills do not develop in isolation; rather, they are part of the child's general cognitive development. What develops prior to age 3 is the ability to understand that objects maintain positions once removed. Such skills as visual closure and object permanence are learned. Shantz (1975) summarizes development in her review of social cognition. At 3 years, the child is able to infer that others see some objects that he or she does not see. By age 5, the child is able to infer another's visual perspective for one object (Flavell, 1977). At about 7 years, the child can recognize another perspective and can mentally rotate objects (Huttenlocher & Presson, 1973). By around age 9, interobject relationships are determined; between the ages of 9 and 10, perspective taking problems are solved (Huttenlocher & Presson, 1973). Development of cognitive mapping skills progresses from concrete to abstract representations of spatial relationships.

THEORIES

Although the development of cognitive mapping skills is becoming better documented, few theories have been proposed to describe this development. Three studies that deal directly with cognitive mapping are Neisser (1976), Downs and Stea (1973), and Kaplan (1973). Neisser (1976) suggests a perceptual cycle, which he applies to cognitive mapping (see figure 5-1) is of a sequence of perceptual learning. First, the activity or event occurs; once the child responds to this event, perception takes place. Perception is the ability to process, integrate, and represent sensations. Perception is a constructive process, not of the immediate stimulus but of anticipations of that stimulus. These anticipations are based on information that is already acquired and/or expected. Finally, exploration of that anticipation takes place. Exploration is in the form of an evaluation in which all appropriate senses participate. Unlike the schemata design that describes perception, the model for cognitive maps stresses the embed-

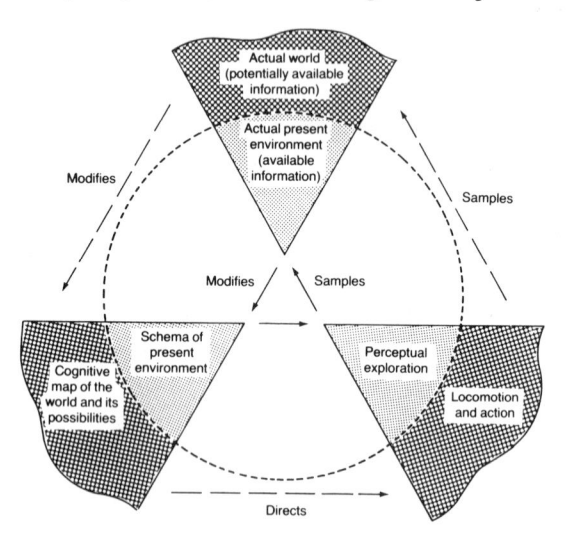

Fig. 5-1. Neisser's schemata as embedded in cognitive maps. (From *Cognition and reality*, by Ulric Neisser. W. H. Freeman and Company. Copyright © 1976. Reprinted by permission.)

ded rather than successive relationship between the perceiver and the object. In other words, objects are experienced in context and though they may be removed from that context and placed within another, the memory of the original context remains.

Another aspect of cognitive mapping on which Neisser focuses is the movement of both the perceiver and the environment. Through movement, new information is constantly made available and can be experienced through many sensory modalities. The perceiver is seen as an active participant, shaping and determining what is perceived, stored, and retrieved.

Downs and Stea (1973) discuss human's acquisition of information as a function of sensorimotor involvement. They define cognitive maps as spatial images or mental plans constructed prior to actual movements, or in the absence of the designated stimulus. Downs and Stea (1973) further suggest that the ability to adapt to the environment depends on the ability to form and use cognitive maps. Cognitive maps direct such activities as motor actions and visual exploration. Cognitive maps allow anticipation and organization of responses to the environment and constitute the basis for our environmental strategies.

Similar to Downs and Stea (1973), Kaplan (1973) suggests that cognitive mapping skills enable decisions to be made that allow us to adapt. Human's adaptation depends on knowledge of the information available from the environment. Kaplan describes four types of knowledge relevant to cognitive mapping: (1) where one is; (2) what is likely to happen next; (3) whether what happens will be good or bad; and (4) what are the possible courses of action. Kaplan discusses cognitive maps as representations or collections of associations, not carbon copies of experience. Kaplan emphasizes the importance of past experience and future expectations, and their integration. This integration of structure allows focus on recurring features within the environment, and on identifying the associating objects and events with limited information.

In general, cognitive maps affect the abilities to move in space, form mental images, take another's perspective, and infer the roles of others. Cognitive mapping skills assume adequate motor movement, selective attention, and memory. Problems in any of these areas result in poorly constructed cognitive maps.

SKILL DEVELOPMENT

In Figure 5-2, the sequential and dependent relationship between the development of motor proficiency, revisualization, mental rotations, and perspective taking is presented. As can be seen, motor proficiency is a prerequisite skill for the development of the other skills; however, it continues to operate after the development of such skills as perspective taking. Revisualization is affected by motor proficiency and in turn affects motor proficiency. Revisualization is a prerequisite to the development of mental rotations and perspective taking and allows mental and spatial manipulations to be performed. Mental rotations and

```
                PERSPECTIVE
                  TAKING

   MENTAL          ↑
  ROTATION         |
        ↖         |
          \       |
           \      |
            \     |
             REVISUALIZATION

                  ↑
                  |
                  |
                  |
                  |
                  |
               MOTOR
             PROFICIENCY
```

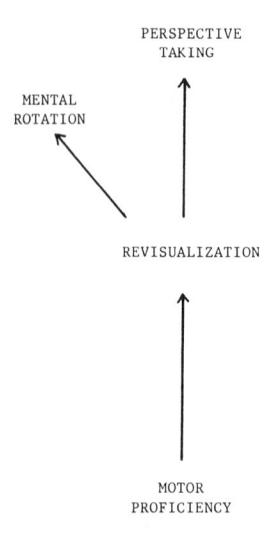

Fig. 5-2. Skills required in the cognitive mapping process.

perspective taking involve different types of spatial manipulations. Mental rotations develop before perspective taking, though whether or not it is a prerequisite of perspective taking is unclear.

Although the diagram depicts a sequential relationship between the development of skills, this process is constructive, ongoing, and integrative. What follows is a summary of the development of the component processes of motor proficiency, revisualization, mental rotations, and perspective taking; the research conducted to document this development with children with learning disabilities is reviewed within each topic.

Motor Proficiency

With respect to normal development, motor movements require the skills to make spatial judgments. Development is not easily quantifiable, marked by both a wide normal range and individual differences. During the first 6 to 8 weeks, the child learns to orient and respond to distance. Soon after, the child begins to turn toward shapes; by 6 weeks, the child responds appropriately to definite cues. The child begins to creep and crawl around 7 months. By 1 year, the youngster walks without support and by 2 years, runs. Development after age 2 is quick. By 3 years, the child is able to throw a ball about 10 feet, to hop a few steps, and to balance heel to toe. By age 4, the child can balance on a thin beam, skip, and learn simple games by following group rules. By age 5, these skills are polished, and complex combinations of motor patterns are learned, such as skipping (Cratty, 1970; Gesell & Amatruda, 1947).

The visual system develops simultaneously with that of the motor system. By 2 months, the eyes follow a moving target. By the third month, the child coordinates the head and eyes. Evidence of size and shape constancy is also seen

Cognitive Mapping

during this time. By 6 months, the child tracks vertical and horizontal lines and is visually attentive at least 50% of the time. By 2 years, the child can distinguish horizontal and vertical and by 5 years, lateral, vertical, and horizontal lines (Cratty, 1970; Gesell & Amatruda, 1947).

Throughout development, motor movements are organized and coordinated. As already mentioned, by the third month the head and eyes coordinate and by the fourth month visual tracking from side to side is observed. By the sixth month the child tracks a toy from where it has been dropped. At 18 months of age the child may refer back to pictures in a book and by the second year eyes and hands coordinate. By 3 years, the child actively plans output and drawings become more accurate and identifiable (Gesell & Amatruda, 1947). Progressively, coordinations require the child to design the visual plan, to coordinate the visual plan with the motor response, and to exercise sufficient motor control.

Motor organization or motor planning is defined by Wedell (1973) as a sequencing of units or single motor acts. All output is motor, and motor organization can be inferred from that output. The child with a motor planning problem may have difficulty in making motor movements, in visually sequencing or organizing, or in coordinating visual and motor.

Bruininks and Bruininks (1977) summarize the available information about the child with learning disabilities and motor performance. These authors suggest that these children's performances are inferior to those of other children when they perform visual motor tasks such as copying designs and write letters (Wedell, 1973), and when they are required to demonstrate balance and agility (Cratty, 1974).

Bruininks and Bruininks' (1977) procedure involved the administration of the Bruininks-Oseretsky Test of Motor Proficiency (Bruininks & Oseretsky, 1976). This test includes many items from the original Lincoln–Oseretsky Motor Proficiency Test with improvement in both developmental norms and standardization procedures. The test provides a general survey of motor proficiency, and includes tasks requiring balancing, speed, agility, bilateral coordination, and visual-motor control. In general, it was found that children with learning disabilities obtained total lower motor proficiency scores than those without learning problems. Performance increased directly with age. Further analysis indicated that children with learning disabilities experienced the greatest difficulty on items requiring balancing, simultaneous coordination of body parts, and visual-motor coordination.

Ayres (1965) also investigated the integration of sensory input. Her sample included 100 children with suspected dysfunctions and 50 without problems. Included in her sample were children with problems other than learning disabilities. The children selected for the study all had verbal IQs of at least 70, perceptual scores lower than verbal scores, and had been identified by their teachers as having learning problems. Thirty-five motor tests were presented; then, a factor analysis was performed. With few exceptions, correlation coefficients were determined for the dysfunction group only. Ayres found that four factors accounted for most of the variance observed within this group. These factors were the ability to plan in-sequence motor movements, to perceive and express spatial relations, to coordinate left and right sides of the body, and to separate figure from ground. Ayres suggested that group performance differences reflected problems integrating or simultaneously processing different sensory information among the children with learning problems.

To summarize, children with learning problems demonstrated poor motor proficiency and motor planning skills when compared to those without learning problems. Two investigators reported that these children had difficulty in coordinating body parts and planning motor movements (Ayres, 1965; Bruininks & Bruininks, 1977). These results must be interpreted with caution in that the subject samples were not always limited to children with learning disabilities (Ayres, 1965).

Revisualization

Cognitive mapping skills involve the revisualization of spatial images. Spatial imagery is the ability to recall information within a visual context. Spatial images are the contents of cognitive maps. The initial image does not necessarily have to be spatial; however, all types of images have spatial representations (Boulding, 1961).

Gesell and Amatruda (1947) summarize the development of spatial imagery. At age 5 months, the child learns to look in directions where objects have been dropped. By 8 months the child reaches for toys out of reach and can estimate distance to a limited extent. By 12 months of age, the child enjoys playing peak-a-boo and seems to understand that actual objects may be present but hidden. By the age of 2 years, the child retains and follows short commands. A child can take short excursions and remember simple routes by age 3 years. By age 5 years, the youngster can generate alternative routes between near and familiar places. Around the age of 8 years, the child is able to form images without movement (Hardwick, MyIntyre, & Pick, 1976).

Piaget and Inhelder (1956) discuss the development of imagery as essential to the development of semiotic or symbolic functions. During the second year, the child experiences what is referred to as deferred imitation. Deferred imitation is defined as imitation that starts after an object disappears, and the child tends to mentally retrieve or represent it. Also, around this time symbolic or pretend play emerges. Most movements are imitative in nature. Drawings or graphic symbols are a step between play and mental imagery, and occur sometime after 2 to 2½ years of age. Like symbolic play, the imitations at this particular period are real and pleasure seeking. Occurring at the end of the sensorimotor stage is the ability to form mental images. These images can be reproductions of sites seen previously or transformations and combinations of images involving movement. These latter images are used in anticipating events. Piaget states that images are not extensions of perceptions, but are associations which are assimilated.

Studies of children without learning problems have focused primarily on the child's ability to revisualize small and large landscapes. Shantz and Watson (1971) found that 48 children, 16 as young as 3½ years, had a sense of spatial arrangements. The children in this sample were between the ages of 3 years, 5 months to 6 years, 5 months. They were presented with a small landscape on which items such as trees were placed appropriately. The child's task was to identify correctly the object's location once the landscape was covered. It was found that children of all ages remembered the location of objects from various positions if they actually moved to each position and viewed the landscape from that perspective.

In a study similar to Shantz and Watson's (1971), Siegel and Schadler (1977) used a landscape for their tasks as well. The responses of 30 kindergarten-children, 15 boys and 15 girls, were studied. The landscapes were scale models (1 inch equaled 2 feet) of the kindergarten classroom and its contents. The models were presented to children at two different times during the school year (1 to 2 months and 8 months). The children were shown the model with 40 items of content and told that it represented their classroom. The children's task was to recreate the arrangement when the original landscape was covered. For half the children, four of the 40 items were placed in various corners on the space where the child was to reconstruct the model. This was referred to as the cued condition. In the uncued condition none of the items was placed.

The results indicated that all children recognized at least 35 of the items regardless of whether cues were provided or not. The boys were more accurate in the placement of the items than the girls. Providing the four cues aided children with 1 or 2 months' experience in their class, but failed to make a difference with children who had been in the class for 8 months. When the relationship or clusters between objects were examined, the children given the four cues performed significantly better. Again, a sex difference was obtained, with boys performing better. Those with 8 months experience, in the cued condition, performed better than those in the other conditions. The results were interpreted as indicating that familiarity with spatial layouts increased the accuracy of spatial representations. Placing landmarks had a dramatic facilitating effect when the content of the clusters was examined.

Another experiment (Kosslyn, Pick, & Fariello, 1974) systematically studied adult and children's retention or memory for spatial relations. There were 14 preschool children (median age 4 years, 11 months) and 14 adults. Kosslyn et al. used a concept of space similar to Shantz and Watson's (1971) and Siegel and Schadler's (1977) landscape tasks. The procedure involved assessing the subjects' abilities to manipulate objects within a 17-square-foot space. The square layout consisted of four quadrants, separated by either opaque or transparent barriers, or by no barrier. The task was to remember the placement of objects, either through individual location or by clustering objects into groups. The results showed that preschool children treated barriers as indicating separate subspaces. These children worked on only one or two spaces at a time. On the other hand, adults dealt with the total space and worked all over the layout. These findings were discussed as indicating that younger children have a limited capacity for processing spatial information, and therefore, process subspaces.

In addition to the difference between subjects, Kosslyn et al. found that the distances between items were perceived as greater if the barrier was opaque, less if transparent, and still less with no barrier at all. With adults, performance was best, and there were no differences between the no-barrier and transparent conditions. They did have difficulty with the opaque barriers. Preschool children, on the other hand, treated all barriers alike.

Herman and Siegel (1978) conducted two experiments to determine the development of cognitive mapping skills (e.g., revisualization of large-scale environments) with children in kindergarten, second, and fifth grades. A small town was constructed within a classroom in a space of approximately 4 by 6 feet. In the first experiment, the children were required to either walk through the model city three times and then reconstruct it from memory; or walk through the model city three times, reconstructing it after each walk. It was found that children's accuracy improved significantly after repeated exposures and that kindergarteners and second graders performed similarly and did not do as well as fifth graders. The authors concluded that the accuracy of the cognitive map improved with sensorimotor experience and age.

In the second experiment, Herman and Siegel (1978) built a city identical to that used in experiment 1 (described above), but the layout was in a gym instead of the classroom. Again, the responses of kindergarteners, second graders, and fifth graders were studied. One half of the children in each grade were assigned to one of two conditions. In the first condition, the children were required to reconstruct the model city three times after walking through the arrangement. In the second condition, the children watched the examiner walk through the model city. Again, the child reconstructed the model after each walk. The performance of the children in these conditions did not differ significantly. In other words, children who watched the examiner walk through the city benefitted as much as those who actively walked through it. Differences as a function of grade were not obtained; however, boys performed significantly better than girls. This sex effect was also obtained by Siegel and Schadler (1977), who used a much smaller landscape.

Herman and Siegel (1978) also evaluated the effects of the layout's location on layout construction. The effects of closed (city within the classroom) and open (city within the gym) environments were compared. Kindergarten children performed in a significantly different manner depending on the situation. Further analyses indicated that the smaller space seemed to facilitate spatial imagery with youngsters at the kindergarten age. The authors suggested that these children had less difficulty forming relationships between objects in a reduced space.

With respect to the data regarding children with learning disabilities, three steps in the revisualization process are suggested. These are, in sequence, recognition, partial recall, and total recall. The only empirical study available was conducted by Bannatyne (1969), and dealt with recognition and total recall.

Bannatyne (1969) used formal tests to study recognition and recall. The method employed was to administer eight tests individually to each child. Then, both between- and within-test correlations were obtained. Although the sample included children with and without learning problems, these groups were not contrasted but rather were combined in the analyses. In this way, additional normative information was obtained, but no specific information about children with learning disabilities was obtained. Two tests pertinent to the discussion here are Bannatyne's Visuo-Spatial Memory Test and the Graham-Kendall Memory Test for Designs.

The Bannatyne Visuo-Spatial Memory Test is a recognition test for which limited reliability and validity data are available. The test consists of 15 designs. Each design is exposed for 4 seconds; then, a clear sheet of paper is interspersed, and a page of eight designs is presented. The eight designs consist of seven distractor items and one figure identical to that of the target item. The child's task is to pick the figure seen previously. The Graham-Kendall Memory Test for Designs is a visual memory test. Salvia and Ysseldyke (1978) suggest that it is reasonably reliable, valid when used with groups, and is a possible diagnostic tool for assessing brain damage.

The results indicated that the correlation between the Bannatyle Visuo-Spatial Memory Test and the Graham-Kendall Memory for Designs Test was low and not significant. This implies that these tests evaluate different abilities (recognition and recall). This was also substantiated when the child's ability to balance was correlated with the Graham-Kendall Memory Test for Designs. This correlation, however, was not obtained with the Bannatyne Visuo-Spatial Memory Test. This latter finding was interpreted as indicating that the Graham-Kendall requires visual motor ability, while the Bannatyne test relies more on visual processing.

It is suggested that when studying the relationships between recognition and recall that the Bannatyne Visuo-Spatial Memory Test and the Graham-Kendall Memory Test for Designs might prove useful. First, however, it would be necessary to obtain information with children without learning problems and then compare the performance of those children to children with learning disabilities. In addition, information about these tests as measuring certain processes should be gathered.

Only two experimenters investigated the ability of children with learning disabilities to revisualize information. Parrill-Burnstein and Becker (1978) used three Piagetian conservation-of-space tasks to evaluate the abilities of children with and without learning disabilities to revisualize spatial boundaries. A total of 169 children were worked with, including 125 children with learning disabilities in grades one through five. The children were presented with two drawings of the same object. On two of the tasks, one of the objects was in the upright position and the other was rotated either 45 degrees or 90 degrees. On the third task only one tilted object was presented. On the upright object a mark indicating a liquid line was drawn. The child's task was to relocate the line on the reoriented object. On the second task, the child was presented with a ball on which a chain was hanging down from the top. The child was to draw the ball and chain when the box was tilted 45 degrees. On the final task, a jar tilted 90 degrees was placed under a faucet, and imaginary water was running into it. The child was to draw the line indicating the orientation of the imagined line when the job was filled.

The results showed that children with and without learning disabilities performed similarly on all items. Furthermore, the three tasks seemed to be equally easy. A significant development grade effect was obtained. Children in the younger group did not correctly revisualize as many of the spatial relocations as did older children. Further examination of the data indicated that performance within each grade was similar for all three groups. The possible implications were that children with learning disabilities did not differ from children without learning problems when a model remained present and the task was to revisualize details within a figure.

In summary, studies regarding revisualization and spatial imagery were reviewed. Limited data regarding the child with learning disabilities were available; therefore, the emphasis was on development in normal children. Briefly, it was reported that children as young as 3½ years demonstrated an understanding of the concept of space and space relations (Shantz & Watson, 1971). It was also found that experience, either visual or motor, helped one to integrate and retain spatial layouts (Siegel & Schadler, 1977). Accuracy was also found to improve with age (Herman & Siegel, 1978), as well as with experience, which could be either visual or motor. With respect to the spatial layout, preschool children seemed to process subspaces rather than the global layout (Kosslyn et al., 1974) and worked better in closed rather than open spaces (Herman & Siegel, 1978). The children perceived distances as greater when barriers, particularly opaque barriers, were used to separate the open and closed spaces. An interesting finding, but difficult to interpret, was with respect to sex. Boys were more accurate in the number of clusters of items formed (Siegel & Schadler, 1977) and in recalling large spatial arrangements (Herman & Siegel, 1978) than girls.

Mental Rotations

The skill of mental rotation develops by age 7 or 8 (Huttenlocher & Presson, 1973). Mental rotation skills and perspective-taking skills are frequently contrasted within the same study. The findings regarding mental rotations are summarized below. An attempt was made in this review to separate these studies from those examining perspective taking.

Huttenlocher and Presson (1973) contrasted mental rotations and perspective-taking skills. A visual array was used. The child was asked what the array would look like if it remained in place or were rotated. There were four conditions (two mental rotation conditions and two perspective-taking conditions). In one of the conditions, one half of the children could see and manipulate the material. In the second condition, the child's view of the material was obstructed (covered). Two trials were evaluated: reproduction and anticipation trials. On reproduction trials, the child selected the array as originally presented; on anticipation trials, the child imagined the array moved. When reproduction trials were examined, performance on the perspective-taking tasks did not differ from performance on the mental rotation tasks. Visible conditions were easier than hidden conditions and third graders made more errors than fifth graders. When the type of error was examined, egocentric errors occurred at the chance level. (An egocentric choice was when the child selected the picture of his original view.) When an array was actually rotated, similar errors were made as when it was imagined moved.

In a most comprehensive set of studies, Hardwick, McIntyre, and Pick (1976) investigated mental rotations and perspective-taking performance. Their subjects were 20 first and fifth graders and college students. Mental rotations were studied in the second experiment. There were two independent groups at each age level. One half of the children in each group were assigned to an obstructed condition and the remaining half to an unobstructed condition. In the unobstructed condition the room remained in view; in the obstructed condition, the apparatus was a collapsible screen and a sighting tube placed on a tripod (for greater detail, see Hardwick et al., 1976). The experiment was conducted in the library room at the child's school. Four standard objects were placed within the room by the examiner to help define the spatial layout. The child's task was to imagine an object moved, and then identify where the remaining objects would be with respect to that move. These authors' findings were consistent with those reported by Huttenlocher and Presson (1973). Mental rotations were easier than perspective taking. The first and fifth graders did better in the mental rotations condition than the perspective-taking condition. Younger children (first graders) did not perform as well as older children (fifth graders and college students) in the perspective-taking condition. Cognitive maps of the first graders were considered less orderly.

To summarize, work with children without learning disabilities suggests that mental rotations are easier than perspective taking; performance improves with age; and possibly as early at first grade, children are able to comprehend spatial layouts. When the surroundings were moved (e.g., Hardwick et al., 1976), few egocentric errors were made in the rotation condition. Older children manipulated the relationship between self and spatial layout better than first and fifth graders (Hardwick et al., 1976). Huttenlocher and Presson (1973) found that children did best when the array to be manipulated remained in view. Hardwick et al. (1973) found that the children in their study also did best when the room was left in view. It is suggested that this latter finding indicated that memory played an important role when using, as well as forming, cognitive maps. These findings with children without learning problems were taken into account when discussing studies regarding children with learning disabilities and mental rotations.

Parrill-Burnstein and Hazan-Ginzburg (1980) examined mental rotation skills of children with and without learning problems. The subjects were 166 children in grades one through five who were equated on achievement level. One hundred and twenty-three of the children had been diagnosed as having learning disabilities, and 43 were without learning problems. Seventy of the children diagnosed as having learning disabilities consisting of verbal and nonverbal problems were from one center and consisted of children at each achievement level who were older than those in the other school for children with learning disabilities (53 children). Children with learning disabilities were in two private educational centers. Those without learning problems were in public schools and in regular classes. Each child was tested individually in a small room in the school by a female examiner.

The stimuli were two boat puzzles and two plexiglass squares. The boat puzzles consisted of two pieces, a bow and a sail. One puzzle was correctly constructed and mounted on one of the plexiglass squares. The other puzzle pieces remained unconstructed and were placed, but not glued, on the second piece of plexiglass. The child's task was to reconstruct the boat as in the orientation of the plexiglass. The moves were made by placing the second plexiglass square directly on top of the constructed and mounted piece. Then, the examiner either slid (moved to one side without rotating) or flipped (rotated) the top plexiglass square. Slides were completed by simply moving the plexiglass in a sliding movement 180 degrees to the left and right, 90 degrees up and down, and on a 50-degree angle to the right and at a 135-degree angle to the left. For flips, the plexiglass was completely turned over and moved with respect to the same degrees as mentioned for slides. In total there were ten moves, five slides and five slips.

The results indicated that all children were equally successful on the slide but not the flip tasks. Flips were significantly more difficult than slides. When flips were analyzed separately, significant school and grade main effects were obtained. Further analyses indicated that children with learning disabilities performed similarly and significantly poorer than those without learning problems. With respect to this task, children in the two learning disabilities groups did not perform differently. Grade trends were not systematic. When children in grades one and two and two and three were compared, they did not differ from each other significantly. All other combinations were significant. Generally, children in the youngest group performed significantly less accurately than those in the older group. These results are interpreted as indicating that achievement level did not mean that all behaviors and skills were consistent with academic performance.

In general, the literature suggested that mental rotations were easier to perform than perspective taking. Furthermore, performance improved with age.

Children with learning disabilities did not perform as expected. These youngsters had difficulty revisualizing or imagining the object moved. This problem was not one of discrimination. The children could duplicate designs as demonstrated during the slide conditions. It was also pointed out in the preceding chapter that children with learning disabilities have problems remembering information. A child cannot mentally manipulate what he or she does not remember.

Perspective Taking

Perspective-taking skills develop around the ages of 9 or 10 (Huttenlocher & Presson, 1973). In the second part of their study, Huttenlocher and Presson (1973) investigated perspective taking using the same platform, blocks, and horse and rig described earlier. Two experiments were conducted. In experiment 1, the horse faced the platform and could be moved separately from the array. For the perspective-taking tasks, the child was asked to recognize the array when the horse remained in place or was rotated 90 degrees, 180 degrees, or 270 degrees. There were two conditions, a visible and a hidden condition. In the visible condition, the child was to imagine the horse moved (the horse was not actually moved). In the hidden condition, the blocks were covered and the horse was actually moved to a position around the platform. The subject was told to figure out what the horse would see from that point.

In general, the results indicated that third graders performed significantly poorer than fifth graders. This was not the case in the hidden condition where performance was poorest for both groups. Children did better in the visible than in the hidden condition. The children made significantly more egocentric errors on the perspective-taking tasks. These authors discussed perspective taking as involving three elements: the ego, the observer or imagined mover, and the array. Mental rotations involved only two of those elements, the ego and the array.

Experiment 2 involved two different perspective-taking problems. The array was hidden after the initial presentation. One condition was a standard perspective-taking task in which the child imagined that his or her position was moved. In the other condition, the array was covered and the child actually moved to the location. No significant differences between the two conditions were found when reproduction trials were considered. With respect to anticipation trials, the child did better in the perspective-moved condition than in the standard perspective-taking condition. As in the hidden perspective condition in experiment 1, the child made more egocentric errors when they did not move (3:1). These authors suggested that during the perspective move tasks, the subject used his or her body to help relocate. They also suggested that the perspective-taking tasks conducted in this way required the same processes as did mental rotation, and eliminated the observer element suggested as part of the perspective-taking task.

In another experiment, Hardwick et al. (1976) compared perspective taking and mental rotations. Half of the subjects were administered a perspective-taking task and the remaining half a mental rotation task. Half of each of these children were in an obstructed condition (the room was not in view), and the remaining half in an unobstructed condition (the room was in view). Perspective taking was found to be more difficult than mental rotations, and performance improved with age. The difference in difficulty between perspective taking and mental rotation was reduced in the obstructed condition where children in the perspective-taking condition performed poorest. Similar to Huttenlocher and Presson (1973), Hardwick et al. (1976) suggested that different processing was required during mental rotation and perspective-taking tasks.

Shantz and Watson (1971) presented two tasks, one of which was a perspective-taking task and the other a mental rotations task. The children were between the ages of 3 and 6½ years. Briefly, the child viewed a total scene; then the scene was covered and the child was asked to imagine different perspectives or rotations. The results showed that children who were successful on the mental rotation task did significantly better on the perspective-taking task. It was also found that children who were presented with the mental rotation task prior to the perspective-taking task did significantly better than when the sequence was reversed. Younger children made the most errors. When errors were made, they were either egocentric or impossible (a view that was not a perspective from any of the four positions).

These authors suggested that although children as early as 3 years, 8 months had the concept of spatial relations, they could not manipulate that space until sometime after the age of 6 years. These authors also presented a trick perspective task. When covered, the contents of the landscape were rearranged. Children who recognized the landscape as different once it was uncovered performed significantly better on the perspective-taking task. These authors concluded that the ability to predict object location occurred prior to the ability to imagine moves.

Salatas and Flavell (1976) presented kindergarten children and second graders with the task similar to that described by Shantz and Watson (1971). Their subjects were 64 children: 32 kindergarteners and 32 second graders. The purposes of the study were to determine the age at which the child learned to coordinate the spatial dimensions, and the age at which children acquired an understanding of viewer perspective. (This task is again discussed when the responses of children with learning disabilities are compared.) The apparatus consisted of three dolls in different colored blankets placed on a square board, with four observers placed one on each side of the square. Three of the observers were Mickey Mouse Club characters who were positioned on three sides of the display. The child sat at the fourth side. Initially, the child was asked to stand behind each observer and select a picture of the view from that position. This will be referred to as the perceptual match task. The child was asked to match the picture exactly. Following this, the child was asked to select pictures of other views of the Mickey Mouse characters without moving.

The results indicated that during the perceptual matching task, kindergarten children were less successful than second graders. On the perspective-taking tasks, kindergarten children selected fewer correct pictures than second graders. The most frequently made errors were egocentric; that is, the children tended to pick views consistent with their actual or original view. This result was consistent with other findings (Hardwick et al., 1976; Huttenlocher & Presson, 1973; Shantz & Wilson, 1971). Further analyses indicated that inconsistent responses were next in frequency. Fewer correct responses followed inconsistent responding. The results were interpreted as indicating that kindergarten children understood the concept that an observer had a view, while consistent recognition that two observers had different views was not established until second grade.

To summarize briefly, Hardwick et al. (1976), Huttenlocher and Presson (1973), Shantz and Watson (1971), and Salatas and Flavell (1976) found that young children had difficulty taking the perspectives of others. They also found that when young children made errors, they frequently made egocentric errors. Also, children in the younger grades had more difficulty than those in the older grades. Furthermore, kindergarten children (Salatas and Flavell, 1976) had difficulty at the perceptual matching level; therefore, we would expect that they would have difficulty mentally rotating objects or taking another's perspective.

Salatas and Flavell (1976) found that kindergarten children had difficulty matching the three-dimensional view with the two-dimensional counterpart (perceptual match). Second graders did not have this difficulty. In another investigation, Parrill-Burnstein and Hazan-Ginzburg (1980) attempted the perceptual matching task with children with learning disabilities. The subjects were 169 children in grades one through five, who were equated on achievement level; 45 children were without learning problems and were in regular classes within the public schools; 124 children were from two private schools for children with learning disabilities. Seventy-four children from one school were older at each achievement level than the 50 children from the second school. With only slight modification, the apparatus and procedure used here was identical to that designed by Salatas and Flavell (1976).

The results were most interesting. Children with learning disabilities matched significantly fewer photographs with physical views than those without learning problems. Further analyses indicated that this performance occurred regardless of the school. Furthermore, when the children with learning disabilities made errors, they tended to select a new view associated with one of the other characters rather than their original view. Few if any egocentric errors were made. A grade effect was also obtained. The trend was linear with the only exception being that children in the fourth and fifth grades performed similarly.

There were a number of implications of these findings. Developmentally, the ability to match one's physical view with a picture of that view occurred by the second grade (Salatas & Flavell, 1976). Yet, children with learning disabilities in the older grades did not seem to have mastered this skill. Furthermore, the error patterns for children with learning disabilities were different from those without learning problems. Rather than making egocentric errors, for the most part they simply substituted another character's view; also, equating on achievement level did not produce other age-appropriate behaviors; and the age differences at the achievement level did not affect performance. Children with and without learning disabilities found the perspective-taking task quite difficult and few if any problems were solved, not allowing determination of differences if present.

The skills involved in the perceptual matching task are prerequisite for mental rotation, perspective taking, and role-taking skills. We do not expect children with learning disabilities to be able to generate or determine options (i.e., other views) when they cannot recognize an option when it is presented. These authors suggest that children with learning disabilities are not able to recognize perspectives because of the type of stimuli used. In other words, it is possible that children with learning disabilities have difficulty shifting from a three-dimensional stimulus (the actual view) to a two-dimensional stimulus (the pictured view).

The literature regarding children without learning problems suggests that mental rotations are easier than perspective-taking skills, and that performance improves with age. Children with learning disabilities do not perform as expected on either the perceptual matching tasks or the mental rotation tasks in the study discussed above. Children with learning disabilities of all ages have difficulty revisualizing or imaging the object moved as well as identifying identical two- or three-dimensional representations. It is possible that the problem is a result of processing the information accurately initially, rather than one of memory.

REMEDIATION AND RESEARCH IMPLICATIONS

Only a few studies have examined the cognitive mapping skills of children with learning disabilities. Generally, it has been found that they have difficulties in motor planning and coordination; in correctly locating objects imagined rotated; and in matching two- and three-dimensional representations. In addition to what these children could not do, they were able to revisualize spatial boundaries if both the upright and rotated objects remained present, and if their task was to revisualize details within the figure rather than to imagine or manipulate the total figure. Educational implications of these findings are that inadequate motor proficiency may be the result of a motor planning problem. Further, children who cannot match two- or three-dimensional information cannot be expected to revisualize, mentally rotate, or take another perspective successfully. They also may not perceive information accurately when spatial planes are changed. These youngsters can be expected to revisualize spatial boundaries within figures and copy designs, both starting points for teaching mental rotation and perspective-taking skills.

Remediation

Remediation implications are organized according to the following topics: motor planning, revisualization, mental rotation, and perspective taking. The following guidelines are assumed to characterize the teaching tasks: (1) information is processed through more than one modality; (2) the child's integrities as well as deficits in learning are considered; and (3) the task analysis approach is applied when suggesting strategies (Johnson & Myklebust, 1967).

MOTOR PLANNING

Most motor theorists have suggested remedial procedures to improve motor skills, particularly gross motor skills (Ayres, 1974; Cratty, 1974). For the most part, these techniques were applied to many children regardless of the type and level of learning disabilities. As a result, the success of such techniques was limited.

For purposes here, motor training and physical skill are not dealt with. Rather, the emphasis is on the cognitive aspect, that of motor planning. Motor planning requires analysis and synthesis of available information. The child breaks the tasks down into sequential components and then reconstructs an activity. The abilities to analyze and synthesize are part of any problem-solving behavior. In the three tasks presented below, the focus of strategy training is on the analysis and synthesis of information. An example of a gross, a fine, and a visual motor activity is presented.

The first activity encourages the development of fine motor planning, and can be employed when teaching a variety of motor skills involving work with one's hands. Present the child with a design that he cannot construct by simply copying. Provide the child with cut-out pieces that when assembled make up the completed pattern (four strips to form a square). Initially, present the child with more than the necessary pieces and ask him or her to select the appropriate ones. Then, ask the child to place on top of the original pattern the corresponding cut-out pieces. Require the child to start at the top, proceed from left to right, and pay particular attention to the exact placement of the pieces. Verbal cues indicating direction and location, such as "Where does the strip go?" and "Does that fit?" can be asked. After the child places the pieces correctly on top of the original figure, the pieces are moved below the figure proceeding from the left to the right. Then, the child is asked to perform the same sequence of steps with other patterns. Eventually, the child is given a new series and asked to reconstruct it without first placing the items on top. This sequence also encourages the development of self-monitoring skills, which are necessary during any cognitive activity.

The second task, a gross motor activity, utilizes touch and verbal cuing as a means of systematically planning a series of actions. The example used is skipping and is not appropriate for children younger than kindergarten age. The child is asked to stand upright and to bend down halfway. Next, the child is instructed to pick up the right leg, making a hopping movement and then dropping the right leg forward. There are approximately 2 feet between the front and back foot. To help the child through with this sequence of movements the clinician literally touches the child and moves him or her into position while providing verbal cues such as "bend down," "lift your leg," and "step forward." These movements are made in a rhythmic fashion and are not chopped into a series of isolated skills. As the child progresses, he or she talks through a new sequence of movements in the same way as the teacher instructed initially.

For visual-motor or drawing activities, Johnson and Myklebust (1967) suggest the use of dots and arrows to guide organization. The child is presented with a figure that he or she has difficulty drawing or copying, such as a square. Dots are placed in the four corners (a green dot in the far left top corner to indicate the beginning point). Arrows indicating direction and location are drawn between the dots. The child is instructed verbally to begin at the green dot, follow the arrows in sequence and not lift the pencil off the paper. Again, appropriate verbal cues are provided. For example, the child is told "start here" (while pointing and mentioning the color of the green dot), "draw up (down)," and "move across." As the child learns this technique, he or she is required to place dots and arrows within other figures. The latter suggestion is a way of evaluating transfer or generalization of learning. Eventually, the child is able to organize figures or letters without the use of such aids.

As can be seen in these three activities, not only is analysis and synthesis of information encouraged, but the child is also required to monitor his or her own errors as quickly as possible, and to learn to perform these strategies without the teacher's aid. Eventually, it is assumed that the child generalizes the training by applying similar strategies to new situations.

REVISUALIZATION

Revisualization of spatial information includes three levels; in sequence, these are recognition, partial recall, and total recall (Johnson & Myklebust, 1967). Activities stressing this analysis are designed. In addition, cues are presented simultaneously and are supplementary rather than competing. Four tasks are described.

The first task is designed to teach the child how to remember. The sequence of recognition, followed by partial recall, and then total recall, is used. The child is shown a series of designs and asked to draw each from memory (total recall). Assume that the child's drawing reflects adequate fine-motor control but poor visual memory. The child is shown a completed figure again, but this time when the figure is removed it is replaced by a card on which part of the figure has been drawn (partial recall). The child is asked to complete the drawing. If the child continues to have difficulty, he or she is shown the completed figure again, but this time it remains present and the task is to copy it (recognition). Then, the sequence is reversed at whatever level the child has difficulty. For example, if the child can recognize and copy, the next step would be to present that same figure partially completed, and finally remove it after presentation.

The second task is aimed at teaching spatial locations. Four to five items are placed in front of the child; all are covered and two are removed. The display is shown again with blank spaces for the missing objects and the child is asked to name the missing items (recall). If the child has difficulty recalling the objects,

Cognitive Mapping

the complete series of items is again presented (though not in sequence) and the child is asked to point to those objects that had been removed initially (partial recall). If problems persist the series of items is presented exactly as it had been initially and the child points to the returned items (recognition). (This allows a determination of the level of the deficit). To remediate, another series of items is presented. The child is asked to point to each item as named by the clinician. (The child may name as the examiner points.) The display is again covered and the sequence outlined above is repeated. Again, verbal and visual information are coordinated to aid the child in recall.

A third activity involves organizing commands requiring movement of the body through space. Organization and visual cuing are used. The child is asked to go to his or her room, make the bed, carry out the trash, and pick up the clothes. First, the commands are organized so that the ones that go together in some way are told together. For example, going to the room, making the bed, and picking up the clothes are all activities that can be performed successively within the same general space, the child's room. If the commands "go to the room," "pick up your clothes," "make your bed," and "take out the trash" are issued, the child has a better chance of success. Furthermore, in this way both memory and time are saved. Also, most commands are verbal; therefore, the speaker should point or require the listener to look in the direction that the command is to be carried out in. In this way, surrounding items or events become cues associated with the command.

The fourth task is modeled after Herman and Siegel's (1978) procedure. The task requires the child to imagine moves to spaces outside the immediate surroundings. Two rooms are selected within the school (e.g., classroom and cafeteria). Two curved paths between them are identified; one frequently traveled and the other infrequently traveled. The child is asked in sequence to describe verbally, then to draw, and, finally, to identify the exact map from among three, and walk the familiar path. The child's description, drawing, and selected map are evaluated in terms of correctness as the child rewalks the path. (Again, the level of functioning is determined.) To remediate, the child walks the unfamiliar path. During the walk the child is asked to point out key objects that will act as cues to help remember the walk. Then, the child is asked to describe verbally, draw, and select the map as had been asked in the first task. While walking the path again, the child's description, drawing, and selected maps are evaluated. Where the child needs help is indicated.

MENTAL ROTATION

Mental rotations allow a child to develop concepts such as visual constancy and figure/ground relationships. The development of this skill is a prerequisite for both perspective taking and role taking. In other words, the child must be able to manage the environment within a spatial layout before relationships between self and others or self and objects occurs. Two activities are presented.

During this activity the child is presented with two identical boxes with one side open. Internal to the boxes and on each of the remaining five sides social situations are depicted and appropriate items glued on. The child is then give the first box. The second box is placed before him or her. The task is to place the second box exactly as the clinician has placed the first one. Next, the five sides are separated from one of the boxes. On the second box, the sides are separated so that when laid flat they are still attached by the center piece. The child is required to take the five separated sides and duplicate the first flat box. Then, the box is imagined moved and the child is to discuss or point to the position that the arrangement is viewed from.

This task also encourages the development of the relationships between mental rotations and perspective taking. It is presented here as an example of combining the two within one remedial procedure. Four to five students are placed at various points within a class or library. A child is placed in the center of the layout. Another child at a specific location is imagined moved. This other child is asked to describe what would surround that child and where the other children will be in relation to the imagined child (mental rotation). If the center child has difficulty, a snapshot is taken of each of the other children's perspectives. Then the imagined child actually relocates. The center child is then asked to elaborate again about the layout surrounding the child. If the center child continues to have difficulty, he or she is given the snapshots and the relationships between the actual moved child and the previous surroundings are discussed while examining the photographs. The child is then required to show and tell where the imagined moved surrounding items would be.

PERSPECTIVE TAKING

The ability to imagine one's self moved and the relationship of objects to that move requires adequate motor planning, revisualization, and mental rotation skills. Only two activities are suggested for perspective taking for three reasons. First, within each activity, the tasks are analyzed and subsequently labeled as to levels of difficulty. Therefore, if the child errors at the first step, he or she should find the next step less difficult and so on. Second, the activities are easily varied and can be used with other materials and themes. Finally, both perspective-taking types of tasks, those internal and external to the immediate surroundings, are addressed through these activities.

Using a familiar room within the school, two children are placed at opposite ends facing each other. Each child is asked to describe what he or she thinks the other sees (expression). If either or both children have difficulty, they are shown three photographs and asked to select the other child's view from among that group. If further help is needed, one child is asked to describe what is actually seen; then the other child is asked to describe what is actually seen. Then, each child in turn is asked to move to a halfway point, though still on the same plane, and to orient his or her body as if facing the same direction as the other child. The final step requires only identification and not imagery as did the first two steps.

The second perspective-taking task requires that four children be seated at a table. A Monopoly board game is suggested for this particular activity. A specific child is asked to name what property another child sees. Some of these will be right side up, some upside down, and some sideways. If the child has difficulty, he or she can be given another board and asked to set it up exactly as the original board is set up. Then, the child is allowed to physically move around the board and look at each view before being asked to describe what items the other children see. It is also interesting to note that two children will see the same properties as sideways; however, the concept of one perspective/one view still holds. If the child finds this confusing, it should be pointed out.

In this section, a number of remedial suggestions were made. The emphasis was on task analysis; intersensory processing; remediation, taking into account integrities and deficits; and the teaching of strategies rather than specific skills.

Research

Many of the suggested studies are simple replications of child development research, but are to be conducted with children with learning disabilities. It is suggested that the performance of children with learning disabilities be compared to the performance of children without learning problems and with other learning problems (e.g., behavior disorders). Inclusion of a normal comparison group is essential. In addition, it is suggested that children of different ages or grades be included. Frequently, the designs employ task analyses and are repeated measures. The task analysis format enables determination of level or type of problem, not just how children with and without learning disabilities differ. Repeated measures allow the child to serve as his or her own control and therefore comparison within as well as between task performances can be made. However, one of the limitations of the repeated-measures design is that it is assumed that performance on a preceding task does not influence performance on a later presented task.

MOTOR PROFICIENCY

As mentioned earlier, few studies were conducted that investigated motor proficiency skills of children with learning disabilities. Yet, many remedial procedures have been instituted.

A frequently used technique with children with learning disabilities is the dots and arrows combination described in the section on remediation. However, as with other remedial techniques, the benefit of this instruction has been observed in the class but not empirically studied. Therefore, it is suggested that the following study be conducted. The design is a mixed design. The conditions are to be followed in sequence. In the first condition, the child is given a design such as a triangle to copy. Next, he or she is given a second sheet of paper on which three dots (in the intersecting angles) and three arrows between the dots are drawn. The child is asked to draw the figure again without being told how to use the cues. In the third condition, the child is told and shown how to use the cues and asked to draw the figure again. Finally, the child is again presented with the original design without any dots and arrows and asked to copy it. The accuracy with which the child draws the design is the dependent measure.

In this experiment, a motor planning task utilizing a maze is proposed. The design is mixed. The child is presented with a series of mazes, which increase in level of difficulty. Each maze is presented three times and the reaction time for each presentation is calculated. The implications are the more familiar the pattern, the less time it takes to complete it; the more difficult the maze, the harder and longer the reaction time. As well as scoring reaction time (the first dependent measure), a second dependent measure, that of correct completion of the maze, is analyzed. Errors such as crossing over lines or entering blind alleys are penalized.

REVISUALIZATION

Researchers have found the children with learning disabilities benefit from specific types of cuing in some situations but not in others (e.g., Parrill-Burnstein & Baker-Ward, 1979). It is possible that emphasizing the relationship between a given item, or items, and its surrounding parts may facilitate the ability to perform revisualization.

In the first study, Siegel and Schadler's (1973) procedure serves as a model. The experiment involves three conditions or corresponding groups. Two of the conditions are considered cue conditions and one is considered an uncued condition. The child is shown a layout of the classroom with representations of the appropriate contents in the proper places. The child is asked to look carefully at the layout. Then, it is covered. Children in the uncued condition (group 1) are given a second set of the same pieces and asked to arrange them appropriately on another but identical space. In the first cued condition (group 2), four objects are placed (one at each quadrant) on the identical space. Then, these children are given a second set of pieces and are instructed to arrange them as best they can. In the final condition (group 3), cues are also provided. In one corner of the imagined space an entire arrangement is constructed, and then the child is given the same instructions as those given to groups 1 and 2. In this way, the effects of type of cuing on spatial imagery in mental rotations is determined.

Four children are seated around a table with a doll house in the center. All children are asked to look carefully at the doll house; then, each child in turn is asked to leave the room. While each child is gone, the house and children are rearranged. When the child returns, he or she is asked to reconstruct the original situation (recall). Following this, the child is shown a series of pictures and asked to pick the one that represents the original layout (recognition). If this proves difficult, the children rearrange in the child's presence and need only recognize the correct arrangement.

The child is required to revisualize the correction of an absurd figure in order to identify the absurdity. First, the child is shown a visual absurdity and asked to state whether or not the figure is weird. After this, the child is asked to point out what is funny about the picture. Finally, he or she is asked to discuss how to correct the absurdity.

This study is designed to assess how well a child remembers routes and plans. Three conditions are proposed: (1) a single walk through; (2) a walk through plus verbal labeling of objects during the walk; and (3) verbalizing the path while walking. Two rooms are selected within the school (i.e., classroom and cafeteria). The control group, group 1, is asked to walk the route and then draw a picture. Those in the second group are asked to identify key objects while walking and then are asked to draw the picture. Those in the third group verbalize their movements as they walk the path, then draw the route. The dependent measures are the accuracy of the path drawn and the types of errors made.

This last study evaluates the effectiveness of recognition, partial recall, and total recall. Three conditions are suggested: (1) the child is shown a series of figures for 5 seconds and asked to draw each from memory; (2) the child is shown the set of figures, which when removed, are replaced with cards with part of the design drawn, and the child is asked to complete the drawing; and (3) the child is asked simply to copy a series of designs. The child with memory problems should have the greatest difficulty when required to totally recall and have little difficulty if any at the level of recognition. However, if the child is having difficulty, visual planning of his or her performance on all three tasks will be poor and the task becomes one of motor planning rather than revisualization.

MENTAL ROTATION AND PERSPECTIVE TAKING

With respect to the research on mental rotations and perspective taking, mental rotations were considered easier than perspective taking problems (Hardwick et al., 1976; Huttenlocher & Presson, 1973). Hardwick et al. (1976) found that children in the first grade benefited the most when allowed to view what was to be manipulated. Many authors found that egocentric errors (selecting self-view) occurred more frequently than any other errors (Salatas & Flavell, 1977; Hardwick et al., 1976; Huttenlocher & Presson, 1973). Shantz and Watson (1971) also found that children who had difficulty remembering locations had difficulty imagining perspectives.

Published research in the area of children with learning disabilities is literally nonexistent. Unpublished data suggest that children with learning disabilities have difficulty at the prerequisite level of perceptual matching and that children have problems mentally rotating objects rather than copying objects (Parrill-Burnstein & Hazan-Ginzburg, 198).

Mental Rotations. Huttenlocher and Presson (1973), in their summary of research on mental rotations, suggest that mental rotation problems are easier to solve than perspective-taking problems. As you will recall from mental rotation problems, these authors used an arrangement of blocks to be rotated as a total unit or group.

Block arrangements are used in this experiment. Unlike in Huttenlocher and Presson's study, here the child is required to recognize or reconstruct the imagined move of the blocks. The child is seated at a table across from the examiner. A pattern of three blocks is presented. The child is asked to imagine that the arrangement is rotated 180 degrees, 90 degrees, or 45 degrees to the right and then to the left. Then the child is asked to either: (1) recognize the picture of the imagined view; or (2) reconstruct with blocks the imagined view. The memory requirement is less for those in condition 1 than for those in condition 2. In condition 1, the child is to recognize the view, and in condition 2, reconstruct it.

Perspective Taking. In one study, we found that children with learning disabilities had difficulty at the perceptual matching level, a prerequisite for perspective taking (Parrill-Burnstein & Hazan-Ginzburg, 1980).

This first experiment is an attempt to better delineate the perspective-taking skills of children with learning disabilities. Two perspective-taking tasks and two perceptual matching tasks are presented. Three objects are placed in three corners of a square board (Salatas & Flavell, 1976). The child is asked in sequence from a group of pictures (1) to select his or her view; (2) to select each of the objects' views; (3) to move to each position and select a picture of that view; and (4) to move to each position and verbalize that view. The first condition assesses the development of "own perspective" while the second assesses perspective taking; the last two tasks assess perceptual matching.

Hardwick et al. (1976) found that for young children, perspective-taking skills were best in the situation in which the view was unobstructed. In the present experiment, the child with learning disabilities is placed in the corner of a large room. Objects are placed in each of the four corners with one being behind the child. The children are assigned to one of four conditions. In the first condition, the child is placed behind a screen and told to imagine being moved to one of four locations. The task is then to select which picture represents the view from that location. In the second condition, the child is also placed behind a screen but this time is asked to verbalize where he or she would be, as well as the other objects in the room, when moved. In the last two conditions, the child is asked the same questions as those described in the first condition, but is given full view of the room.

To summarize, many of the research suggestions are replications of studies that have been conducted with children without learning problems. The reasons for this were explained within the text. Within each of the studies, it was important that developmental information be obtained; that children with learning disabilities be compared with children without learning disabilities; and that the performance of children with learning disabilities be further delineated and defined.

REFERENCES

Ayres, A. J. Patterns of perceptual-motor dysfunction in children: A factor analytic study. *Perceptual and Motor Skills,* 1965, *20,* 335–368.

Bannatyne, A. D. A comparison of visuo-spatial and visual-motor memory for designs and their relationship to other sensorimotor and psycholinguistic variables. *Journal of Learning Disabilities,* 1969, *2*(9), 451–466.

Boulding, K. E. National image and international systems. *Journal of Conflict Resolution,* 1961, *3,* 120–131.

Bruininks, V. L., & Bruininks, R. H. Motor proficiency of learning disabled and nondisabled students. *Perceptual and Motor Skills,* 1977, *44,* 1131–1137.

Cratty, B. J. *Movement behavior and motor learning.* Philadelphia: Lea & Febiger, 1964.

Cratty, B. J. *Social dimensions of physical activity.* Englewood Cliffs, New Jersey: Prentice-Hall, Inc. 1967.

Downs, R. M., & Stea, D. (Eds.). *Image and environment.* Chicago: Aldine Publishing Company, 1973.

Flavell, J. H. *Cognitive development.* Englewood Cliffs, New Jersey: Prentice-Hall, Inc., 1977.

Gesell, A., & Amatruda, C. S. *Developmental diagnosis* (2nd ed.). New York: Hoeber-Harper, 1947.

Hardwick, D. A., McIntyre, C. W., & Pick, H. L. The content and manipulation of cognitive maps in children and adults. *Monographs of the Society for Research in Child Development,* 1976, *4*(3), Serial No. 166.

Herman, J. F., & Siegel, H. W. The development of cognitive mapping of the large-scale environment. *Journal of Experimental Child Psychology,* 1978, *26,* 389–406.

Huttenlocher, J., & Presson, C. C. Mental rotation and the perspective problem. *Cognitive Psychology,* 1973, *4,* 277–299.

Johnson, D. J., & Myklebust, H. *Learning disabilities: Educational principles and practices.* New York: Grune & Stratton, 1967.

Kaplan, S. Cognitive maps in perception and thought. In R. M. Downs & D. Stea, *Image and environment: Cognitive mapping and spatial behavior.* Chicago: Aldine Publishing Company, 1973.

Kosslyn, S. M., Pick, H. L., & Fariello, G. R. Cognitive maps in children and men. *Child Development,* 1974, *45,* 707–716.

Neisser, U. *Cognition and reality.* San Francisco: Freeman and Company, 1976.

Parrill-Burnstein, M., & Baker-Ward, L. Learning disabilities: A social cognitive difference. *Learning Disabilities: An Audio Journal for Continuing Education,* 1979, Vol. III (10).

Parrill-Burnstein, M., & Hazan-Ginzburg, E. *Social cognition and cognitive mapping: Understanding the impact of the learning disability.* Unpublished manuscript, Emory University, 1980.

Piaget, J., & Inhelder, B. *The child's conception of space.* London: Routledge & Kegan Paul, Ltd., 1956.

Salatas, H., & Flavell, J. H. Perspective taking: The development of two components of knowledge. *Child Development,* 1976, *47,* 103–109.

Salvia, J., & Ysseldyke, J. C. *Assessment in special and remedial education.* Boston: Houghton-Mifflin Company, 1978.

Shantz, C. U. The development of social cognition. In E. M. Hetherington (Ed.), *Review of child development research* (Vol. 5). Chicago: University of Chicago Press, 1975.

Shantz, C. U., Watson, J. S. Spatial abilities and spatial egocentrism in the young child. *Child Development*, 1971, *42*, 171–181.

Siegel, A. W., & Schadler, M. The development of young children's spatial representations of their classrooms. *Child Development*, 1977, *48*, 388–394.

FURTHER READINGS

Adams, J. Visual and tactual integration and children with learning disabilities. *Journal of Learning Disabilities*, 1978, *11*(4), 197–204.

Ayres, A. J. *Sensory integration and learning disorders*. Los Angeles: Western Psychological Services, 1974.

Ayres, A. J. Learning disabilities and the vestibular system. *Journal of Learning Disabilities*, 1978, *11*(1), 18–29.

Ames, B. L. Children with perceptual problems may also lag developmentally. *Journal of Learning Disabilities*, 1969, *2*(4), 205–208.

Bibace, R., & Hancock, K. Open forum: Relationships between perceptual and conceptual cognitive processes. *Journal of Learning Disabilities*, 1969, *2*(), 17–29.

Bluestein, N., & Acredolo, L. Developmental changes in map-reading skills. *Child Development*, 1979, *50*(3), 691–697.

Carr, H. A. *An introduction to space perception*. New York: Longmans, Green & Company, 1935.

Cox, M. V. Perspective ability: The conditions of change. *Child Development*, 1977, *48*, 1724–1727.

Cratty, B. J. *Perceptual and motor development in infants and children*. New York: The Macmillan Company, 1970.

Cratty, B. J., & Martin, M. N. *Perceptual-motor proficiency in children: The measurement and improvement of motor attributes*. Philadelphia: Lea & Febiger, 1969.

Dolan, A. B., & Matheny, A. P. A distinctive growth cure for a group of children with academic learning problems. *Journal of Learning Disabilities*, 1978, *11*(8), 490–494.

Doman, R. J., Spitz, E. B., Zucman, E., et al. Children with severe brain injuries: Neurological organization in terms of mobility. In E. C. Frierson & W. B. Barbe (Eds.), *Educating children with learning disabilities*. New York: Appleton-Century-Crofts, 1967.

Dunsing, J. D., & Kephart, N. C. Motor generalization in space and time. In J. Hellmuth (Ed.), *Learning disorders* (Vol. 1). Seattle: Special Child Publications, 1965.

Feldman, A., & Acredolo, L. The effect of active versus passive exploration on memory for spatial location in children. *Child Development*, 1979, *50*(3), 698–704.

Flavell, J. H., Omanson, R. C., & Latham, C. Solving spatial perspective-taking problems by rule versus computation: A developmental study. *Developmental Psychology*, 1978, *14*(5), 462–473.

Friendland, S., & Meisels, S. J. An application of Piagetian Model to perceptual handicaps. *Journal of Learning Disabilities*, 1975, *8*(1), 20–24.

Feffer, M. H. The cognitive implications of role taking behavior. *Journal of Personality,* 959, *27,* 152–168.
Gruber, J. J. Implications of physical education programs for children with learning disabilities. *Journal of Learning Disabilities,* 1969, *2*(11), 593–599.
Inhelder, B., & Chipman, H. H. *Piaget and his school: A reader in developmental psychology.* New York: Springer-Verlag, 1976.
Kephart, N. C. The perceptual-motor match. In W. M. Cruickshank & D. P. Hallahan (Eds.), *Perceptual and learning disabilities in children: Psychoeducational practices* (Vol. I). New York: Syracuse University Press, 1975.
Kurdek, L. A. Structural components of intellectual correlates of cognitive perspective taking in first-through fourth-grade children. *Child Development,* 1977, *48,* 1503–1511.
McAninch, M. Body image as related to perceptual-cognitive-motor disabilities. In J. Hellmuth (Ed.), *Learning disorders* (Vol. 2). Seattle, Washington: Special Child Publications, 1966.
Pick, H. L., & Olsen, M. G. Environmental differentiation and familiarity as determinants of children's memory for spatial location. *Developmental Psychology,* 1975, *11*(4), 495–501.
Sandberg, B. Rotation tendency and cerebral dysfunction in children. *Perceptual and Motor Skills,* 1977, *44,* 343–356.
Shepard, R., & Metzler, J. Mental rotation of three-dimensional objects. *Science,* 1971, *171,* 701–703.
Siegel, A. W., & Schadler, M. The development of young children's spatial representations of their classrooms. *Child Development,* 1977, *48*(2), 388–394.
Siegel, A. W., & White, S. H. The development of spatial representations of large-scale environments. In H. Reese (Ed.), *Advances in child development* (Vol. 10). New York: Academic Press, 1975.
Steinberg, M., & Rendle-Short, J. Vestibular dysfunction in young children with minor neurological impairment. *Developmental Medical Child Neurology,* 1977, *19,* 639–651.
Tolan, E. C. Cognitive maps in rats and men. *Psychological Review,* 1948, *55,* 189–208.
Trickett, E. J. Toward a social-ecological conception of adolescent socialization: Normative data on contrasting types of public school classrooms. *Child Development,* 1978, *49*(2), 408–414.
Vellutino, F. R., Steger, B. M., Moyer, S. C., et al. Has the perceptual deficit hypothesis led us astray? *Journal of Learning Disabilities,* 1977, *10*(6), 375–385.
von Hilsheimer, G., & Kurko, V. Minor physical anomalies in exceptional children. *Journal of Learning Disabilities,* 1979, *12*(71), 462–469.
Wedell, K. *Learning and perceptuo-motor disabilities in children.* New York: John Wiley & Sons, 1973.

6
Social Cognition

Social cognition is a problem-solving activity that presupposes intact processing of the skills discussed in earlier chapters: attention, concept organization, memory, language learning, and cognitive mapping. Social cognition is one component of a more global and constructive process. Two other components are input (stimulus) and overt responses (product). The relationships between these three components is depicted in Figure 6-1. To elaborate briefly, the stimulus provides the child with available social cues, which are picked up by an active perceiver (Neisser, 1976). The social cues provide information about feelings, beliefs, and attitudes (Flavell, 1977). How these cues are accumulated, related, and integrated is social cognition. The child's social cognition is reflected in his or her observable behavior, which is referred to as the product. Three products of the social cognitive process are symbolization (i.e., flag), conceptualization (i.e., red), and social competence. Social competence is the focus here.

Social competence is defined as the ability to interact appropriately with others and interpret the behavior of others accurately. Three skills basic to social competence are role taking, person perception, and perspective taking. Role taking is the ability to understand the social positions of others. Person perception is the ability to identify and process relevant cues about another. Perspective taking is the ability to imagine physical manipulation. Accomplishment of these skills can be analyzed into four sequentially dependent components. These are: selective attention, response generation, response execution, and the appropriate response to feedback. Available research is organized according to this analysis.

```
                    STIMULUS
                   SOCIAL CUES
                    (INPUT)
                      ↑↑↑
                      │││
                      ↓↓↓
               SOCIAL COGNITION
                   (PROCESS)
              ↙        ↓        ↘
    SYMBOLIZATION   SOCIAL    CONCEPTUALIZATION
                  COMPETENCE
                  (PRODUCTS)
```

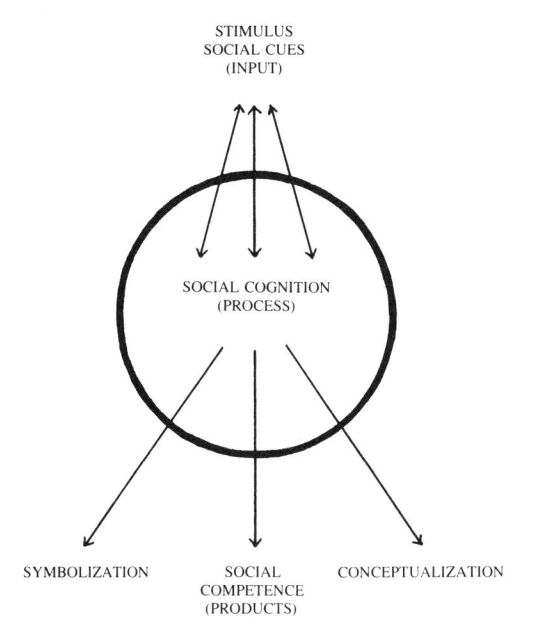

Fig. 6-1. An analysis of the components involved in the social cognitive process.

SOCIAL COGNITIVE DEVELOPMENT

The development of social cognition parallels that of cognition. Consistent with other problem-solving abilities, the efficiency of processing required at each stage of social cognitive development increases with age. Chandler (1977) and Shantz (1975) summarize social cognitive development. Their focus, and the focus here, is on the development of social cognitive skills such as perspective taking, person perception, and role taking. Limitations of this research are dealt with in depth by Chandler.

Before the age of 6, the child's perspective-taking skills are limited. Although another's perspective is recognized, no other information is utilized. After the age of 6 and through middle childhood, the child is able to take another's perspective through imagery as well as recognize the reciprocal relationship between self and others. In the next few years, the development of the skill of role taking and complex social behaviors occurs. Throughout life, the skills of perspective taking, person perception, and role taking continue to develop.

Perspective Taking

In the chapter on cognitive mapping, the spatial ability of perspective taking was discussed. Perspective taking involved the child's ability to take another's physical position through imagery, and view concrete objects from that other's perspective (Hardwick, McIntyre, & Pick, 1976). Social perceptions, unlike cues associated with perspective taking, are those that provide information about social thinking. Social perceptions may be verbal or nonverbal in nature. Social cues that are verbal in content are associated with language. These cues may be receptive (e.g., observing another verbal language), inner (e.g., integrating received information), or expressive (e.g., observing one's own language). Both what is spoken and how it is spoken shape the contents of the reaction or the response. Nonverbal cues are both temporal and spatial; they involve facial expressions, body movements, and body postures. Cues of this type provide information about the location and arrangement of social figures, the relationship between two or more figures within the context, and the relationship of each figure or combination of figures to the general theme. Social perceptions are basic to person perception and role taking.

Person Perception

Person perception refers to how one describes and categorizes the behaviors of others (Shantz), 1975). Livelsey and Bromley (1973) suggest that person concepts underlie person perceptions. Person concepts are single representations that are organized and integrated into constructs, which, if confirmed, generalize to more than one person. The development of person concepts, constructs, and rules allow one to predict, explain, and manage the behaviors of others.

Role Taking

Role taking requires adequate perspective-taking skills and person-perception skills. In role taking, a reciprocal relationship between the self and others occurs. Initially, through imagery, the self takes simultaneously his or her own position and the other's position. Once this is accomplished, inferences based on the beliefs, feelings, motives, and attitudes from both perspectives are formed (Flavell, 1974). Flavell (1977) centers his work on the spatial aspects of role taking. He discusses the child as both an observer and an object of observation. He suggests that successful execution of any specific social activity requires that the preconditions referred to as existence, need, and inference be met. Shantz (1975) includes a fourth precondition, that of application. Existence refers to the child's basic knowledge that a particular social situation can or does exist. Need refers to the sensed desirability of attempting an act of social cognition. In other words, the social situation requires that some inference be made in order to act appropriately. These inferences refer to the skills required to carry off such an act of social thinking successfully. Shantz' (1975) precondition of application requires that the child evaluate and determine the consequences of having acted. Appropriate social cognition requires that perspective-taking skills, person-perception skills, and role-taking skills develop as expected.

THEORIES OF COGNITIVE DEVELOPMENT

Many of the models developed to describe cognitive theory are appropriate when applied to social cognition. Cognitive theorists pertinent to this discussion are Bruner, Piaget, and Gagné. The Hypothesis Testing Model is also applicable. Bruner (1973) focuses on learning styles that develop in response to the environment. He suggests that learning can be accelerated through appropriate intervention. Three levels of acquisition are specified. At the first level, that of enactive representative, the child relies on physical and motor involvement in forming concepts. At this point, the child clearly relies on the observable and salient cues depicted by the physical characteristics of figures. Role taking and perspective taking are not operational at this level. At the next level, that of iconic representation, the child begins to develop and use strategies that enable him or her to take the physical positions of others through the use of imagery. At the final level, that of symbolic representation, the child forms abstractions and generalizes learning to similar events. The child develops and applies constructs about his or her social world.

The stage theorists (Piaget & Inhelder, 1969) introduce a slightly different perspective. According to this theorist, the child progresses through stages and learning is hierarchical. At each stage, the child's level of cognitive ability is reflected in observable behavior. The child learns to assimilate and accommodate new information into an initially loose schema. Changes in structure occur as a result of adding and modifying present information.

Piaget suggests five stages or developmental levels. The sensorimotor stage occurs before the age of 2. The child anticipates responses and may repeat a response in expectation of a specific action. Between the ages of 2 and 7 years, children are classified as preoperational. At the preoperational stage, children are egocentric and recognize only their own perspectives. Literal interpretations are made of events, the child's perceptions are bound by the physical characteristics of the situation.

Early to middle childhood corresponds to the concrete operations stage. At this stage, the child develops and refines problem-solving strategies. Events are anticipated and consequences predicted with increased accuracy. At the final stage of formal operations, logical inferences based on the ability to take and manipulates others' views simultaneously with one's own view occurs. The child receives information regarding feedback, which is based only in part on the actual situation. Prior experiences are recalled through imagery and allow maximum evaluation of present situations. Problems are solved through logical verbal and nonverbal reasoning.

Another developmental theorist, Gagné (1969), stresses the effects of cumulative learning. He suggests that his model be considered a description rather than a theory of learning. The child is assumed to require simpler skills, which, although not hierarchical, are integrated and combined into more complex rules and generalizations. Applying Gagné's model to the development of social cognition, the child first associates a specific social stimulus (e.g., a group of children standing together) with specific social responses (e.g., walking over to the children). After these S-R associations are formed, they are combined with other associations and simple concepts or constructs result. These constructs, such as "polite," are applied successfully to more than one social figure or situation. These generalizations are rules that continue to develop and expand as they are applied.

Another descriptive model (Levine, 1975; Gholson, 1980) describes hypothesis-testing behaviors. Hypothesis testing theorists assume the person as an active processor of information who selects, tests, and evaluates hypotheses in order to learn. Hypothesis-testing as a task can be analyzed into four sequentially dependent components. In sequence, these are selective attention, response generation, response execution, and feedback (Parrill-Burnstein, 1978). Problem solving as a process can be analyzed into these components. Therefore, social cognition as a problem-solving activity can also be analyzed into hypothesis testing behaviors. These components—selective attention, response generation, response execution, and appropriate response to feedback—are defined in sequence.

With selective attention, the child is attending to and integrating relevant social cues into social perceptions. Response generation is making inferences and drawing conclusions about the social perceptions. These inferences take the form of hypotheses or response alternatives. Response execution is the hypothesis selected and expressed. Feedback is the response of others to the child's actions.

The following is an example of this analysis applied to a social cognitive situation. A child observes a group and attends to the figures within the group (selective attention). The child decides that he or she can run, walk, or call to the group (response generation). The child selects a response, such as walking up to the group, and acts (response execution). If the child is pushed down, feedback is negative and that response should be eliminated and another selected. If he or she is included in the group, feedback is positive and the response is repeated in a similar or same situation. This analysis will be used when organizing available research regarding social perception and social cognition.

In the earlier chapters, the information reviewed suggested that children with learning disabilities had problems in attention, concept organization, memory, and the formation of cognitive maps. Work in attention indicated that children with learning disabilities did not always differentiate relevant cues, particularly if those cues were not salient or obvious. In addition, children with learning disabilities did not generate as many response options as those without learning problems. Furthermore, when responses were generated and executed, the children did not respond appropriately to feedback.

Findings regarding memory pertinent to this discussion were those indicating that young children with learning disabilities fail to use strategies spontaneously (Torgesen & Goldman, 1977). In social cognition as well as other problem-solving activities, the child must be flexible enough to apply certain strategies. If feedback is positive, the child must maintain that strategy; if feedback is negative, the child must eliminate it.

In addition to problems with attention and memory, it was observed that children with learning disabilities had difficulty taking the perspectives of others. The child with learning disabilities was observed to have difficulty correctly revisualizing the transformed locations of cues when the orientation of the array was changed (Parrill-Burnstein & Hazan-Ginzburg, 1980). In general, the child with learning disabilities had problems with those cognitive mapping skills that underlie successful social cognitive processing (e.g., person perception and role taking).

For appropriate social cognition, the information processes of attention, memory, concept organization, and cognitive mapping must be intact. Therefore, it is possible that when studying social cognition, we are studying the impact of the learning disability.

STUDIES OF SOCIAL COGNITION AND LEARNING DISABILITIES

Social cognition was studied in several ways. Studies of children with learning disabilities focused on the cognitions of self toward others and the cognitions of others toward self. The cognitions of others toward self is relevant to the cognitions of self toward others in that the type of response another makes elicits specific responses from the other. Reactions of others also provides feedback to the child with learning disabilities about how he or she is received. This type of feedback should in turn influence the behaviors of that learning-disabled child. To better understand the influence of this feedback, it is important to examine the cognitions of others toward the child with learning disabilities. The perceptions of others about the child with learning disabilities were elicited when employing such procedures as rating scales, sociometric techniques, taped presentations, and objective codings of behavior. Direct measures of the perceptions of the learning-disabled child toward others are few. Data regarding person perception and role taking were not available.

In the following review, research will be summarized according to two response types: those elicited and those emitted by children with learning disabilities. The task analysis approach suggested at the beginning of this chapter will be used to organize available information regarding social perception and social cognition. The results will be described in greater detail as they relate to selective attention, response generation, response execution, and appropriate response to feedback.

Responses Elicited by Children with Learning Disabilities

The relevant others whose perceptions of learning-disabled children have been studied include parents, teachers, peers, and objective observers. The bulk of this research is Bryan's (for a review, see Bryan, 1978). She suggests that children with learning disabilities have problems in interpersonal relationships. Generally, it has been found that children with learning disabilities are rated as less popular and less attractive, and elicit more help than children without learning problems. Bruininks (1978) and Scranton and Ryckman (1979) also found that children with learning disabilities were less popular than children without learning problems. Limitations of these findings, however, are suggested for two reasons. First, the children worked with were restricted to those receiving itinerant help. Second, most frequently, conclusions were based on the behaviors of a small number of children.

Feedback

Several types of responses to feedback are elicited by children with learning disabilities. Most of these responses are negative in nature. Children with learning disabilities utter more competitive statements, are ignored more frequently by classmates, helped more frequently by professionals, and rated among the least popular by peers. Yet, they are reinforced in a similar fashion as those without learning problems. To ignore responses is to extinguish those behaviors. The implication is that nonreinforced responses increase in frequency initially and taper off if not attended to, which is not the case with children with learning disabilities. Children with learning disabilities respond with behaviors that are not always expected by those without learning problems.

Bryan (1974a) analyzed the classroom behaviors of children with learning disabilities. Her subjects were 10 boys in a third-grade class, 5 with learning disabilities and 5 without learning problems. The subjects were matched for grade, sex, and race. The method involved observing each pair for 5 school days over a period of 5 months. The observer spent 25 days in the 5 third-grade classes. In addition, the children were observed while they were working with a learning disabilities specialist. The results indicated that children with learning disabilities were more likely to be ignored by their classmates and teachers than those without learning problems.

In another study, Bryan and her associates (Bryan et al., 1976) observed 17 children with learning disabilities while they interacted with a youngster in their class. Two observers observed the youngsters and coded their responses in terms of the types of statements made, the responses of one child to another, and the patterns of verbal interaction. The results indicated that children with learning disabilities received more rejecting statements than those without learning problems. Also, the child without learning problems uttered both competitive and considerate statements. These results indicated that the inappropriate social behaviors of children with learning disabilities were reinforced intermittently or on a variable reinforcement schedule. Variable schedules maintain behaviors at high rates.

In terms of positive and negative reinforcement, children with learning disabilities received similar amounts of reinforcement compared to those without learning problems when interacting with the regular classroom teacher (Bryan, 1974a). In other words, reinforcement from the teacher, both positive and negative, was equally distributed to the children within the two groups. (This is in contrast to findings of Chapman, Larsen, and Parker, 1979). Implications of these findings were that although children with learning disabilities demonstrated more inappropriate social behaviors, some of their behaviors were positively reinforced and others negatively reinforced or ignored (e.g., reinforcement was not a contingent upon the learning-disabled child's behavior). Also, teachers did not differ in the type of reinforcement patterns distributed to children with and without learning disabilities; rather, the content and quality of the interaction was different.

Chapman, Larsen, and Parker (1979) observed dyadic teacher-child interactions. Four teachers were involved in observations lasting 13 weeks. The children were 110 first graders. Fifteen percent of these children had been diagnosed as having learning disabilities; 17% were diagnosed as low achievers; 42% were identified as medium achievers; and 26% were identified as high achievers. Five different interactions were coded: response opportunity (the child's attempts to answer questions posed by the clinician); recitation (the child's making an oral presentation); procedural contact (interaction between the child and teacher about individual needs such as supplies); work-related contacts (interactions about homework); and behavioral contacts (teacher disciplining the child). Results indicated that learning-disabled children received more praise, more criticism, and more teacher feedback when the teacher initiated the interaction. Learning-disabled children also received more praise and criticism when they initiated the interaction. In general, children with learning disabilities elicited more responses from the teachers than children in the other groups.

In summary, when the reinforcement patterns of the child with learning disabilities were examined, it was found that inappropriate responses were maintained by extinction, positive feedback, and variable reinforcement schedules. When the child worked with a learning disabilities specialist, the learning disabilities specialist reinforced, in a positive fashion, more of the child's responses, resulting in more appropriate behaviors. These data suggested that the learning-disabled child elicited similar amounts of positive and negative feedback and that the differences obtained may have been due in part to the manner in which reinforcement was delivered.

Selective Attention

The social cues to which others attended affected their social cognitions about the learning-disabled child at a most basic level of processing. For the most part, children with learning disabilities were viewed by others as different, less popular, and more difficult to manage; in addition, they were associated with reduced expectations.

A series of sociometric techniques was used by researchers to understand the reactions of peers to the students in their class with learning disabilities. Siperstein, Bopp, and Bak (1978) studied the social status of children with learning disabilities. Their subjects were 117 children, 22 of whom had learning disabilities and who were receiving itinerant help during part of their regular school day. The children were asked to name the same-sex peer whom they liked best. Also, they were asked to select the best athlete, the smartest, and the best-looking classmate. The results indicated that children with learning disabilities were less popular and were not considered stars of the class; moreover, they were not rated as more isolated than or physically different from their fellow classmates.

Bryan conducted a number of studies using the sociometric technique. In one of her studies (Bryan, 1974b), she asked 84 children with learning disabilities and 84 without learning disabilities in grades three, four, and five to do such things as select: (1) three classmates who were friends; (2) three children who were not friends; (3) the one child they thought was having difficulties sitting still in class; and (4) one who was handsome or pretty. The items were grouped into two categories, social attraction and social rejection. The results indicated that children with learning disabilities received significantly more votes of rejection and fewer votes of social attraction when compared to the others in the class. Girls with learning disabilities, particularly white girls, received the highest rejection ratings. In a later study (Bryan, 1976), these findings were replicated. The implications were that personality characteristics were reliable across classes and time.

Bruininks (1978) studied the actual social status, self-concept, and perceived status of children with learning disabilities. Subjects were 162 elementary school children in grades one through four. Twenty-three were diagnosed as having learning disabilities. A normal comparison group of 139 children was included; these children were from regular classrooms. Bruininks found that children with learning disabilities were generally rated as having lower social status (less popular) than children without learning problems. Also, children with learning disabilities frequently overestimated their popularity. These results were interpreted as reflecting problems in perceived and actual self-concept.

Scranton and Ryckman (1979) worked with 42 children in grades one through three who were receiving resource help for learning disabilities. Sociometric techniques were employed. Responses to questions such as whom the child liked best and whom would the child like to sit next to and play with most were studied. The children were also asked questions stated in negative sentence structures, such as whom they would not like to sit next to, whom they would not like to play with, and whom they did not like. Scranton and Ryckman found that for positive items, girls without learning disabilities were rated highest. Significant differences between those types of ratings and learning conditions were also obtained. Girls with learning disabilities received more negative statements, which accounted for this significant effect.

The impressions of mothers, parents, and teachers have also been elicited. With respect to mother-child perceptions, Doleys, Cartelli, and Doster (1976) observed mother-child interactions for a total of 20 minutes. There were 27 mother-child pairs, 9 children without learning problems, 9 children considered noncompliant, and 9 children with learning disabilities. The observations were of two types: (1) directed play by the mother; and (2) free play with mother's instructions. Each phase lasted 10 minutes. Four different results were analyzed: rewards, commands, frequency of questions asked, and number of criticisms given. The results indicated that mothers of children with learning disabilities rated their children as having more problems than those without learning problems, but as having fewer problems than those children who were considered noncompliant. Also, the mothers of children with learning disabilities rewarded their children more frequently and asked more questions. A limitation of these findings and many others to be reviewed is the lack of attention paid to the role of the child's behavior in eliciting these reactions.

Using the rating scale technique, Strag (1972) elicited the responses of both parents about their child with learning disabilities, mental retardation, or without problems. The scale consisted of 30 items covering a wide variety of behaviors. When the responses of parents of children with learning disabilities were compared to those of the parents of children without learning problems, it was found that the learning-disabled children were rated as significantly more depressed, less considerate of others, unsuccessful at eliciting affection, and more clingy. Comparisons between learning-disabled children and severely mentally retarded children indicated that children who were retarded were significantly more physically dependent and had more difficulty receiving affection.

Teacher impressions were also polled. Foster, Schmidt, and Sabatino (1976) investigated teacher expectations with respect to the label "Learning Disabilities." Their subjects were 44 elementary grade classroom teachers. The teachers saw a 12-minute color videotape of a beginning fourth-grade boy. The tape showed the child taking the reading subtest from the Wide Range Achievement Test and the general information subtest from the Peabody Individual Achievement Test; performing various perceptual-motor tasks; and participating in a brief play period. The teachers were told that the child either did or did not have a learning disability. The results showed that teachers who were told that the child had a learning disability had lower expectations than those teachers who were told that the child did not have learning problems. These authors discussed the negative implications of labeling.

In summary, those without learning problems viewed the learning-disabled child as different. Teachers, parents, peers, and naive observers focused on the negative or inappropriate cues emitted by the child with learning disabilities. Perceived differences at the level of attention affect the accurate processing of social cognitive cues.

Response Generation and Response Execution

When using strategies, children must be able to generate as many feasible options as possible. If a response is incorrect, other possibilities must be available for the child to sample. If the child returns a previously tested response to his or her pool of possible options (sampling with replacement), then there are fewer response options generated, and a greater chance of resampling incorrect options. Children without learning problems demonstrated a greater variety of response options than those with learning disabilities. This was observed when studying the statements emitted by children when interacting with peers and with younger children. When interacting with younger children, those without learning problems modified the complexity of their language consistent with the younger children's level of comprehension. These children took into account the information processing levels of those with whom they were interacting (Bryan, 1978).

RESPONSES EMITTED BY CHILDREN WITH LEARNING DISABILITIES

Children with learning disabilities displayed more inappropriate social behaviors than children without learning problems. The verbal and nonverbal cues they emitted, the activities in which they engaged, and their unexpected reactions to situations distinguished them from others. Yet, the availability of data suggests that they received similar reinforcement patterns from teachers, discussed similar amounts of information as peers, and were not separated by others on the basis of physical characteristics.

Selective Attention

Basic to one's cognition is the ability to maintain and sustain attention to relevant information. Problems in focusing on important social cues affect the learning-disabled child's ability to solve social cognitive problems.

Bryan and Wheeler (1972) found that children with learning disabilities spent less time on tasks that were relevant to their assignments and more time on spent less time on tasks that were relevant to their assignments and more time on nonrelevant tasks than did children without learning problems. Presently, this is the only study available that discusses the child's attention within the classroom.

Parrill-Burnstein and Baker-Ward (1979) presented a series of tasks to children with and without learning disabilities to evaluate attention, memory, and integration of social cognitive information. Their subjects were 118 children, who were equated on achievement. Seventy-six of these children had learning disabilities and were from two private school settings for children with learning disabilities; 39 of these children were performing at the same achievement level as the 37 children in the other school, but were doing so at a younger age level. Forty-two children were without learning problems and served as the comparison group. On one task the children were required to describe a pictured scene. The children were presented with a picture depicting both foreground and background in terms of inside and outside scenario. Irrelevant objects were placed in the four corners of the picture. The central theme conformed in design to the criteria specified by Myklebust (1965) for his Picture Story Language Test (PSLT), and the PSLT scoring system was used.

The results showed that children with learning disabilities performed similarly to those without learning problems when productivity and syntax (as defined with the PSLT) were scored. The difference between the groups was significant when the children were scored according to the level of concrete-abstractness. Children with learning disabilities made significantly fewer inferences and conclusions about the scene when compared to children without learning problems.

In another experiment within the same study, Parrill-Burnstein and Baker-Ward (1979) compared attention to facial features as reflected in the task requiring that children recognize faces seen previously. The subjects were 130 children, 35 in one school for children with learning disabilities, 50 were without learning problems and were achieving at the same levels as those in the second center (45 children), but were doing so at a younger age. Children at the first center are referred to as "younger LD"; those at the second center are referred to as "older LD." In all of the studies, the children with learning disabilities were in full-time special education placement during the school day. During the pretest, younger children with learning disabilities recognized significantly fewer faces than older children with learning disabilities or those without learning problems. Those from the older group of children with learning disabilities did not differ from those without learning problems. After this initial phase, the children were told to make a judgment of "mean" or "nice" on each exposure. After this type of strategy training, all children performed similarly. The implications were that younger children with learning disabilities who were achieving at the same academic levels did not focus initially on relevant social stimuli or cues but could be encouraged to do so with appropriate instruction.

To summarize, younger children with learning disabilities did not attend to or focus on relevant stimuli when compared to older children with learning disabilities or those without learning problems who were performing at the same academic levels. Yet, after receiving instructions to direct attention to relevant information, younger children with learning disabilities improved and performed similarly to those in the other two groups. It is also suggested that younger children with learning disabilities may not focus on relevant information or use strategies to facilitate adequate selective attention in the classroom.

Response Generation and Response Execution

With respect to response generation and execution, children with learning disabilities differed significantly from those without learning problems. With respect to verbal behavior, children with learning problems displayed a more restricted array of responses (Bryan et al., 1976). Children with learning disabilities emitted significantly more competitive statements and fewer considerate statements than those without learning problems. It was possible that children with learning disabilities resampled from the set of negative options (competitive statements) while those without learning problems were able to generate other options, including positive statements.

On the discrimination learning task, children with learning disabilities also generated significantly fewer hypotheses or options (Parrill-Burnstein & Baker-Ward, 1979). The differences observed were due to the performance of older children with learning disabilities who were performing at the same achievement levels as younger children with learning disabilities and children without learning problems. Many of these children with learning disabilities repeated disconfirmed and inappropriate responses. Generally, children with learning disabilities generated and executed significantly fewer response options than those without learning problems.

Chapman et al. (1979) also found that children without learning disabilities emitted more responses than children with learning disabilities and without other learning problems.

Feedback

These data suggested that children with learning disabilities responded differently to negative and positive feedback. According to hypothesis testing theorists, the appropriate response to feedback is to retain a correct response and eliminate an incorrect response and sample from among confirmed responses. Parrill-Burnstein and Baker-Ward (1979) studied reinforcement patterns when presenting children with a two-choice discrimination learning problem. Their subjects were 138 children: 89 with learning disabilities and 49 without learning problems who were equated on achievement level. The children with learning disabilities were in two schools for children with learning disabilities. Forty-five children in one school were shown to be younger when equated on achievement level with the 44 children in the other school. It was found that children with learning disabilities did not respond as expected to feedback. In general, these youngsters were sometimes correct and sometimes incorrect in their responses to feedback information provided. Furthermore, those in the two different learning disabilities populations performed significantly differently. Older children with learning disabilities who performed at the same achievement levels as the younger children in the other center eliminated responses most of the time. This was appropriate only after negative feedback. Children with learning disabilities in the other school retained responses when appropriate and eliminated responses when inappropriate. When eliminating responses, children with learning disabilities resampled incorrect responses.

Bryan (1974a) showed that children with learning disabilities received more negative feedback when working with the regular classroom teacher, and demonstrated significantly more inappropriate behaviors than with the learning disabilities teacher. It should be noted that inappropriate social behaviors were measured by on-task attention; it is questionable whether or not this is a measure of social behaviors. The implications of these findings were that negative reinforcement increased inappropriate behavior and positive reinforcement increased appropriate behavior.

In a study described earlier, Bryan and her colleagues (Bryan et al., 1976) found that children with learning disabilities uttered more competitive statements when compared to those without learning problems. These children were also the recipients of more rejection comments. In another study also cited above, Bryan and Wheeler (1972) had observers code the behaviors of four children in each of five classes, two children in each class with learning disabilities and two children in that same class without learning problems. Children in this study were observed every 10 seconds for 5 minutes. The tasks were coded in terms of the task orientation, nontask orientation, waiting, and interaction. These authors found that when production was compared, children with learning disabilities had as much quantity to their description and interaction as those without learning disabilities. The difference was not in terms of quantity, but rather in the quality of the interaction. In general, it was found that children with learning disabilities did not respond as expected to the feedback provided. These children continued to retest a response that was rejected (feedback), and did not always maintain a response that was accepted. Teachers have often noted these behaviors in their classes.

CONCLUSIONS

Children with learning disabilities did not appear to efficiently or appropriately solve social cognitive problems. Differences were observed at each level of the task components analyzed. Consistent with other information reviewed in the earlier chapters, children with learning disabilities differed in terms of selective attention to relevant social cues, generation of social response options or alternatives, the number of social behaviors executed, and appropriate social responses to feedback. At a most basic level, that of selective attention, children with learning disabilities were observed to emit different verbal and nonverbal cues than those without learning problems.

With respect to response generation, it was found that children with learning disabilities generated fewer response options than those without learning problems. This affected resampling following negative and positive feedback. In terms of response execution, children with learning disabilities tended to repeat disconfirmed responses or to resample from the set of disconfirmed responses.

Of particular interest was the finding associated with feedback. Other people often provided negative feedback when interacting with children with learning disabilities. Others tended to ignore, help, exclude, and reinforce on variable or intermittent schedules the responses of children with learning disabilities. Furthermore, older and younger children with learning disabilities who were achieving academically at the same levels performed differently when responses were negatively reinforced, positively reinforced, and ignored. The initial responses of the younger children with learning disabilities were appropriate after given both negative and positive feedback. Children with learning disabilities who were older changed responses after both types of feedback. Children from both of these groups did not resample appropriately following negative feedback. These findings were interpreted as reflecting limited response generation and therefore constrained response execution.

In addition to the responses of children with learning disabilities following positive and negative feedback, their reactions following extinction were also analyzed. Children with learning disabilities increased inappropriate social responses after extinction. The expected decrease in inappropriate responses following extinction did not occur. It was also found that children with learning disabilities received similar reinforcement patterns from their teachers as did those without learning problems. Thus, inappropriate social behaviors were maintained on variable or intermittent reinforcement schedules.

In summary, when equated on achievement level, younger children with learning disabilities responded more appropriately following positive reinforcement. Through instruction, a younger group of children with learning disabilities successfully integrated available stimulus information and improved recognition memory; finally, production of verbal expression was similar for children with and without learning disabilities; however, ideation and integration of social cognitive cues differentiated the groups. These characteristics of task performance should be taken into consideration when planning appropriate strategies for remediation.

IMPLICATIONS FOR RESEARCH AND REMEDIATION

When planning remediation of social cognitive problems and designing research in this area, the following were taken into account: (1) most incidental or instructional learning requires simultaneous integration of verbal and nonverbal information; (2) children with learning disabilities had difficulty at each level of information processing analyzed, particularly that of responding appropriately

Social Cognition

following feedback; (3) a component analysis approach was effective when teaching younger children without learning problems complex strategies (e.g., Parrill-Burnstein, 1978); (4) more appropriate responding was observed following positive reinforcement and more inappropriate responding was observed following a negative reinforcement and extinction; and (5) variables such as task characteristics, level and type of processing, and prerequisite skills influenced problem solving.

The following remediation suggestions were categorized according to three cognitive skills: recognizing social cues; relating social cues; and role taking. Levels of selective attention, response generation, response execution, and feedback were specified as appropriate.

Recognition of Social Cues

Social cues include facial cues, body postures, and the position of figures within and between the spaces. Three tasks are suggested.

First, present the child with a series of facial expressions and ask him or her to label each expression (stimulus differentiation and selective attention) and state social situations where such an expression could occur (response generation). Then, discuss the social cues that are available about the expression (e.g., mouth and eyes). Inferences and conclusions should be drawn on the basis of those cues discussed.

A second task includes presentation of facial expressions as part of an ongoing theme. Ask the child again to describe the various figures' expressions and their appropriateness of inappropriateness to that context. When responses are inconsistent or incorrect, alternative responses should be substituted (response generation and feedback).

Another task, recognition of social cues in various combinations reflecting the essence of the social scene, is encouraged. Present the child with verbal and/or visual absurdities (e.g., a child in a boat fishing for berries). Ask that the child state the absurdity (selective attention). If the child has difficulty, ask that he or she describe what is shown or said. Then have the child identify the absurdity. Ask that an appropriate response(s) be stated to correct the absurdity (response generation). The response options or alternatives stated should be based on the context in which the absurdity occurs. These alternative responses should be evaluated with respect to the degree of appropriateness to the depicted scene (feedback).

Relating Social Cues

Relating and integrating social cues enables inferences and conclusions to be drawn. Three tasks are suggested to develop these abilities.

Cues are related as part of a general single theme as well as part of the sequence of themes. To encourage the forming of relationships within a single theme, show the child a pictured theme of an ongoing activity. Ask that facial expressions and important body movements be identified. Then, discuss the relationship between the facial expressions and the body movements as they relate to each figure and between figures. Discuss other situations where these same cues may also be observed (response generation).

Using another single-pictured theme, show the child the stimulus and ask him or her to discuss what is depicted (stimulus differentiation). If the child has difficulty (e.g., mentioning the parts in random order or not naming the figures shown), block off most of the part of the picture with a piece of paper, exposing only one section at a time. Ask the child to discuss each part as shown (selective attention). Such cue questions as "what," "where," "who," "when," and "how" should be provided. Exposing two or more parts simultaneously, ask the child to describe and relate those parts. Continue this until all the parts are shown, described, and related. After all the parts of the picture have been presented, ask the child to state an appropriate title (feedback). The title represents the general theme. Next, instruct the child to relate each of the initially blocked off parts to the title or general theme (response generation and feedback). Finally, a new and more appropriate title should be stated.

Another task requiring relationships between social cues involves sequence cards. On such cards, each picture represents a single idea or theme. Ask the child to arrange the series and then verbalize the scene as presented. If the child has difficulty, place the first card in the correct sequence and remove all others (selective attention). Ask the child to describe the situation shown and speculate about what possible pictures might logically follow this card (response generation). Then, ask the child to select the next correct card from among those remaining (response execution). Evaluate the feasibility of the speculations generated in terms of their correctness or incorrectness to the second correct card. Discuss correct (positive feedback) and incorrect (negative feedback) responses including *what* about the response was appropriate or inappropriate. If more than one picture is correct, the best choice should be identified and discussed. Repeat this sequence with the other remaining cards in the series.

Another task requiring integration of social cues involves the story-telling situation. First, require the child to tell or read part of a story; then, have the child make up what he or she thinks would follow (response generation). Discuss how these verbalizations are continuations in logical expressions of the initial story (feedback). Have the child change his or her response if inappropriate and change to a more appropriate response before continuing. Instructing the child on how to determine verbal and visual cause-and-effect relationships also involves integration of social cues. Present the child with verbal "if" statements and have him or her complete the statement with possible consequences or effects (response generation). These effects are solutions and should be discussed in terms of their accuracy (feedback).

Role Taking

To encourage role taking, three tasks are suggested. Present the child with a picture of a figure or figures observing an activity. Ask the child to verbalize what is depicted (stimulus differentiation and selective attention). Instruct the

Social Cognition

child to pretend that he or she is the observer of an activity and ask what that person is feeling or thinking. If the child has difficulty determining the others' feelings, the teacher should state these logical feelings as well as the available cues that help determine them. The child or teacher states that the figure wishes to become part of the group, and then the teacher asks the child what he or she might do. After determining what possible options could be taken, the child is asked to select and verbalize a particular option. Negative and positive feedback should be provided. Ask the child to state what responses received negative and what responses received positive reinforcement. If feedback is negative, the child should be told to eliminate that response and select another. If correct, the child should be encouraged to use that response again.

Other role-taking activities involve presentation of a pictured theme. The child is asked to label the figure as well as discuss the relationship between figures. Then, the relationship between figures and the general theme are to be discussed. Hypotheses about feelings, motives, and attitudes of others are elicited. Cues making this information available are identified and discussed.

Having the children act out various social interactions (e.g., borrowing school supplies or asking another child over after school) would also help encourage role-taking development. During this role-taking activity each child is assigned a role and is asked to discuss how he or she feels in that role. After the child responds appropriately in that role, ask him or her to take the others' perspectives and again state feelings, motives, and beliefs associated with the new role. Children are encouraged to switch roles. Children observing these interactions are asked to identify important social cues emitted by each of the children as they interact.

To date, successful remedial procedures are few (e.g., Minskoff & Minskoff, 1976). With a few exceptions (Johnson & Myklebust, 1967), most educators teach specific skills rather than strategies. Research with children without learning problems suggests that training of this type does not generalize the tasks that differ in both format and stimuli from the original training problem (Campione & Beaton, 1972). Application of the component analysis approach seems useful when teaching children either concepts or strategies (Lerner, 1976). Through strategy training, children with learning disabilities should be able to analyze the sequence or component skills necessary to solve social cognitive problems, as well as determining the interrelationships between components.

RESEARCH

Research findings were that children with learning disabilities were less popular, received more criticism and negative feedback, and had difficulty attending selectively, generating responses, and responding appropriately to feedback. These research findings were taken into account when designing the following studies. Research, similar to remediation, is organized according to recognition of social skills, relating social cues, and role taking. In all experiments, it is suggested that a comparison group of children without learning problems be employed; that children in the category of learning disabilities be differentiated; and that children with and without learning disabilities be equated on SES, IQ, and either achievement level or chronological age.

Recognition of Social Skills

When equated on achievement level, younger children with learning disabilities do not attend to or integrate as many relevant cues as children without learning problems or older children with learning disabilities who were at the same achievement levels. To evaluate a procedure to encourage the integration of facial cues, the following experiment is suggested.

Three conditions are proposed in this repeated-measures design: baseline, manipulation, and posttest. In condition 1, the child is shown a series of 20 pictures of faces and then is presented with three faces (two distractors and the original face) and asked to select the one seen before. After collection of these baseline data, the children are presented with a new set of 20 faces (condition 2) and are asked to group the ones that go together. Following this, recognition is tested in the same way as during condition 1 (condition 3).

Comparisons between condition 1, recognition, and condition 3, recognition, are made. Differences as a function of grade, school, and condition are analyzed.

Relating Social Cues

Children with learning disabilities have problems relating social cues. Differences as a function of the nature of the social cue have not yet been evaluated. This is the purpose of this next experiment.

The experiment is conducted in a single phase. The child is presented with the stimulus of an activity (e.g., children playing basketball). This picture stimulus is removed; the child is presented with four cards, one of which follows the initial stimulus card logically and three distractor items. The distractor items can vary from the original stimulus by being inconsistent in background, color of clothes, and activity depicted. The child's response is recorded as correct or incorrect and the errors are analyzed as inappropriate background, color, or activity. These are compared for children with and without learning disabilities, with different types of learning disabilities, and by age or achievement level.

Role Taking

In order to interact appropriately with others, it is assumed that the child must be able to take another's perspective or role. To evaluate this assumption, the following experiment is suggested.

The child is presented with a series of pictures, each showing two children engaged in conversation. The child is presented with problems verbally, such as "John wants to borrow a pencil from Sally." Then, the child is posed with the following question: "What should Johnny do?" The child's responses are recorded (response generation). (Responses generated should include more than one appropriate response.) Then, the child is asked to choose a response and is given negative feedback. Such negative feedback might be that when selecting the response of taking the pencil, the child is told that Sally would keep the pencil. The child is asked again what John should do. The next alternative is recorded as new-appropriate, new-inappropriate, old-appropriate and old-inappropriate (the last two are retested responses). Differences as a function of number of responses, number of appropriate responses to feedback, and the type of resampling following negative feedback are analyzed.

In general, the research implications suggested are to evaluate some of the basic assumptions underlying teacher impressions of children with learning disabilities. It is also suggested that research be developed to investigate remedial techniques presently in practice or suggested elsewhere (Gable, Strain, & Hendrickson, 1979).

REFERENCES

Bruininks, V. L. Peer status and personality characteristics of learning disabled and nondisabled students. *Journal of Learning Disabilities,* 1978, *11*(8), 484–489.

Bruner, J. S. *Beyond the information given.* New York: W. W. Norton & Company, 1973.

Bryan, T. An observational analysis of classroom behaviors of children with learning disabilities. *Journal of Learning Disabilities,* 1974a, 7(1), 26–34.

Bryan, T. Peer popularity of learning disabled children. *Journal of Learning Disabilities,* 1974b, 7(10), 621–625.

Bryan, T. H. Peer popularity of learning disabled children: A replication. *Journal of Learning Disabilities,* 1976 9(5), 307–311.

Bryan, T. Social relationships and verbal interactions of learning disabled children. *Journal of Learning Disabilities,* 978, *11*(2), 58–66.

Bryan, T., & Wheeler, R. Perception of learning disabled children: The eye of the observer. *Journal of Learning Disabilities,* 1972, 7, 367–373.

Bryan, T., Wheeler, R., Felcan, J., et al. Come on dummy: An observational view of children's communications. *Journal of Learning Disabilities,* 1976, 9(10), 661–669.

Campione, J. C., & Beaton, V. L. Transfer of training: Some boundary conditions and initial theory. *Journal of Experimental Child Psychology,* 1972, *13*, 94–114.

Chandler, M. J. Social cognition: A selective review of current research. In W. F. Overton & J. M. Gallgher, (Eds.), *Knowledge and development* (Vol. I). New York: Plenum Press, 1977.

Chapman, R. B., Larson, S. C., & Parker, R. M. Interactions of first-grade teachers with learning disordered children. *Journal of Learning Disabilities,* 1979, *12*(4), 225–230.

Doleys, D. M., Cortelli, C. M., & Doster, J. Comparison of patterns of mother-child interaction. *Journal of Learning Disabilities,* 1976, *9*(6), 371–375.

Flavell, J. H. The development of inferences about others. In T. Mischel (Ed.), *Understanding other persons.* Oxford, England: Blackwell, Basil and Mott, 1974.

Flavell, J. H. *Cognitive development.* New Jersey: Prentice-Hall, Inc., 1977.

Foster, G. F., Schmidt, C. R., & Sabatino, D. Teacher expectancies and the label "learning disabilities." *Journal of Learning Disabilities,* 1976, *9*(2), 111–114.

Gable, R. A., Strain, P. S., & Hendrickson, J. M. Strategies for improving the satus of social behaviors of learning disabled children. *Learning Disabilities Quarterly,* 1979, *2*(3), 33–39.

Gagné, R. M. Contributions of learning to human development. *Psychology Review,* 1969, *75,* 177–191.

Gholson, B. *The cognitive-developmental basis of human learning: Studies in hypothesis testing.* New York: Academic Press, 1980.

Hardwick, D. A., McIntyre, C. W., & Pick, H. L. The content and manipulation of cognitive maps in children and adults. *Monographs of the Society for Research in Child Development,* 1976, Vol. *4*(3), Serial No. 166.

Johnson, D. J., & Myklebust, H. *Learning disabilities: Educational principles and practices.* New York: Grune & Stratton, 1967.

Lerner, J. W. *Children with learning disabilities.* Atlanta: Houghton Mifflin Company, 1976.

Levine, M. *A cognitive theory of learning: Research on hypothesis testing.* Hillsdale, New Jersey: Lawrence Erlbaum Associates, 1975.

Livesley, W. J., & Bromley, D. B. *Person perception in childhood and adolescence.* New York: John Wiley & Sons, Ltd., 1973.

Minskoff, E. H., & Minskoff, J. C. A unified program of remedial and compensatory teaching for children with process learning disabilities. *Journal of Learning Disabilities,* 1976, *9*(4), 215–222.

Myklebust, H. R. *Development and disorders of written language: Picture Story Language Test* (Vol. 1). New York: Grune & Stratton, 1965.

Neisser, U. *Cognition and reality.* San Francisco: W. H. Freeman & Co., 1976.

Parrill-Burnstein, M. Teaching kindergarten children to solve problems: An information processing approach. *Child Development,* 1978, *49*(3), 700–706.

Parrill-Burnstein, M., & Baker-Ward, L. Learning disabilities: A social cognitive difference. *Learning Disabilities: An Audio Journal for Continuing Education,* Vol. III (10), 1979.

Parrill-Burnstein, M., & Hazan-Ginzburg, E. *Social cognition and cognitive mapping: Understanding the impact of the learning disability.* Unpublished manuscript, Emory University, 1980.

Piaget, J., & Inhelder, B. *The psychology of the child.* New York: Basic Books, 1969.

Scranton, T. R., & Ryckman, M. A. Learning disabled children in an integrative program: Sociometric status. *Journal of Learning Disabilities,* 1979, *12*(6), 402–407.

Shantz, C. U. The development of social cognition. In E. M. Hetherington (Ed.), *Review of child development research* (Vol. 5). Chicago: University of Chicago Press, 1975.

Siperstein, G. N., Bopp, M. J., & Bak, J. J. Social status of learning disabled children. *Journal of Learning Disabilities,* 1978, *11*(2), 49–53.

Strag, G. A. Comparative behavioral rating of parents with severe mentally retarded, specific learning disability, and normal children. *Journal of Learning Disabilities*, 1972, *5*, 631–635.

Torgesen, J., & Goldman, T. Verbal rehearsal and short-term memory in reading disabled children. *Child Development*, 1977, *48*(1), 56–60.

FURTHER READINGS

Borke, H. Interpersonal perception of young children: Egocentrism or empathy. *Developmental Psychology*, 1971, *5*, 263–269.

Bruininks, V. L. Actual and perceived peer status of learning disabled students in mainstream programs. *Journal of Special Education*, 1978, *12*, 51–58.

Chandler, M. J. Social cognition and lifespan approaches to the study of child development. In H. Reese (Ed.), *Advances in child development* (Vol. 11). New York: Academic Press, 1976.

Cullinan, D., Epstein, M. H., & Dembinski, R. J. Behavior problems of emotionally handicapped and normal pupils. *Journal of Abnormal Child Psychology*, 1979, *7*(4), 495–502.

Donally, C. Social and emotional factors in learning disabilities. In H. Myklebust (Ed.), *Progress in learning disabilities* (Vol. II). New York: Grune & Stratton 1974.

Coopersmith, S. *The antecedents of self-esteem.* San Francisco: W. H. Freeman & Company, 1967.

Crowne, D. P., & Stephens, M. W. Self-acceptance and self-evaluative behavior: A critique of methodology. *Psychological Bulletin*, 1961, *58*(2), 104–121.

Doyles, D. M., Cartelli, L. M., & Doster, J. Comparison of patterns of mother-child interaction. *Journal of Learning Disabilities*, 1976, *9*(6), 371–375.

Feffer, M. Developmental analysis of interpersonal behavior. *Psychological Review*, 1970, *77*(3), 197–214.

Feffer, M., & Gourevitch, V. Cognitive aspects of role-taking in children. *Journal of Personality*, 1960, *28*, 383–396.

Smith, I. L., & Greenberg, S. Hierarchical assessment of social competency. *American Journal of Mental Deficiency*, 1979, *83*(6), 551–555.

Von Isser, A., Quay, H. C., & Love, C. T. Interrelationships among three measures of deviant behavior. *Exceptional Children*, 1980, *46*(4), 272–276.

Wallbrown, F. H., Fremont, T. S., Nelson, E., et al. Emotional disturbance or social misperception? An important classroom management question. *Journal of Learning Disabilities*, 1979, *12*(10), 645–648.

7
Issues

A number of issues are at present receiving increased attention in the fields of abnormal psychology, special education, and learning disabilities. Ten of these are discussed briefly under the categories of theory, remediation, and research. These issues are only a few of those visible at this time and are chosen for their present and future influence. These issues appear to be of major concern to teachers, parents, and legislators and reflect a philosophical change in terms of designing better research, implementing more appropriate remediation, and in formulating more accurate theories.

THEORY

Theoretical issues are: (1) the noncategorical approach to educating mildly handicapped children (collapsing across the categories of behavior disorders, learning disabilities, educable mental retardation); (2) the controversy over learning disabilities as reflecting a delay in development or as constituting a difference in cognitive processing; (3) the feasibility of developing different models or applying available models of expected development to describe the development of children with learning disabilities; and (4) the application of an information processing model, hypothesis-testing, to describe the behaviors of children with learning disabilities.

Noncategorical Approach

In a recent report, Garrett and Brazil (1979) present data suggesting a philosophical move toward a noncategorical approach to educating mildly handicapped children. This noncategorical approach is not implemented by federal policy; rather than collapsing across categories, boards of education are increasing their use of categories. This is not unexpected in that Public Law 94-142 (Federal Register, 1976) requires that children with special needs be differentiated and labeled in order to qualify for appropriate services.

Data reviewed in this text suggest that rather than grouping children with learning disabilities with those with other kinds of learning problems (e.g., behavior disorders and mild mental retardation), further differentiation within the category of learning disabilities would be more appropriate. Reasons for this position are: (1) the variability observed within the category of learning disabilities (e.g., Parrill-Burnstein & Baker-Ward, 1979); (2) the different perceptions and overt responses of parents (Doyles, Cartelli, & Doster, 1976), teachers (Gajar, 1979), and peers (Bryan, 1978; Siperstein, Bopp, & Bak, 1978) to children with different kinds of learning problems; and (3) the differences in terms of the primary deficits, for example, behavior disorders reflecting psychological and academic failure; learning disabilities reflecting central processing dysfunctions and academic failure; and mental retardation reflecting general developmental delays (Gajar, 1979).

Differences versus Delays in Performance

Children with learning disabilities do not solve problems in the same ways as children without learning problems do. These problems are interpreted as either a difference or a delay in performance. Research supports both positions. However, not all children with learning disabilities show the same developmental trends as children without learning problems. When differences are obtained, trends frequently are inconsistent and variable. Interpreting these results as indicating delays in performance implies that the children may have acquired only more basic skills and are not yet prepared to learn material presented at their chronological age level. This implication poses certain problems. For example, teachers and parents frequently are baffled by the inconsistent and variable performance of their children with learning disabilities. These same children do not necessarily learn better through repetition or after further maturation; problems persist throughout development and require different teaching approaches.

Recent work in our laboratory supports the hypothesis that learning disabilities represent a difference and/or a delay in performance. Significant differences are obtained when learning disabilities and normal children are equated on achievement (Parrill-Burnstein & Baker-Ward, 1979; Parrill-Burnstein & Hazan-Ginzburg, 1980). On the other hand, much of the work on attention supports the interpretation of a delay in performance (e.g., Dykman et al., 1971). Both overt responses and physiologic changes are observed to approach normalcy as the children with attentional deficits increase in age.

Along these same lines, the most recent issue of the *Diagnostic and Statistics Manual of Mental Disorders (DSM* III) describes two categories applicable to learning disabilities: Attention Deficit Disorder and Specific Developmental Disorder. It is emphasized that children with these disorders do not simply grow out of their disabilities; symptoms persist into adulthood, although these children may learn to compensate for their learning problems.

If the performance of children with learning disabilities is interpreted as a delay, implications for remediation are considerably different than if performance is interpreted as a difference. Interpreting performance as a delay would suggest that teaching instructions and materials appropriate for children without learning problems would be appropriate for children with learning disabilities. The difference would be in that the instructions and materials used would be the same as that for a younger child without learning difficulties. Interpreting performance as a difference would imply that the instructions and materials used would need modification, taking into account such variables as the child's learning assets and deficits, rate of performance, and levels of tolerance for input (Johnson & Myklebust, 1967). It is quite possible that, when compared to children without learning problems, some children with learning disabilities demonstrate delays, others differences, and still others delays and differences in performance; appropriate remediation should reflect these individual differences.

Application of Expected and/or Different Models of Development

Should expected or different models of development be used to describe the development of children with learning disabilities? The answer to this question depends on whether or not the task performance of the learning-disabled child is interpreted as indicating a delay and/or difference in problem solving, in development, and in information processing. If the task performances of children with learning disabilities is interpreted as indicative of a delay, then models of expected development are appropriate for describing how these children learn. In this way, normal models of development provide an index of what behaviors are expected or occur consistently during specific age periods. Models of expected development also provide the sequence of the emergence of specific skills. This latter application is used for determining gaps and not just discrepancies in performance.

If the performance of children with learning disabilities is interpreted as indicative of differences in performance, then the development of models stressing differences in development is appropriate. The major assumption is that performance is not depressed, but rather discrepant with regard to the normal pattern. Developing a model stressing differences in development would allow better descriptions of deviant behaviors as well as differences in the sequence and acquisition of skills and strategies. As stated earlier, it is quite possible that some children with learning disabilities have delays in performance. Other children

Issues

with learning disabilities may have differences in performance. Still others may demonstrate both differences and delays in performance. Both models stressing expected differences in development may be necessary to describe the behaviors of children with learning disabilities.

The Hypothesis-Testing Model

Some children with learning disabilities may have difficulty solving problems because of information processing deficits. Applying the Hypothesis-Testing Model, the deficit(s) may be at the level(s) of: selective attention, response generation, response execution, and/or appropriate responses to feedback. Research using the Hypothesis-Testing Model suggests that children with learning disabilities show deficits at specific levels or combinations of levels of this information processing analysis of problem solving. On the basis of this analysis, the most impaired areas were determined to be in responding appropriately to feedback, and in attending to and integrating relevant stimulus information. Deficits at these specific levels influenced performance at higher levels and resulted in inappropriate behaviors in complex problem solving.

To summarize, variability within the category of learning disabilities suggests the need for further differentiation within the category. This is not consistent with the noncategorical approach proposed to educate these children. Furthermore, normal developmental data, and data based on the development of abnormal models may both be useful to better understand these deviant or different behaviors of children with learning disabilities. One information processing model of learning, the Hypothesis-Testing Model, can be used to describe and clarify the unexpected behaviors of children with learning disabilities and possibly those with other types of learning problems.

REMEDIATION

Remediation should be systematically planned, implemented, and evaluated. An approach to designing or planning remediation is task analysis; implementation frequently involves the two-pronged approach. Evaluation of successful remediation requires that the child generalize the training to new problem-solving situations. Research regarding children without learning problems suggests that to accomplish this, strategies, that is, organized sequences of behaviors that lead to solution of problems, be taught. This approach frequently involves the task analysis approach and improving deficits through instruction emphasizing learning strengths. Task analysis, the two-pronged approach to learning, and generalization are discussed briefly.

Task Analysis

The task analysis approach is incorporated into the classic remedial procedures of Johnson and Myklebust (1967), and a recent procedure referred to as Cognitive Behavior Modification (Finch & Spirito, 1980). Task analysis stresses a hierarchical and sequential relationship between the steps necessary to solve the problem. Task analysis may be employed when teaching a specific skill or strategy. When a specific skills is taught, such as learning to remember a group of objects, the child is exposed to an additive sequence of steps analyzed as necessary to acquire that skill. In strategy training, a series of tasks is analyzed into similar sequences and trained. When teaching strategies, the clinician relates tasks by their similarities in stimuli, responses, and format (Campione & Beaton, 1972).

To date, teaching specific skills has not been successful in remediating deficits in performance (e.g., Velluntino et al., 1977). If generalization is to occur, strategies need to be taught or trained. Task analysis and strategy training are a potentially successful combination.

Two-pronged Approach

When remediating problems, the clinician or teacher can focus instructions in different ways, depending on their philosophical orientation. Teachers or clinicians can teach skills (1) focusing on the child's learning integrities; (2) focusing on the deficit; or (3) using the learning strengths or integrities to remediate the learning deficits. This latter position, first articulated by Johnson and Myklebust, is referred to as the two-pronged approach.

The logic for stressing the two-pronged approach is as follows. If the child is taught only to use his learning strengths, the gap or discrepancy between his learning deficits and those integrities increases, but if training focuses on the deficit areas, the child's frustration may compound his or her learning difficulties. Working the integrities in learning into a lesson to remediate the deficits in performance, however, may result in faster acquisition with less failure and frustration. For these reasons, the use of two-pronged approach to remediation is strongly advocated.

Generalization

The success or lack of success of remedial procedures is determined by the extent and type of generalization obtained. Generalization occurs when skills or strategies learned on a specific task are observed on a task not taught. The task not taught is referred to as a transfer task. For generalization to occur, Campione and Beaton (1972) suggest that the training and transfer tasks need to be as similar as possible in terms of stimuli and format.

Keogh and Glover (1980) have expressed concern that the training given children with learning disabilities does not generalize to new tasks. In evaluating treatment procedures, these authors suggest that three questions be considered: (1) how broad are the intervention effects?; (2) does intervention affect educationally relevant variables?; and (3) how sensitive is the intervention technique to the setting in which it occurs, as well as to outside influences?

In order to achieve generalization, Meichenbaum (1980) suggests the following: (1) feedback must be immediate and explicit; (2) multiple stimuli should be used; (3) direct instructions to generalize the strategy to a certain type of task should be specified; and (4) general strategies to supplement specific strategies are to be taught.

To summarize, three components of remediation were described briefly: analysis; the two-pronged approach to teaching; and training to obtain generalization. It was suggested that task analysis be used to teach strategies. Further, it was stressed that the procedure implemented should take into account both the child's learning deficits and integrities. Finally, it was emphasized that the goal of teaching and training is transfer or generalization. Stressing similarities between training and transfer tasks in terms of format and stimuli are suggested (Campione & Beaton, 1972).

RESEARCH

Three issues are discussed here as they relate to research. These issues include discussion of (1) comparison groups; (2) equating groups on important variables; and (3) longitudinal and cross-sectional developmental research.

Comparison Groups

The type of comparison group used when studying the responses of children with learning disabilities should be determined by the research questions addressed in the study. If the research were designed to determine if children with learning disabilities perform similarly to children with other learning problems, comparison groups of children diagnosed as behavior disordered and mentally retarded would be appropriate. Some data are available comparing children with different kinds of learning problems (e.g., Gajar, 1979). In addition, including comparison groups of this type would provide information about the feasibility of a noncategorical approach to education. If asking if children with learning disabilities are similar to children without learning problems, employing a normal comparison group would be appropriate. Empirically addressing this latter question provides data about the use of expected models of development to describe the performance of children with learning disabilities.

Equating Groups

Defining the characteristics associated with research participants allows the comparison of results across studies. Defining populations similarly with respect to the variables of IQ, chronological age or achievement age, sex, and SES would provide these necessary data. These defining variables also apply to comparison groups which are included in the study.

If equated on achievement age with children without learning problems, the performance of children with learning disabilities should be similar to the performance of children without learning problems if a delay is present. If significant differences between these groups are found, then a difference rather than a delay in performance may be implied. When significant differences are obtained when children with learning disabilities are equated on age, systematic and linear trends could indicate depressed performance interpreted as delay; differences in performance are implied if differences are variable.

Equating on the basis of IQ scores allows control of differences due to initial differences in learning abilities. An important consideration here is the measure used and scores reported to evaluate learning abilities or IQ. For example, if the WISC-R is used, which score (the Verbal, the Performance, or Full-Scale) should be the basis for equating? Another point: Should the IQ measure test the same ability as required in the task (e.g., Columbia Mental Maturation Scale and a card-sorting task)? An additional issue is the minimum cutoff IQ score when defining learning disabilities. In the literature reviewed, the lower limits or minimum cutoff points for IQ ranged between 70 and approximately 90.

The Study of Development

Development can be studied with the same individual over time, referred to as longitudinal research; or it can be studied at the same time with children at different ages, stages, grades, etc. The latter way of studying development is referred to as cross-sectional research. Both types of research designs provide much needed information in the field of learning disabilities. To date, developmental research about children with learning disabilities has been cross-sectional. With this approach, performances of children at various chronological ages are compared and trends are inferred. Longitudinal data would allow the study of changes over time; that is, *how, when,* and *what* occurs within the same individual as he or she increases in age (and grade or stage). It is possible that data of this type would present a different picture of the development of the learning disabilities child than cross-sectional research.

To summarize, such research issues as the use of comparison groups, the definition of the learning disabilities population, and the choice of research strategy were described briefly. For a more comprehensive review of research variables, see Torgesen (1975).

The ten issues discussed here briefly are yet to be resolved. Before definitive answers can be formulated, additional research is required. Research allows important variables (i.e., reinforcement, stimulus presentation, stimulus complexity) to be controlled or manipulated systematically and under standardized conditions. Using research findings, implications for remediation can be drawn. As we continue to understand and increase our knowledge of the problem-solving skills of children with learning disabilities, more successful remedial procedures can be designed and implemented.

REFERENCES

Bryan, T. Social relationships and verbal interactions of learning disabled children. *Journal of Learning Disabilities*, 1978, *11*(2), 58–66.

Campione, J. C., & Beaton, V. L. Transfer of training: Some boundary conditions and initial theory. *Journal of Experimental Child Psychology*, 1972, *13*, 94–114.

Diagnostic and statistics manual of mental disorders (3rd ed.) (DSM III). Washington, D.C.: American Psychiatric Association, 1980.

Dykman, R. A., Ackerman, P. T., Clements, S. D., et al. Specific learning disabilities: An attentional deficit syndrome. In H. R. Myklebust (Ed.), *Progress in learning disabilities* (Vol. II). New York: Grune & Stratton, 1971.

Federal Register, Vol. 41, No. 23, Monday, November 29, 1976. Public Law 94-142, Section 5(B).

Finch, A. J., & Spirito, A. Use of cognitive training to change cognitive processes. *Exceptional Education Quarterly*, 1980, *1*(1), 31–39.

Gajar, A. Educable mentally retarded, learning disabled, emotionally disturbed: Similarities and differences. *Exceptional Children*, 1979, *45*(6), 470–472.

Garrett, J. E., & Brazil, N. Categories used for identification of exceptional children. *Exceptional Children*, 1979, *45*(4), 291–292.

Johnson, D. J., & Myklebust, H. *Learning disabilities: Educational principles and practices*. New York: Grune & Stratton, 1967.

Keogh, B., & Glover, A. T. The generality and durability of cognitive training effects. *Exceptional Education Quarterly*, 1980, *1*(1), 75–82.

Meichenbaum, D. Cognitive behavior modification with exceptional children: A promise yet unfulfilled. *Exceptional Education Quarterly*, 1980, *1*(1), 83–88.

Parrill-Burnstein, M., & Baker-Ward, L. Learning disabilities: A social cognitive difference. *Learning Disabilities: An Audio Journal for Continuing Education*, Vol. III(10), 1979.

Parrill-Burnstein, M., & Hazan-Ginzburg, E. *Social cognition and cognitive mapping: Understanding the impact of the learning disabilities*. Unpublished manuscript, Emory University, 1980.

Siperstein, C. N., Bopp, M., & Bak, J. Peers rate learning disabled children on who is the smartest, best looking, and most athletic. *Journal of Learning Disabilities*, 978, *11*(2), 98–102.

Torgesen, J. Problems and prospects in the study of learning disabilities. In E. M. Hetherington (Ed.), *Review of child development research* (Vol. 5). Chicago: University of Chicago Press, 1975.

Velluntino, I. R., Steger, B. M., Mayer, S. C., et al. Has the perceptual deficit hypothesis led us astray? *Journal of Learning Disabilities,* 1977, *10*(6), 375–385.

Index

Accuracy
   cognitive tempo and, 33, 34, 36–37
   personality factors and, 36–37
Activity level, attention and, 22–25
Appropriate level, attention and, 22–25
Appropriate response to feedback, 2–3
Associations in gestalt perceptual theory of learning, 16–17
Attention (inattention), 15–48
   cognition and, 33–43, 46–48
   cognitive tempo and, 33–40
   conditional discrimination and, 25–27
   dysfunctive reaction time task and, 21, 22, 25–27
   in gestalt perceptual theory of learning, 16–17
   implications for research, 47–48
   information processing theory of, 17
   learning disabilities and, 19–21
   memory and, 30–32, 45–47
   in orienting responses theory, 18–19
   perception and, 21–30, 44–45, 47
   remediation of problems with, 44–47
   selective, 2, 18–20, 61
      complex concept selection and, 61
      hypothesis testing behavior and, 65–66
      recall of children with learning disabilities and, 98–104
      recognition memory of children with learning disabilities and, 106–109
      social cognition and, 180, 184–187
   selectivity theory of, 16, 17
   simple reaction time tasks and, 21–25
   specificity, theory of, 16
   verbal regulation and, 40–43
   vigilance and, 27–30, 46
Attention Deficit Disorder, 7, 19
Attentional Deficit Hypothesis, 19–21

Babbling, 118

Cardiac deceleration, attention and, 22–23, 25
Card sorting tasks, concept formation and, 71–72
Concept organization, 81–84
Central recall, 96
Central-incidental learning task, 30–31
Cognition
   attention and, 33–43, 46–48
   language and, 119–123

207

Cognitive Behavior Modification, 202
Cognitive development
　hypothesis testing theory of, 5–6
　language and, 119
　social, 177–178
　stage theory of, 3–4
　theories of, 3
Cognitive mapping, 10, 149–172
　development of, 149–50
　mental rotations and, 149, 158–161
　motor proficiency and, 149, 151–154
　perspective-taking and, 149, 161–164
　remediation of problems with, 164–169
　research implications, 169–172
　revisualization and, 149, 154–158
　theories of, 150–151
Cognitive style, cognitive tempo and, 39–40
Cognitive tempo, 33–40
　cognitive style and, 39–40
Comparison groups, 203
Complex concept selection, 59–64
　learning disabilities and, 75–78
　mediation and, 61–63
　selective attention and, 61
　stimulus differentiation and, 59–64
Complex concept selection tasks, 55
Concept formation, 69–72
　card sorting tasks and, 71–72
　language development and, 122
　learning disabilities and, 78–79
　Twenty Questions Game and, 69–71
Concept formation tasks, 55
Concept identification tasks
　learning disabilities and, 79
　simple concept selection and, 72–74, 79–80
Concept organization, 8, 55–85
　of children without learning problems, 58–74
　complex concept selection and, 59–64, 75–78
　concept formation and, 69–72, 78–79
　hypothesis testing behaviors and, 65–69, 76–78
　implications for research, 83–85
　implications of research, 81
　learning disabilities and, 74–80
　remediation of problems with, 81–82
　simple concept selection and, 72–74, 79–80
　strategies and, 56–58
Concept shift learning
　learning disabilities and, 75–76
　mediation and, 61–63
　selective attention and, 61
　stimulus differentiation and, 59–60
Conceptual Style Test (CST), 35–36
Concrete operational period, 121, 179
Conditional discrimination, attention and, 25–27
Constraint Seeking Questions, in Twenty Questions Game, 69–71

Deferred imitation, 154
Depth of processing model of memory, 92
Development, study of, 204–205
Diagnostics and Statistics Manual of Mental Disorders (DSM III)
　Attention Deficit Disorder in, 7, 19
Dichotic listening tasks, 32
Dimension Checking Strategy, 64–68
Dimension preference tasks, simple concept selection and, 72–74
Disinhibition, 7, 19
Distractibility, 7, 19
Distraction, vigilance task performance and, 29
Dysfunctive reaction time task, attention and, 21, 22, 25–27

Egocentric speech, 119, 120
Encoding, 91
　improvement of, 109–110
　research on, 111–112
Exploration, 150
　in orienting responses, theory of, 18
Extradimensional shifts, concept organization and, 59–64

Index

Faces, recognition of, 97
Feedback
  appropriate response to, 2–3
  hypothesis testing behavior and, 67–69, 77, 78
  recall of children with learning disabilities and, 105–106
  social cognition and, 180, 182–183, 188–190
Focusing strategy, 64, 68
Formal operations period, 121, 179

Generalization, 202–203
Gestalt Perceptual Theory of Learning, attention in, 16–17

Hagen's central-incidental attention task, 30–31
  memory skills of children with learning disabilities and, 98–100
Hyperactivity
  attention and, 7, 19–21
  impulsivity and, 39–40
Hypothesis Checking Strategy, 64–66
Hypothesis Seeking Questions in Twenty Questions Game, 69–71
Hypothesis testing behaviors, 5
  complex concept selection and, 63–64
  concept organization and, 65–69, 76–78
  feedback and, 67–69, 77, 78
  learning disabilities and, 76–78, 82–85
  mediation and, 66–67
  remediation of concept organization problems and, 82–83
  selective attention and, 65–66
  social cognitive development and, 180
  stimulus differentiation and, 65
  Subset-Sampling Theory of, 63–64
  syntactical development as, 125
Hypothesis testing model, 201
Hypothesis testing theory, 5–6

Imitation, deferred, 154
Impulsive-reflective dimension, 46–47
  Matching Familiar Figures Test (MFFT) and, 33–40
Impulsivity, hyperactivity and, 39–40
Inattention, *see* Attention
Incidental recall, 96
Informational organization, 130
Information processing theory, 1
  of attention, 17
Inner speech, 119, 120
Instruction, neo-Piagetian theory of, 4
Instructional theory, 4–5

Knowledge-based model of memory, 93

Landscapes, revisualization of, 155
Language, 8, 117–144. *See also* Speech
  cognition and, 119–123
  development of, 117–119
  Piagetian theory of development of, 119–121
  phonology, 123–124
  pragmatics, 129–131
  semantics, 126–129
  syntax, 124–125
  thought and, 121–123
Language disorders (or deficits), 8–9, 131–144
  phonologic, 131, 138–139
  pragmatic, 137–138, 140–141
  remediation implications, 138–139
  research implications, 141–144
  semantic, 134–137, 140
  syntactic, 131–134, 139
Learning disabilities
  Attentional Deficit Hypothesis of, 19–21
  cognitive tempo and, 38–39
  complex concept selection and, 75–78
  concept formation and, 78–79
  concept organization and, 74–80
  concept shift learning and, 75–76
  differences versus delays in performance in, 199–200

Learning disabilities *(continued)*
  hypothesis testing task and, 76–78, 82–85
  models of development and, 200–201
  recall and, 98–106
  remediation issues and, 201–203
  research issues in, 203–205
  simple concept selection and, 79–80
  social cognition and, 181–186
  theoretical issues in, 198–201
  theories of, 6–11
Lincoln-Oseretsky Motor Proficiency Test, 153
Listening, dichotic, 32

Matching Familiar Figures Test (MFFT), 33–40
Matching-to-sample task, verbal regulation and, 41, 42
Mediation
  complex concept selection and, 61–63
  hypothesis testing behavior and, 66–67
Memory, 8, 91–113
  attention and, 30–32, 45–47
  components of, 91
  depth of processing model of, 92
  development of, 95–98
  knowledge-based model of, 93
  implications for research, 111–113
  long-term and short-term, 92
  metamemory model of, 93–94
  Piagetian theory of, 94–95
  remediation of problems with, 109–111
  social cognitive development and, 180–181
Mental rotations, 149
  development of, 158–161
  remedial procedures to improve, 167–168
  research implications, 171–172
Metamemory, 93–94
Minimal brain dysfunction (MBD), attention and, 21–25
Minimally brain damaged (MBD), distraction and, 29

Modeling
  hypothesis testing behavior and, 83
  Twenty Questions Game and, 70
Motor developments, cognitive mapping and, 10
Motor planning, remedial procedures to improve, 165–166
Motor proficiency, 149
  development of, 152–154
  research implications, 169–170
Movigenics, 10
Multisensory processing, 7

Neo-Piagetian theory, 3, 4
Noncategorical approach to educating mildly handicapped children, 198–199
Northwestern Syntax Screening Test, 104

Orienting responses, theory of, attention in, 18–19
Overstimulation, 7

Perception, attention and, 21–30, 44–47
Perceptual dysfunction, 7
Perceptual learning
  gestalt theory of, 16–17
  specificity, theory of, 16
Perseveration, concept organization and, 64, 66
Person perception, 178
Perspective-taking, 149
  development of, 161–164
  mental rotation skills and, 158–161
  remedial procedures to improve, 168–169
  research implications, 172
  social cognitive development and, 177–178
Phonemes, 123
Phonology, 123–124
  deviant, 131
  remediation of problems with, 138–139
  research implications, 141–142

Index

Piagetian theory, 3, 4
　imagery development in, 154
　language in, 119–121
　memory schema in, 94–95
　social cognitive development in, 179
Picture Story Language Test (PSLT), 187
Portable Rod Frame Test, 39
Pragmatics, 129–131
　disorders in, 137–138
　remediation of problems with, 140–141
　research implications, 143–144
Preoperational period, 121, 179
Presuppositions, 129–130
Primacy effect, 95
　learning disabilities and, 98
　serial position curves and, 31–32
Problem-solving analysis, 2
Psychological presuppositions, 130

Question games, concept organization and, 82, 84

Reading ability, cognitive tempo and, 38
Recall
　central, 96
　incidental, 96
　learning disabilities and, 98–106
　in Piaget's memory schema, 95
　serial, 96
Recency effect, 95
　serial position curves and, 31–32
Recognition (recognition memory)
　learning disabilities and, 106–109
　memory development and, 96–97
　in Piaget's memory schema, 94
Reconstruction in Piaget's memory schema, 95
Reflective-impulsive dimension, 46–47
　Matching Familiar Figures Test (MFFT) and, 33–40
Rehearsal strategies, memory development and, 95–96
Remediation, current issues in, 201–203
Response execution, 2
　social cognition and, 180, 186, 188

Response generation, 2
　recall of children with learning disabilities and, 104–105
　social cognition and, 180, 186, 188
Response latency, attention and, 22–25
Response latency variability, attention and, 22–25
Response sets, 64
Retrieval, 91
Reversal shifts, concept organization and, 59–64
Revisualization, 149
　development of, 154–158
　remedial procedures to improve, 166–167
　research implications, 170–171
Rod Frame Test, 39
Role taking, 178
　encouragement of, 192–193
　research on social problems and, 194–195

Search in orienting responses, theory of, 18
Selective attention, 2, 18–20, 61
　complex concept selection and, 61
　hypothesis testing behavior and, 65–66
　recall of children with learning disabilities and, 98–104
　recognition memory of children with learning disabilities and, 106–109
　social cogntition and, 180, 184–187
Selectivity Theory of attention, 16, 17
Self-regulation, 46. *See also* Verbal regulation
Semantic Features Hypothesis, 127–128
Semantic presupposition, 129–130
Semantics, 126–129
　disorders in, 134–137
　research implications, 143
　remediation of problems with, 140
Sensorimotor period, language learning and, 119–120, 179
Sentence utilization, pragmatics and, 129
Serial position curves, 31–32
Serial recall, 99
　memory development and, 96

Simon Says Game, 46
  verbal regulation and, 41–42
Simple concept selection
  Concept Identification Tasks and, 72–74, 79–80
  concept organization and, 72–74, 79–80
  learning disabilities and, 79–80
Simple concept selection tasks, 55
  selection of strategies in, 58
Simple reaction time tasks, attention and, 21–25
Social cognition, 10–11, 176–195
  development of, 177–178
  feedback and, 180, 182–183, 188–190
  learning disabilities and, 181–186
  remediation of problems in, 190–193
  research implications, 193–195
  response execution and, 180
  response generation and, 180
  selection attention and, 180, 184–187
  theory of, 179–181
Social competence, 176
Social cues
  remediation of social problems and, 191–192
  research on social problems and, 194
Spatial imagery. *See also* Revisualization
  development of, 154
Specificity, theory of, attention in, 16

Speech. *See also* Language
  egocentric, 119, 120
  inner, 119, 120
Speech acts, pragmatics and, 129
Stimulus differentiation, 2
  complex concept selection and, 59–60
  hypothesis testing behaviors and, 65
Storage, 91
  improvement of, 110–111
  research on, 112–113
Strategy development, 56–58
Sub-Problem Analysis, 59
Subset-Sampling Theory, 63–64
Syntax, 124–125
  deficits in, 131–134
  remediation of problems with, 139
  research implications, 142–143

Task analysis approach, 202
Thought, language and, 121–123
Transformational grammar, 125
Twenty Questions Game, 69–71, 82

Verbal labeling
  hypothesis testing behavior and, 67
  as rehearsal strategy in memory development, 95
Verbal regulation, 40–43, 46
Vigilance, attention and, 27–30, 46